WHILE THE CITY SLEPT

A Saint John Mystery

Thomas L. Shanklin

The Saint John Crest on the Flag

Motto

O Fortunati Quorum Jam Moenia Surgunt
Has been translated two ways:
O Fortunate Ones Whose Walls Are Now Rising
O Happy They, Whose Promised Walls Already Rise

ISBN-13: 978-1979113045
ISBN-10: 1979113041

Published by
Thomas L. Shanklin
16114 Pennington Road
Tampa, Florida 33624
mysterywy@gmail.com

In Memory of
Captain Thomas Spragg
Loyalist who arrived in New Brunswick
In 1784

And

In Honour of all those
Who have built and preserved the historic city
Of Saint John

INTRODUCTION

Saint John is my city. New Brunswick is my Province. Canada is my ancestral home.

My father, born at Hatfield Point, moved into the city with his parents and siblings around 1906. He was ten years old. To his dying day at the age of 106 in 2002, my father, Harold MacKenzie Shanklin, would say that "when they moved from upcountry into Saint John, he thought his life was over." He so loved Belleisle Bay. But he also loved Saint John.

So it was no coincidence that from the day I was born, my father told me his boyhood stories. I wrote about them in my book "Downeast-UpCountry." [1] I was probably one year old when my father brought me to New Brunswick. I have spent nearly every summer of my life vacationing in Saint John and Upcountry. These vacations were opportunities for me to see the Old Saint John, meet numerous relatives and re-live my father's childhood.

Saint John is a part of the fabric of my life. It is woven deep into my soul and heart. My year would not be complete without a visit to Saint John. I come. I camp at Rockwood Park. I sit and watch the Bay. I drive the streets. I remember what used to be. I sit in the fog. Saint John infuses me with new life for another year. The air off the Bay of Fundy renews my soul.

This book is a figment of my imagination. It draws from my familiarity with Saint John. I have used city street names, descriptions of real buildings and family names that dot the landscape of New Brunswick.

The events described in this book come from my imagination. I created the story as a way of remembering. But I ask the reader to not merely remember but to honour and preserve what is left of Saint John. We can allow the decay of our past to create our present. But more importantly, we can remember our past and its good and bad moments and infrastructure and build upon it in positive ways.

---

[1] "Downeast-UpCountry: A Place, A Family, A Time" Available from the author, on Amazon and in bookstores and historical societies.

All characters in this story have been created by me. Any resemblance of them to any real person, dead or alive, is purely by coincidence.

The one real incident that I describe is the fire that destroyed St. Paul's Anglican Church in the Valley. I took the photograph of the fire that is included on the cover. I was in Saint John in 1981. When the fire broke out, I was standing in the parking lot next to Old Stone Church. I watched for hours as the fire destroyed historic St. Paul's. It is my understanding the fire was started by blow torches that were used to remove old paint in preparation for new and restoration. The church was about to celebrate a major anniversary. As I watched, I cried. When I saw the fire ascend into the steeple, I knew all was lost. There was no way to save the church. Consequently, there was little way to save the historic area. With the loss of St. Paul's came the loss of some historic buildings in the neighbourhood.

Truly Morrell is based on a chance meeting I had with Vern M. Garnett one day as I lingered in Kings Square in the summer of 2017. He has been a major source and encouragement to me in writing about Saint John. He, as I, mourn the loss of so much that was unique to the city.

The Victorian city that I experienced as a young boy in the early 1950's is nearly gone. Just remnants remain. I walk the Old Market, sit at Fort Howe, and drive Germain Street every summer. I note the magnificent beveled glass doorways of buildings that have survived. I grieve over the state of disrepair of the North End. The home where my family ancestors lived, 31 Metcalf, and where I spent many happy vacation days, still stands. They lived there from around 1906 to the 1960's. But it is a forlorn reminder of what was. I remember the North End with the hustle and bustle of people going about their daily lives. Errand boys ran to the Dominion store. Children played in the street and walked to Alexandra School. Wisps of smoke billowed out of chimneys announcing that a delicious meal, perhaps of fresh salmon bought at the old market, was being prepared. And of course, blueberries that had been picked the day before at Rockwood Park, were bubbling away as housewives made blueberry buckle or blueberry belly bang. [2]

---

[2] Blueberry recipes from New Brunswick natives and North Enders are included in the appendix of this book.

I encourage the reader to go with me on an imaginary mystery assuaging my grief over the loss of so much that was Saint John.

I encourage the reader, if from Saint John, to consider what the city has been and *can again be*: a vibrant, interesting, historic city important to Canadian history and future.

Thomas L. Shanklin
February 2018

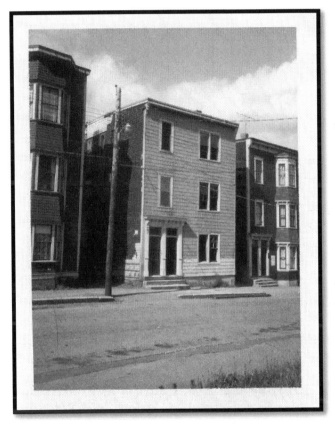

31 Metcalf Street Circa 1960
My Grandparent's home for many decades
Where I spent many childhood vacations.

THE SHROUD DESCENDS

The city slept. Truly Morrell had retired early hoping that he would awaken on the other side of dawn. Instead a dream had nudged him out of a restless sleep. He had spent an uneasy day morphed into an uneasy night. Now at three in the morning, he arose to greet the dawn. There was no need to try for more sleep. And the dawn would not awaken him. He was already awake. Truly Morrell had awakened from an uneasy sleep.

While the city slept, Truly dressed. "My plaid woolen shirt will do," he thought as he pulled on his boots. A quick comb through his white beard was enough to get him on his way before the dawn broke. He liked greeting the dawn. It made him feel as if he were in some control of the day rather than the dawn controlling him. There were enough things about the day and the city that were out of control. Truly didn't need to feel any more out of control.

He had grown up in the old city. The North End of Saint John was home even though he no longer lived there. His family had moved from upcountry decades before. It was a time when the city teemed with activity. Victorian houses marched up and down the craggy hills and narrow streets. Neighbors knew neighbors. Errand boys ran here and there gathering whatever the ladies of the home needed for the evening meal. They would run to the local Dominion Store or in summer to the Old Market across town where farmers from the country had brought in their bounty. That was all gone now. Tourists had replaced the daily living. Even those who daily lived and worked in the city had gone.

Truly paused. He took a quick look in the hall mirror before stepping onto Germain Street. "Better take a hat," he whispered. "Not much hair left up there to filter the wind. Or the fog." He grabbed his wool hat and pulled the brim down to touch the top of his ears. The heavy door with its leaded bevel glass swung shut behind him.

He stood for a moment breathing in the moist sea air coming off the Bay of Fundy. The mist in the air was just enough to wet his whistle as he set out. He let the houses lean in and embrace him as he walked along. There was a friendliness to their presence. They reminded him of his childhood when the city was whole. It wasn't that the city had disappeared. It just was that the city wasn't anymore. So much had happened since he was a boy in the 1950's.

9

Truly set a brisk pace across the streets and the viaduct. He was headed for Fort Howe. At this hour of the morning, he could be alone with his thoughts and memories. And he could greet the dawn before the dawn enveloped the city in its glare and changed it into something Truly didn't want to see. The city had changed. The dawn revealed too much for him. The fog and the darkness of the early morning night were more of a comfort than the bright dawn.

The city slept. Truly took advantage of the sleeping city to alleviate the unease that had awakened him. He wanted to be sure to arrive at Fort Howe so that he could claim his city one more time before it faded in his memory.

"The Three Sisters Light must be doing double duty tonight," he whispered as the fog horn sounded off in the distance. The harbour, one of the best on the east coast of Canada, was also one of the most treacherous. The fog, combined with the shoals coming in and around Partridge Island, needed navigation by someone who had befriended them many times sailing in with a ship.

"Those old captains," thought Truly, "had to really know how to navigate and sail." There was no GPS for them to guide them safely into harbour and anchorage at the foot of Kings Street. He knew that for a fact. When his grandfather handed him his sextant he had used during his sailing days he told Truly many stories about being captain of those schooners. Those stories were not only part of Truly's soul, they were part of the city. He told those stories to anyone who would listen. He didn't want the city to be lost to forgotten memories.

Truly looked down King Street as he crossed over. "The few farmers left will come soon to stock their stalls in the Old Market." He whispered. No one was listening. Few cared. Truly cared.

Fort Howe overlooked the harbour and the city. It was the perfect vantage point for Truly to see the city. At this hour of the morning it was also a place where he could be alone with his memories. He could see what he remembered. He could see what he didn't want to see. He could see what he hoped might someday again be.

There was no one at Fort Howe. The lovers hanging out had left. The insomniacs had drunk their last cup of Tim Horton coffee and gone home. Those searching for something, be it a sexual encounter or some other satisfaction, had either given up or met their match and gone home. Truly was alone.

There was almost always a wind at Fort Howe. Even when the fog had rolled in, like this night, there was a hint of a wind off the Bay of Fundy. This was no different than any other night.

Truly stood alone. The fog had rolled in and enveloped the city like an heirloom quilt. It tamped down the noise of the fog horn off in the distance and the screeching railroad cars groaning as they were tugged and pulled by some late night engineer manning a diesel. "I wonder where they are going at this hour," thought Truly.

More importantly, Truly stood there breathing in the moist fog air. In his mind the fog was mingled with the blue smoke of bustling traffic rising from the Main Street below. He saw it through the fog.

Even at this early hour he could smell the activity. He could hear the noises of people awakening to a new day. He could see the buildings leaning to and fro along Main Street as they awaited the activity that kept them alive and viable.

As he saw the city through the thick fog that had enveloped it and blotted out the city as it had become, Truly heard the clock chime in the towner of Saint Luke's Anglican Church. With much of the old buildings along Main Street demolished, Saint Luke's had escaped the wrecking ball. It stood firmly anchored at the head of Main Street and the head of Douglas Avenue. Truly could see it. He had seen it so many times that he didn't need to have the fog lift to see it. The chimes comforted him that it was still there. The little congregation lingered on. There had been talk of demolishing that building. But the congregation resisted and persisted.

"Now what would they do with that property," thought Truly, "if that church were torn down? Build another hotel?" He shuddered at the thought only to realize that probably the property would be left vacant. "Another site to add to the decay of the North End," he whispered.

As sun began to rise and dawn arrived to wipe away the city Truly had seen floating in the midst of the fog, he was jolted back into reality. The city he once loved, still loved was no more. Just a remnant of the city's Victorian former self remained. Just enough to satisfy the tourists arriving on cruise ships, but not enough to satisfy those who had lived among and loved what had been.

The fog lifted. The city arose from its sleep. But while the city gave the appearance of not sleeping, it slept. And this sleep caused the city to be passed off and passed by.

Truly watched as the Harbour Station arena appeared in place of the magnificent railroad station. He watched as the Red Rose painted logo was covered by brick and nameless paint. He watched as the schooners and ships creating activity in the harbour sailed out to sea with the fog. It seemed there was no stopping the decline and destruction. There was nothing else he could do. But was there? He wept.

View of Saint John from Fort Howe
Summer 2017

WHAT DO YOU SEE?

"You know," said Truly, "I really don't know why the cruise ships stop here in Saint John. There's not that much to see." He commented to the tourist couple who had stopped him as he walked across Kings Square. "Where are you folks from?"

"We're from Barcelona," replied the woman. "The square is beautiful." The husband was more interested in the square than the conversation.

"The flowers are beautiful," said Truly. "They are always beautiful. In fact, they are the one thing around here that hasn't changed. Year after year they are the same. Flowers love the climate here. The impatiens, nasturtiums, geraniums and begonias just love this sea air. It never gets very warm here in summer. Our growing season is short, but the plants sure take advantage of it. Did you see the vegetables at Pete's Fruitque in the Old Market?"

"We did," replied the woman. Her husband motioned for the two of them to stand side by side so he could take a photograph.

"The Old Market," replied Truly, "used to be filled end to end with local produce. Pete's and a few others are the only ones who bring their bounty in now. At least it gives the visitors some idea of what it used to be like. It didn't take long for the Old Market to change into a tourist trap."

"How do you mean?" said the woman.

"Twenty years ago," he continued, "Back in the 1950's, the Old Market was still a bustling place for those shopping for their food. There was fish from the sea, dulce from Grand Manan, home baked goods and vegetables. Some of it is still there but you have to look beyond the tourist things to see it. People now buy Saint John sweatshirts instead of baskets of food."

"I bought one," said the husband. "He had taken the photo of Truly and the woman and turned his attention to the conversation. He was somewhat of a history buff.

"I bet," said Truly, "you think that you are photographing something very unique?"

Old City Market, Circa 1960

"Yes," he replied. "This square is unique. The flowers, the monuments, the bandstand; it is so beautiful."

"Thankfully," continued Truly, "the city has treasured the square as a gem. Not so much regards the rest of the city."

"Really?" said the man.

"Yes," continued Truly. "If you had come here before 1960, you would have seen a Victorian City. You would have thought you had stepped back in time, perhaps even that you were visiting London or the British Isles."

"We come from a place, Barcelona," she remarked, "that honours the past. Before anything is torn down and replaced by a new building, a serious study is done as to the value of the building. We have some of the most treasured buildings in the world. Have you ever heard of Gaudi?"

"The architect who designed such unusual building?" said Truly.

"Yes," she continued. "He designed the Sagrada Famila church that is still under construction. When it was first begun, people thought he had lost his mind designing such an unusual building. There is nothing like it in the world. Now people see his vision. Being inside is like standing in a forest of cement and colour. No one would dare think about destroying it. It's famous."

"I have seen photographs of it," replied Truly. "We used to have some buildings here that were treasures. Instead, in the name of progress, the city has seen fit to encourage businesses to move to the outskirts. People can drive there. The centre of the city has lost many of its buildings. This square is almost all that remains. I remember. I wonder what tourists think they are seeing."

"I'm seeing a beautiful square," replied the husband as he pointed his camera at one of the floral plantings. "This is beautiful."

"They are the same year after year," replied Truly. "It is amazing how they manage to make the square look the same year after year. It is the one thing the city hasn't touched. Did you notice the monuments?"

"Yes," replied the wife. "I bet there are some stories behind them."

"Indeed," said Truly. "That one over there," he pointed to the one with the skater relief. "That one is part of the city's unique history. Charles L. Gorman was our World Champion Speed skater. He competed in the 1924 and 1928 Winter Olympics. In the 1920's he was the speed skater in North America to beat. In the 1920's he was often referred to as the "Man with the Million Dollar Legs" and the "Human Dynamo" We used to have great ice on the rivers here but in recent years the winters haven't been as cold. My father, in fact, was born upcountry about 25 miles from here. He used to tell about folks driving cars across the river on the ice. Some folks even skated all the way to the city and back. It was a different time."

"Wow!" replied the husband. "Where's that monument?"

"Over there in front of what used to be the Admiral Beatty Hotel," said Truly, "That has even changed. It used to be the premier place to stay in the city but with motels and hotels springing up on the outskirts, people no longer stay there. It wasn't the place to be seen anymore. It's now a residence, kind of like senior housing. Walk around the square. You'll get a little of the flavor of what it used to be like here before the progressives decided new was better than old. Make sure you take a gander at that cathedral-like monument over there." He pointed to the pink monument."

Gorman Speed Skater Monument

"What's that?" asked the wife.

"That," said Truly, "is the story of a man who dove into the Bay of Fundy to save a man drowning. The man was saved but the man rescuing lost his life. It is quite a story. It must have been such a shock and moving experience to the people of the city long ago that they wanted to remember the valour of someone giving their life for another. There's a relief of the man swimming in the ocean and underneath is the inscription, *"Greater love has no man than this than to give his life for another."*

John Frederick Young Memorial – King's Square

The couple stood in silence. They realized that where they were standing was a place of history. "The Loyalists came here in 1784," said Truly. "They were loyal to the crown of England. They came from the south, New York area in particular. And here they brought their customs, dreams and desires. They built a nation and a city that reminded them of where they came from. Much of it is gone. The city has even removed the Loyalist Man image from city promotions."

"I'm sorry," replied the wife. "Thank you for telling us about the city. You obviously love it. You mourn the changes, I guess. And you want people to remember. Thank you for telling us about your city. I hope others on the ship have had an opportunity to meet someone such as you who tells them what they are seeing and not seeing."

"Thank you for listening," said Truly. "I love this city. It is my heart and home. I mourn it every day that passes and more is torn down. I do my best to encourage the city to restore rather than destroy. At least I have the memory of what the city looked like when I was a child and before the "fog" of progress rolled in and obliterated much that I loved.

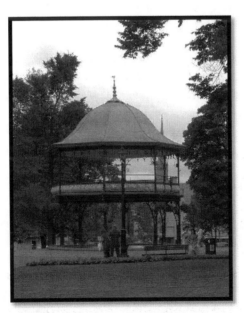

King Edward VII Memorial Bandstand

THE FOG

Fog! It is part of the architecture of Saint John. People who talk about fog in London or San Francisco haven't seen the Saint John fog. It is as sneaky as a cat stalking its prey and as warm as an heirloom quilt on a chilly summer night. Fog!

Truly Morrell loved the fog, tourists, not so much. The city people come to see disappears when the fog rolls in. For Truly it doesn't matter that the fog rolls in. The city is still there. The Victorian architecture he grew up with reappears in the fog. It is a comfort to know that one is able to descend into the memories of a city long gone and ignore the most recent announcement that this, that or other building is going to suffer the wrecking ball in the name of progress. Fog.

Cruise ships take a chance docking in the Saint John Harbour. They don't mention in their travel and excursion promotions that Saint John is no longer Saint John. All they care about is filling up their rooms. As long as Saint John gives some impression of what it once was, they will dock and people will take excursions.

Truly has spent many summer afternoons at Fort Howe watching the cruise ships come and go. If he lingered long enough sooner or later a taxi would arrive filled with cruise ship tourists. They'd get out, point their cameras and experience the brisk wind off the Bay of Fundy. Truly was always amused. It didn't matter if the weather was sunny or foggy, they always behaved the same.

Foggy days were particularly amusing. Tourists would pose for group photos with the fog as a backdrop. Sometimes Truly would engage them in conversation.

"Too bad you are here on a foggy day," he would say.

"Did you grow up here?" they would ask.

"Ayuh," he'd reply as he stroked his long white beard. "Over there in the North end. Metcalf Street. Went to Alexandra School."

They would nod and turn again to take more pictures of the fog.

"There's a city down there," he would quip with a twinkle in his eye. "Too bad you weren't here thirty years ago. There was a city there then but it was a different city. It was a city steeped in history, Victorian architecture, hustle and bustle. Long gone."

The tourists would pile back into the cab and head back to their cruise ship abode, all the time thinking that they had seen something and photographed something for the ages.

They had. Fog!

Truly would go back to his memories. On many summer afternoons he watched the fog roll in over the course of a half hour, as if something behind was pushing it to its destination. It began with a hint of what was to come. A mist would gather over the harbour. Slowly at first, Nova Scotia off in the distance would disappear. Occasionally the Digby Ferry coming in from crossing the bay would appear out of the descending mist.

Sailors beware was a common thought for those who lived by the sea. As if the shoals around Partridge Island and in the bay weren't enough, the fog added an extra ounce of challenge to make safe harbour. It was always a good idea to sail in before the fog totally obliterated the way and the tide descended to its lowest point.

Truly watched. The phenomenon fascinated him. He wondered what was the right conditions that caused the fog to appear over the water and envelope the city. Didn't matter. The fog was a friend, his friend.

The fog was thickest when it finally reached Fort Howe. The bright lit "SAINT JOHN" sign announcing arrival to cruise ships disappeared. Just a hint of its light below the edge of the Fort gave notice that I was there.

Then all sorts of living creatures could do their living under the cover of the fog.

Fog – View of Saint John from Fort Howe

FIRE!

Noll Huggard stood alongside Old Stone Church. The spire of St. Paul's Anglican Church in the Valley that had been poking up through the early morning fog, began to appear as if it was descending from heaven. Few moments before all he could see was the heavy fog lingering in the valley and the spire signaling that something was there to be seen.

Noll knew what was there. He had spent his life walking the streets of Saint John. The old city, in his mind, had never disappeared. It was etched in his memory forever. Whether the fog was there or not, Noll was there. It embraced what was left of what once was.

"The fog is lifting," he said to himself as he panned from side to side observing the city coming to life. It was mid-August. Tourists had been streaming into the city. "to see what's left," he whispered.

Noll had been born and raised upcountry. The locals know what you mean when you say, "upcountry." It is that beautiful area along the Belleisle Bay, Washademoak, Kennebecasis and the Saint John River. The rivers hug the shoreline and embrace the villages that were settled by Loyalists two hundred years before.

Hatfield Point, once known as Spragg Point, was Noll's hometown. It was the last stop for the riverboats coming from Saint John. He was born in the house next to the wharf where the boats stopped. On warm summer afternoons the event of the day was the arrival of the boat. He always anticipated who might be coming for a visit or what news might be brought from the big city. He lived upcountry but the city was not far away in distance, mind or heart.

He stood by Old Stone church. He had stopped there many times to watch the city emerge from the fog. This day was no different. His mind wandered. He thought about upcountry. He remembered the day the whole family had moved into the city. They rented a second floor cold water flat in the North End, Metcalf Street. He lived there still. The flat might have been cold water but it was elegantly Victorian with fireplaces in the parlors, dining room and kitchen. The woodwork was pristine. Hardwood floors welcomed woolen carpets. The curved stairway up from the sidewalk had a distinct odor of first generation linoleum. It was home just as Saint John had become his home.

Noll was so filled with the sights and memories of his upcountry and Saint John home that he could never leave. All his life he lived out the proverbial saying, "you can take the boy out of upcountry and Saint John, but you can't take upcountry and Saint John out of the boy." No matter how much urban renewal, destruction and new building happened, Noll remembered.

The fog that allowed Noll to sink into his memory of the way the city was, descended down the steeple of the Anglican Church in the Valley. Gradually, foot by foot, the 150 year old church emerged. Its steeple a beacon to all who lived in the area. Noll felt secure and safe knowing the church was still there. Saint John had not left him.

It was difficult to notice. In the brilliant sun that emerged, the church appeared to be safe for another day. No one had given any thought to closing it. The City Council had plied their urban renewal by tearing down Main Street buildings, the Train Station and everything else in their path around the valley. They left the Anglican Church in the Valley to live another year, decade or day.

While the City Council may not have had Valley church, as they called it, in their sights. Others had different plans. As Noll stood there he noticed that there seemed to be a haze hanging over the church. Initially he thought it was just the fog lingering on into the morning sun. "It'll dissipate soon," he thought. Just as that thought crossed his mind, the haze turned into smoke and smoke turned into fire alarms.

"The church is on fire," he spoke out loud. "The church is on fire." With the arrival of fire fighters and ladder trucks, Noll's plans for the day changed. He found himself transfixed on the activity across the valley. He lost all sense of time. All he could think of was the history of that church. He feared it might be meeting its demise.

The firefighters clambered all over the building. In no time they had water trained on the roof. A crowd of onlookers gathered nearby. The Rev. Cannon Jacob Kierstead of Old Stone Church came out. "Dear God in heaven," he said to Noll. "How long has this been going on?"

"Just started, Father," he said. "I was watching the fog lift when I noticed a haze hanging over the building. In no time flames broke out."

"And," said the Father, "it's an old wooden building. Dear God in heaven," he repeated. This time it was a prayer more than an exclamation over the situation. "Dear God in heaven."

"They might save it," said Noll. "They got here right away. The water has been pouring down on the roof. I hope they save it."

"Indeed," said Father Keirstead. "Our churches have enough on their plate without fire too. It will either be a blessing in disguise or the end of them."

"You mean?" asked Noll.

"I mean," continued Father, "that sometimes a curse can be a blessing. Sometimes a fire can be an opportunity. It all depends upon how the congregation reacts and responds to this. They could see it as a chance to start new or an excuse to wallow and mourn."

Just then they heard a bang as the fire ripped through the roof. "Look," said Noll as he pointed. "Look! It is going up in the steeple."

"Dear God in heaven," said Father Keirstead. "Dear God in heaven. It is done."

"The steeple is like a chimney," whispered Noll. He didn't let Father see that he was crying. So many of the parts of the city that he dearly loved had disappeared. Now, it appeared, another was done.

The fire ripped up the steeple in nothing flat. What took two hours to burn up until then, took only minutes for the flames to race up the steeple and lick at the sky. It was a beautiful sight in its own way but a desperate one.

"She's gone," said Father Keirstead. "She's gone. The Church in the Valley is gone. They might as well let her burn to the ground now. The steeple's gone. The roof fell in. There's nothing more to do. The fire just enabled more urban renewal and tearing down of the history of our city."

Noll wept.

Fire of St. Paul's Church, Summer 1981

IN THE ASHES

Saint John was no stranger to fire. It had experienced fire before, the most famous being the Great Fire of 1877. It destroyed two fifths of the city. Fires were a common occurrence in the 19th century. Building codes were non-existent. Firefighters were volunteer. Equipment was horse driven and primitive. The most useful tool was a leather bucket and a hat.

After the Great Fire of 1877, the city rebuilt itself in the style of the day. Much of that style was out of necessity. People needed places to live and quickly. The houses in the South End took on the shape of two or three story box structures that belied their opulence that lived on the inside. Because of their plain appearance they were seen as necessary housing rather than architectural treasures to be preserved. So when the time and money was right, some of the houses were replaced with fashionable brick and mortar Victorian homes. Eventually those homes, in the eyes of city officials and residents became, obsolete. Local residents often cease to see the beauty of the city, the landscape or architecture. Fires were seen as an opportunity to deal with a blight that had descended upon the city over years of neglect, fog and apathy.

What was once treasured as "home" became something to be ignored or razed. It is easy to become blind to ones surroundings.

This was somewhat the situation with St. Paul's Anglican Church in the Valley. The building was being taken for granted. It was the beloved home of a worshiping congregation while at the same time a place that had become so familiar that cracks in the infrastructure were not seen. All wooden buildings need constant maintenance and when that is differed a building reaches a point of no return. That wasn't quite the situation of Valley church but it was at a point when restoration was needed if the congregation was to observe its 150th anniversary.

A fund raising had been undertaken to prop up the beloved old building with new paint, roofing and grace. Workmen had been storming over the exterior for days. Old paint was removed. New paint was being applied. Scaffolding surrounded the steeple which was being prepared for restoration. The congregation was abuzz with excitement.

Then one early morning as the fog that had offered opportunity lifted, fire broke out. Some blamed the workmen. Some thought they had seen blow torches being used to remove paint. Others just chalked it up to chance. Some even said that God had intervened to teach a lesson to the congregation and to "light" a fire of the Holy Spirit under them.

Once the embers had cooled to ashes, the job of salvage, resurrection and investigation began. There wasn't much to salvage. A few things necessary for Anglican worship had survived. The fire licked around the altar but did not destroy it. Members of the congregation rescued the cross, candlesticks and communion ware. The pews were buried under the collapsed roof. A hymnbook and prayer book here and there was saved. The pipe organ had melted into a mass of tin and lead never to play a note again.

Truly Morrell had heard whispers around the city that the fire may have been set. At Old Stone Church the congregation prayed for their neighbor church and offered them a place for worship. Before night descended and the city was once again sleeping under its blanket of fog, arrangements had been made for the homeless congregation.

Only one issued remained. Where was the good Rev. Gwyn Davies? He was much beloved and respected. But he was nowhere to be found. This was most unusual. Father Gwyn was always available. The fact the fire occurred in his own parish made it stranger that he had not appeared. He was always the first one in the trenches to come to the aid of others. Now he needed others to come to his aid. The congregation was left to fend for itself while the fire marshal sifted through the ashes.

The embers cooled. Rumours heated up.

RUMOURS

Truly Morrell was no stranger to rumours. His long white beard attracted the attention of friends, foe and tourists. He was always willing to chat. And he was always up for a conversation about the old city as it once was and the city as it had become. He knew many people in the city. He knew the truth tellers. He knew the naysayers. He knew those out for a quick buck. He knew. He could spot them from a mile away. And sometimes that was exactly where he chose to be, a mile away from many.

"That's one less building they have to worry about," Truly commented to Annalee Gaudet. "I figured someday they would get around to razing that neighbourhood around Valley Church. Now they have a good excuse. I bet they'll still have a fight on their hands from the congregation. They might want to try to rebuild."

Annalee was on her lunch hour from the New Brunswick Museum. She had walked up King Street. It was a beautiful summer day. Many people had shucked their fog-resistant clothing for shorts and sandals.

"They sure look funny," she commented.

"What?" said Truly. His mind was on the fire. In a way he was grieving once again for the old city he once knew. Truly knew how to grieve. He had just lost his wife of many years. Any loss reminded him of that great loss.

"They look funny wearing shorts, t-shirts and sandals." She repeated. "When I was a child we would come into the city and I never saw anyone dressed like that. I guess the weather has changed a bit."

"Couldn't tell by me," replied Truly. He stroked his beard and looked at the ground as if to find some solace from the sadness he was experiencing. "I don't know what is coming of us," he said.

"Us?" she asked.

Annalee was always full of questions. She was the archivist for the museum. It was easy to spot her. Archivists have that air about them. Though only in her early 30's, she dressed the archivist part. Her hair was pulled back tight and wound into a bun. Her black suit, shoes and white shirt were job appropriate and drew one's attention to the flash of red lipstick. It was the only colour she wore, if you don't consider black and white colours. She could be spotted from a mile away. Strangers would whisper, "Here comes a funeral director, or librarian, or…"

She reached for her black cane. The cane was necessary to steady herself. An old injury had made her a little wobbly and wobbly on the old city streets doesn't bode well. It makes it easier to reinjure whatever was injured in the first place.

As she stood, Truly repeated himself. "That's one less building," he said with a twinge of sadness.

"How do you mean?" said Annalee.

"The Church in the Valley," he replied. "They've had their eye on that part of town for some time. Get that building out of the way and then they have an excuse to get rid of some of the other old houses. They don't respect what is. All they can think about is what can be."

"They?" she said.

"The powers that be," he replied. "We vote them into office. They think they have gotten a free ticket to do whatever they want. They seem themselves a progressive. I call them deconstructionists. All they want to do is tear down. Much of the time they don't even have a plan of what they are going to do once history is torn down."

"I see," said Annalee in her most official archivist tone. "I see. People have the same attitude about their own history. Occasionally we get donations at the archivers relating to Loyalists, Irish, or city history. Too often that history remains stashed in attics somewhere and ending up lost to fires or the garbage heap." She turned to leave.

"Annalee," said Truly, "Will you stay in touch with me if you hear news of more plans to tear down parts of the city? I want to know. I'm not sure what I will do. I'll do something."

"Truly," she replied. "I am always happy to chat with you. You are my best supporter. You can be my best source for things needing to be archived. Have a lovely afternoon in the square," she said as she turned to head down King Street to the Museum.

"If you set any fires," she whispered in passing, "make sure it's one of those awful modern utilitarian buildings." She joked.

He knew she wasn't serious but the thought had crossed his mind. He would never do that. He would make it known that those replacement buildings didn't hold a candle in historical value to the ones that were torn down.

"Never," he whispered back. "Never."

THE CLERGY

In many ways the clergy of Saint John had become historical themselves. There was a time when everyone darkened the doors of the city churches. Times had changed. The city churches had become redundant. Clergy had been relegated to weddings, funerals and crisis. The Valley Church fire gave the clergy a reason to exist.

The Rev Canon Caleb Hatfield of St. Luke's Anglican shuddered to think what would happen if his church caught fire. His congregation may have dwindled down to a faithful few but the church and all it stood for remained a beacon of hope for the North End. It stayed cemented to its corner lot at the head of Douglas Avenue and Main Street.

Douglas Avenue held on to its 19th century glory. Most of the Victorian houses with their gingerbread adornment and widow's walks remained vigilant. They were treasured for their history. They kept up the appearance that Douglas Avenue was one of THE places to live in the city. It was, if one could afford the upkeep. The condition of the homes revealed who could and who could not.

Main Street was a different matter. Main Street Baptist, an imposing brick structure, was on its last legs. Someone had painted graffiti around its doors. The businesses that had lined that end of Main Street down into the North End and around into Indiantown were mostly gone. Dykeman Hardware around the corner held fast. The rest of the businesses that marched along both sides of Main Street from Saint Luke's over to King Street were gone. Marigolds in the summer made do. They were planted each summer to take away the impression that nothing was happening. They were a distraction from what once was. Trollies, buses, and pedestrians no longer strolled along making their way over town to the Old Market or just to sit in one of the city's squares and watch people go by.

Lord Beaverbrook Arena on one side had been built after the razing of the historical buildings as an attempt to bring about urban renewal. It failed. Across the way from the rink stands a single 19th century building that once housed a bank. It was a reminder of when this part of the town was a bustle of activity.

Truly Morrell sometimes walked this stretch of Main Street. He would grieve the loss of a part of the city he loved. As he walked he would remember the businesses, the residents and the times he would encounter an old friend. He always stopped to reminisce. Reminiscences always turned into talk about how to save what was left of the city. [3]

Main Street Circa 1940's
From "The Lost Blog"

Occasionally Truly ran into Noll Huggard. Noll spent much of his days walking the city. He never had much to say. An occasional 'ayah' would suffice. If he did engage in conversation with Truly or a stranger it usually involved some mindless tittle he had observed. It was difficult to know just what was on Noll's mind. He always seemed to be on retreat into another world. His family didn't even know.

Truly and Noll were out walking Main Street two days after the Valley Church fire. Noll walked along with his head down and hands behind his back. Thinking. Truly was alert for any sign of what might happen next. The Rev. Canon Caleb Hatfield was also out. He often walked Main Street. It felt as if his walks gave him a purpose to his mission.

"Morning, Reverend," said Truly, as they met at the corner of Magazine and Main. "How's your day going?"

"Sad today," said The Reverend. "Sad. I worry about this city and what it is coming to. We lost another treasure in a fire. Didn't we?"

---

[3] A list of businesses that existed in the North End and other parts of the city is provided in the appendix.

"Yes we did," said Truly. "I watched it go down from the lot next to Old Stone Church. I cried. I don't know what we can do. Our city is disappearing right before our eyes." He looked toward Saint Luke's. "Your church," he hesitated, "I mean, 'our' church, Saint Luke's is one of the must unsung and undiscovered treasures in our city. Tourists come and have no idea what they are missing by not seeing inside."

"You are right," said the Reverend. "It is one of the most beautiful churches in the city. And the few faithful left are some of the most beautiful in the city. They love that church. Some of them have family history that goes way back to when the church was built. Their ancestors were shipbuilders, sailors and captains. They knew how to build ships. And they knew how to build churches."

"Indeed," said Truly. "Hello Noll," said Truly. The Reverend and Truly had strolled on down Main a bit. Noll had been sitting on a bench. He had overheard some of the conversation and, in his usual mute way, he nodded agreement. At least they took his acknowledgement of their passing as agreement.

"Saint Luke's had a fire in the 1800's," said the Reverend. "The congregation rebuilt bigger and more beautiful. A fire is nothing to celebrate but sometimes a fire is the only way a congregation finds its faith and purpose. I don't mean to say we should burn down every church so it can rise from the ashes like the Pheonix, but..."

"Yes," said Truly. "Sometimes there is a blessing mingled with a curse. I don't know about Valley Church. They've been through a lot. The city has coveted that property for decades. It might have been just a matter of time before one of those urban renewal people came along and managed to get them to move." He paused. "Or take over their property by imminent domain."

The Reverend walked along in silence thinking about what Truly had just said.

"I am trying to keep the fires burning in the hearts of my people. Sometimes the building is more important than the fire of faith." He commented. "But they are good people. They love their building. They love their God. They love this city. Maybe their seeing what has happened to Valley Church will light a fire under them."

"Have you been in contact with The Rev. Gwyn Davies?" asked Truly.

"No." replied the Reverend. "In fact I don't think they have been able to locate him. I find it rather odd that he wasn't at the fire supporting his congregation as they watched the church burn. He has been a good and faithful servant. I hope they find him soon."

"In the ashes?" asked Truly.

"Maybe," replied the Reverend, "But I hope not. I hope he's just off somewhere in shock."

"Old Stone Church," continued Truly, "has offered the Valley Church congregation the use of their building while they decide what to do next."

"I had heard that," said the Reverend. "It is the kindest thing that anybody could do for them. People are good. They often come to the rescue of others in distress. It will relieve the immediate burden off their shoulders as they figure out their path forward."

Their conversation had walked the length of Main and the two of them stood across from Saint Luke's. "I'm not sure," said Truly, "what is more out of place here. Saint Luke's or McDonalds across the street? McDonalds surely doesn't add much to the historical atmosphere of this gateway to the North End. It used to be called Portland, you know."

"Yes I do," replied the Reverend. "And when they finally had all those Main Street buildings razed and valuable property to sell, the city encouraged McDonalds to build. As if that would bring about urban renewal. All it has brought is more traffic to its drive-up, litter and decay. Thankfully St. Luke's is an imposing structure that can "lord" it over McDonalds and all those who pass by. St. Luke's is hard to ignore. Don't you think?"

"I do," replied Truly. "And I hope the city ignores any idea of every tearing it down.

They crossed the street. "I'll be going in now," said the Reverend. "Would you like to come in and sit a spell?"

"My pleasure and delight," said Truly, "I'm always up for a good moment of silence in such a beautiful place before I head back over town." The Reverend unlocked the door. They entered in and were immediately enveloped in the silence of spiritual beauty. They stood. The city as it had become disappeared from their minds and hearts as what once was came back to life.

"I'll be going now," said the Reverend as he headed toward the Vestry. "Sunday is soon upon us and I must offer some words of hope and comfort in the wake of the fire. You stay as long as you wish. I'll also work at gathering the clergy together. We'll not let this fire go down as just another loss. Have a blessed quiet time here and a lovely rest of your day," he said as he waved from the door to the vestry.

"Yes, Father," whispered Truly. "I truly will." He loved to use his name occasionally to emphasize his own attentiveness to the moment.

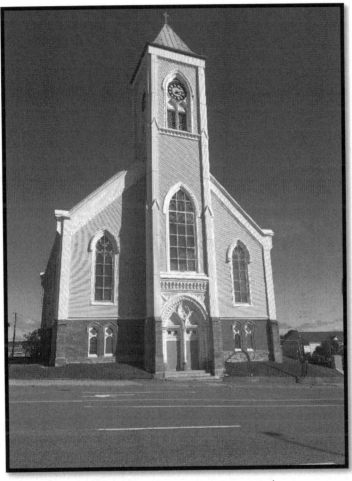

St. Luke's Anglican Church [4]

---

[4] Photograph taken September 2017 by Cathy Szelistowski of Tampa, Florida while visiting Saint John. She also attended Sunday worship.

THE GATHERING

"So what are we going to do?" said Reverend Canon Caleb Hatfield as he called the meeting to order.

"That's the question of the century," said Rev. Jacob Wentworth. "We ask that question all the time at Old Stone Church. So far the answers have been few and far between. "Thoughts and prayers," are their solutions to problems. I keep saying 'fine and good' but what hands and feet are you going to put to your 'thoughts and prayers' that might make a difference. We need to have more than just 'thoughts and prayers.' Thoughts and prayers are only as good as we are willing to participate in them."

"Agreed," said Hatfield. "We all know that. But we've had that discussion one too many times. Maybe it is time for the clergy of this town to move from thoughts, prayers, and redundancy to walking the talk? What do you think?"

Rev. Hatfield was also a shaker in the community. He and Rev. Wentworth met weekly at Reggie's for breakfast. Reggie's had become the local gathering spot for anyone with any kind of clout in the city. It was just a few steps from the Old City Market and across the street from Brunswick Square. When the venerable Manchester, Robertson and Allison department store went out of business and was replaced by the towering Brunswick Hotel and shopping mall, several of the clergy had met. They knew then that King Street's ambiance would be changed forever. It was. Replacing an historic department store that required you to walk uphill to shop with a non-descript, architecturally bland building achieved its purpose. Less ambiance, less of an incline on King Street and less business in centre city.

"Agreed," said Wentworth. "Coffee?" he asked as he went to get some.

"Yes," replied Hatfield. "And while you're at it, order me some oatmeal, brown sugar and heavy cream. You've got to have heavy cream to make oatmeal good."

"Keep that up," said Rev. Hatfield, "and we'll be burying you with the ashes of Church in the Valley. Probably somewhere up country with the rest of your ancestors."

"Bayview Cemetery, Hatfield Point, Kings County," replied Hatfield. "And by the way, do we have to keep up this Hatfield and

Wentworth routine when it's just the two of us? I'm Cal to you. You're Jake to me. Okay?"

"Ayah," said Wentworth as he left to get the coffee and place the order. "But don't say it too loud when we're in uniform. We must keep up appearances."

Wentworth placed the order at the high top counter in front of the cooks. He returned with the coffee, silverware and napkins. "Sure a nice thing Reggie's father did for him. Not every parent would be so creative as to open a breakfast and lunch restaurant named after their son AND make the son the manager." Reggie was sitting two tables over. From there he greeted every person. Occasionally he would clear a table or initiate a conversation.

"Food's up!" yelled Maude from behind the high top counter. "Food's up Reverend!" she repeated.

"I wish she would leave off "Reverend," said Hatfield. "I know we stand out like a sore thumb hitchhiking for a ride. Let's ditch the uniform when we know we are going to meet here. Okay?"

"You got it, Cal," said Wentworth as he got up to retrieve the oatmeal, bacon, eggs and home fries. Don't forget, I'm Jake."

It didn't take Cal long to dive into the food. He always did love breakfast.

"Hey, hey," said Jake, "aren't young going to say grace? We're on display, you know. People are watching."

"Okay, okay," said Cal. "I'll say it," he whispered.

"Gracious giver of all good,
Thee with thank for rest and food,
Grant that all we do or say
In thy service be this day."

"Where'd you come up with that?" said Jake.

"John Wesley," said Cal. "He was Anglican you know. Only thing is, Good and food don't rhyme. I always want to say 'fud.' Short 'u." He laughed.

"You're a funny guy," said Jake. "That's why I like you so much. It's also why your congregation loves you. And it's why we make such a good team in getting the clergy together to bring about change, or should I say, bring about saving the old city from itself destruction. While the city sleeps and sinks under its own weight, we will do our best. If the population isn't going to rise to the occasion, we will."

"So what's the plan," said Cal as he took a big spoonful of his heavy creamed oatmeal.

"I say," replied Jake, "we get the clergy together as a first step. We present the issue."

"Which is?" said Cal.

"Where is Rev. Gwyn Davies? For one thing. His church is in ashes and he is nowhere to be found."

"Maybe in the ashes," said Cal.

"That's to be discovered," said Jake. "We can have thoughts and prayers for him. On a more pressing issue we need to discuss how to save this city's Victorian ambiance and charm while the progressives and urban renewal group try to save it by destruction and new building. They think, you know, that getting rid of the old, historic parts of the city will stop the mad dash of businesses to the suburb. They can't see that it is the Victorian charm and history that draws people to the Centre city. We need to save them from themselves. Let's make a list of who to invite."

"Okay," said Cal. "I think we need to contact each one of these face to face to explain the urgency. An opening with them could be, 'how can we help Valley Church now that it is no more? Once we get them talking about that, subtly shift the conversation to how the loss of Valley Church is just one example of how we are losing the history of Saint John. Here's who I think ought to be invited. I'll contact these: Rev Gwyn Davies of Valley Church, if I can find him now that his church is in ashes. Sister Honora Collins of Sisters of Charity of the Immaculate Conception and the Rev. Monsignor William Sweeney of the Cathedral of the Immaculate Conception. He's from County Killenney, you know. He ought to understand the importance of preserving history. He can also speak to the Irish in Saint John."

"Great," said Jake. "And how about contacting Rabbi Zeke Rosenfeld of Beth Torah Congregation. He knows just how to approach the authorities and make change happen. Did you know that when he was a young man he helped desegregate Tuscaloosa, Alabama? He grew up in Montreal and knows just what it is to live with people who judge, separate and resist change. He's also respected in the city. He is much beloved."

"Ask him," said Cal, "if he would be part of a trio, you, me and Zeke, to coordinate preserving Saint John while encouraging Saint John to prosper.

"I'll do it," said Jake, we'll be a powerhouse to be reckoned with. And I'll ask Rev. John Bruce of Church of Saint Andrew and Saint David on Germain Street. He already knows what it is to deal with historic buildings. And there's also Elder Laurence Colwell of Germain Street Baptist. They've been struggling for years. Ever since Victoria Street Baptist in the North end folded and was torn down, Colwell has struggled with the tension between history and mission. He grew up on Victoria Street, you know. He'll identify with what we are trying to accomplish."

"And don't forget," said Cal, 'to contact Rev. Stuart Somerville over at Centenary Church. They've got that 1800 seat Gothic revival church and a dwindling congregation. I am sure that he is constantly fretting over how they can continue while avoiding the deterioration of that magnificent building."

"Done!" said Jake as he sopped up the last of his eggs with the toast. "Done! Let's plan to meet here again in a week to report in. And just to cover our bases, let's schedule a meeting of the entire group for two weeks from today. Late August is a good time to get them going before they all get into the swing of homecomings, Thanksgiving and Christmas. And if you can think of any other person we might invite, ask them. I can think of Truly Morrell and Noll Huggard off the top of my head."

"Truly, definitely," said Cal. "As for Noll, he knows the city backwards and forwards. I'm sure he can walk it in his sleep. I'm not so sure about his being helpful. Pretty quiet fellow, you know."

"But," said Jake, "when he does speak or offer an opinion it is reasoned and to be listened to."

"It's a deal," said Cal. "Gotta go. I'm always fanning the proverbial flames at St. Luke's. I "work the crowd" to keep them fired up. I don't want them to think that they are a part of Saint John that is disappearing. Have a great day," he said, as he grabbed his scarf and stepped out into the mid-morning fog that had begun to lift.

Saint John weather was always deceptive. Fog could roll in without any warning. Or the sun could shine bright and hot in late August. Cal nodded at the people on the street as he briskly walked toward Main Street. It was how he got his exercise and reminded himself of what once was along that major artery from Centre city to the north end. He loved seeing Saint Luke's from the vantage point of Main. It reminded him of its prominent place in the history of the city. And he was determined to make sure St. Luke's kept its perch on the hill overlooking the harbour as well as its influence over the people.

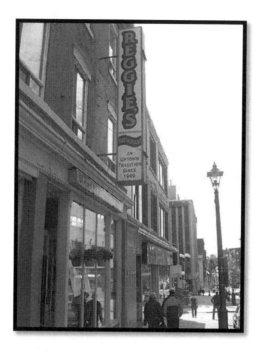

Reggie's Restaurant[5]

[5] Photographs in public domain.

SIFTING THROUGH

The RCMP had a constant presence around the remains of the Anglican Church in the Valley. They were there to make sure the police lines were maintained as much as to protect what might remain of anything worth salvaging. They also were there just in case anyone had died in the fire. Rev. Gwyn Davies, for instance. It had been a week since the fire and he was still nowhere to be found.

The Vestry had met to discuss what to do next as much as to mourn their loss. Abner Short, the senior warden, had opened the meeting with prayer but it shortly, no pun intended, turned into a melee of grief and confusion. Fire Marshall Belyea had been invited to the first meeting after the fire. He was there as much to report the extent of their loss as to inventory what might be the cause of the fire. And he was most interested in the behavior of those present. The brick Christ Fellowship Hall adjacent to the skeletal remains of the church had survived. The meeting was held there.

Rumours had been circulating through the city as fast as the fire in the church's steeple. The rumours had been smoldering for days as soon as the fire was out. Not much was gained. All the rumour mongering did was to make the congregation less united and more susceptible to bringing itself down into the left over ashes. The angry, sad and confused comments at the meeting made it clear that no one could see a clear path forward. Many just wanted to go backwards into the history of their minds, hearts and memories of what once was.

"Alright," said Abner, "let us take some time in silence to listen to our hearts before we listen to each other."

"We've had enough time for silence," yelled a woman from the back of the room. "I want to get over there and see what is left of the Altar Guild supplies. Those RCMP won't let us cross the line."

"I want to find the hymnbooks that I donated in memory of my parents," yelled a man.

Before Abner could say another word the room erupted in chaos. Fire Marshall Belyea watched with great interest. "Who really cares about their church," he thought. "Who might be the arsonist, if there is one? Who is really interested in his job of sifting through the ashes?"

Maude Short, Abner's wife, walked to the front of the room and raised her hand in a Boy Scout quiet salute. She stood there surveying the faces of the congregation that she had been a part of since childhood. She watched as Nellie Somerville sat quietly. Tears streamed down her face. Gordon Spragg sat with his arms folded in defiance. He didn't really want to be there. He figured there was no use holding the meeting at all. "The church is gone," he told his wife Elisabeth. "It's gone. Let's forget it and move on." In some ways she agreed with Gordon. But she felt the old memories of what was tug at her heart strings.

"What are we going to do?" she said to Gordon. "Let the congregation disperse like the Jews in exile? This city needs us. They don't need more ashes spread around on the old city streets to allow cars to drive around between what once was and what is now."

"What do you mean by that?" he said.

"I mean," she continued, "the city has torn down too many of our old historic buildings already. Our church may be gone but we are still here. We can stay together and be the spark that lights a new fire."

"That's just what we don't need," said Gordon. "We don't need another fire."

"I mean," she said, "we can be the people who promote restoration, preservation and renewal. Our congregation now needs renewal. Our city needs someone to speak up for its past, its present condition and the future."

Maude Short was still standing up front with her Boy Scout quiet salute. One by one, members noticed her. She was a familiar influence in their congregation. When she stood to speak, or in this case, to not speak, they eventually listened. The room quieted.

"My brothers and sisters," said Maude, "we have worshiped together for many years in a beautiful building. The Church in the Valley has stood as a beacon of peace, love and hope for our city. It has graced the scenery of our neighbourhood for almost 150 years. Have we learned nothing in all those years? You all know the church is not a building. It isn't even a steeple, although steeples in Saint John proclaim to the world that we are here. Unfortunately we have lived as if those steeples no longer exist. We have become accustomed to their presence. Just like someone who builds their house on a hillside with a fantastic view. After some years, the view disappears. The homeowner doesn't notice the view any more. That has happened to us. Our church is gone. Suddenly we notice. The city notices. And the city is looking to us to do something.

This might be the opportunity we have been looking for to have a fire lit under us. Maybe it is our turn to step up, speak up and build up what is left of our beautiful Victorian city and history. How many here are Loyalist descendants?" she asked, as she perused the gathering. About two thirds of the people gathered raised their hands.

"Exactly," she continued. "We are proud of our ancestors. They must be proud of us by how we deal with the loss of our church. We must make them proud by preserving what is left of our city. We must build out of the ashes a city that honors our past and looks to the future." She sat down.

Abner leaned over, kissed his wife and whispered, "Where did that come from? I didn't know you had that in you." He turned to address the gathering. Maude had so shamed and inspired the gathering that they sat in stunned silence.

"Now," said Abner, "We have a mission to do. We can yell all we want about rebuilding, tearing down, disbanding or uniting with a congregation. Yelling gets us nowhere. Silence might. Heartfelt discussion and caring will. And while we are gathering our hearts, minds and love, Old Stone Church has offered their sanctuary as a place to worship. We can join with them and hold our own services there. The way will become clear. Agreed?"

Abner could see a movement of the gathering to agreement or at least to a point whereby they would listen.

"Now," he continued, "The first order, and really the only order tonight, is to listen to the report of Fire Marshall Belyea. You will have a chance to ask questions when he is finished. Then we will plan for another meeting within a week. We will get our ducks in order. Rockwood Park ducks come running when people show up with bread? It doesn't matter how visible the signs are to "Do not feed the ducks," people still feed the ducks and the ducks come in mass for the tossed out bread. We must be like those ducks. We must be like those who ignore the "do not feed the ducks" sign. When the Spirit calls, we must come. When God speaks, we must come together. When an opportunity is given to us, such as this fire, to feed the city with food so badly needed before our history disappears, we must respond. Let us spend time listening. Fire Marshall Belyea, the floor is yours."

SIFTING THE ASHES

Belyea had put on his dress uniform for the evening. As he listened to the gathering he thought that his visit might have been more effective if he had come covered in ashes in his Fire Marshall Inspector duds. But he realized that looking official might have more effect on those gathered to hear what he had to say.

"First I want to say," He began, "how sorry I am that you have lost your church. I have visited your beautiful church many times. I was always awed by the beautiful wood construction, stained glass windows and altar. They don't build churches like that anymore. They are either too costly or modernism wins over."

Belyea set a large canvas satchel on the table. Whispers filtered through the room as if ashes from the fire were descending.

"I wonder what he's got there," whispered Maude Short to her husband Abner.

"Cremains," he replied.

"Don't be funny," she said. "He wouldn't bring cremains. Furthermore, who would they be? Father Gwyn?"

"Silly," said Abner. "Probably show and tell. Maybe he's going to give us a lesson in sifting through ashes after a fire. First thing is to wait till the ashes go stone cold. Dead."

The rest in the room bobbed their heads here in there in order to get a better look at what Belyea had brought. Truly Morrell had slipped into the back of the room. He was standing in the shadows toward the back. Truly often attended meetings. His interest intensified whenever there was talk about Saint John history and historical buildings. Noll Huggard was also there. He had slipped in the side door. He just happened to be out on one of his walkabouts when he saw people gathering. He might not have much to say but he was curious. No one ever knew what he was thinking until after having observed the city, he might make a comment or two.

Fire Marshall Belyea began. "When one goes through a fire scene," he said, "one is looking for what can be saved, remains of a past life, memories that might be gone forever. We are also looking for what caused the fire. Sometimes we find who caused the fire. Sometimes we find remains."

A shudder went through the crowd. "He's not going to tell us he found Father Gwyn, is he?" whispered Elisabeth Spragg to her husband, Gordon. Tears began to stream down her face again.

"Get over it," said Gordon. "If he did, then we know. If not, then we don't know where he is. Besides, there's nothing you can do about it. Stop your whimpering."

Elisabeth dabbed at her tears with an old lady tatted hankie that her mother Fanny had made for her years before. Elisabeth kept it in her purse as a reminder of her mum. People didn't know that she really kept it in her purse because she felt guilty about the way she had treated her mother before she died. Each dab of the tears with the hankie brought more tears, tears that were as much for her mother as for the lost church.

Belyea continued. "I can report that we are still sifting through the ashes. No one died in the fire."

Those words brought a sigh of relief from the gathering. Truly listened carefully. "That's a relief," he thought, "but that still leaves the mystery of where Rev. Gwyn has disappeared to."

"You all must be thinking," said Belyea, 'Where is Rev. Davies?' I don't have an answer to that question. At least I can tell you that he is not in the ashes of the church. We found no remains of any living creature beyond a half burned rat or mouse. No one died in the fire."

"Then what's the fire all about?" said Gordon as he jumped up and waved his finger in the air.

"I see you have one of those fingers too," replied Belyea. "See mine? Please sit down so that I may continue."

A rumble went through the crowd as if it were the beginnings of a wave at a soccer game. They were anxious to see if the Fire Marshall would score or not regarding the fire. Not the least of their interest was the cause of the fire. Would their insurance cover the loss?

Gordon sat down and placed his "finger" in his pocket to alleviate any chance of his doing a repeat of his crowd inciting behavior.

"No one died in the fire," repeated Belyea. "We are always thankful for that. What did die is one of our most beautiful and historic churches in the city. The Anglican Church in the Valley is no more. When the inspection is done, you will have thirty days to tear the rest down and clear the site. What you do after that is your business."

"Get on with it," whispered Gordon under his breath just loud enough for his wife to hear. She jabbed him in the side and grabbed his arm with the stowed finger just in case he had any more ideas.

Belyea opened the top of his canvas satchel. He reached in but didn't immediately pull out anything. "As I said," he continued, "we are most interested in where the fire started and if it is a crime scene. Sometimes the cause of a fire is useful to an insurance company. They don't want to be paying claims if arson or negligence caused the fire."

Belyea paused to find what he was searching for in the satchel. He pulled out a short piece of wood that only looked like charcoal. "This" he said, "as he held it up is part of the cross beam that was over the altar. I brought this to show you because this was probably nearest where the fire started. But I also bring it to you to tell you something very mysterious."

Placing the burned crossbeam on the table, he continued. "One of the most mysterious things about the fire is that your altar survived. Not only did your altar survive, the altar with its cloth hangings survived! In addition to that, your communion ware and the reserved sacrament of your Lord made it through the fire unscathed."

Belyea reached into the satchel and pulled out a chalice that had looked like the Altar Guild had just polished it. The gathering gasped. "And," he continued, "I found this in a locked niche that had fallen from the wall and was lying on the floor."

"The Tabernacle," whispered Abner. "The Tabernacle survived the fire."

"Inside the locked niche," said Belyea.

Abner interrupted him. "Sir," he said, "That's the Tabernacle where the consecrated hosts are stored."

"Inside the Tabernacle," Belyea corrected himself, "we found this." He reached into the bag and pulled out a silver lidded box and sat it down next to the chalice.

"May I see?" asked Abner Short as he approached the table.

"Of course," replied Belyea.

Abner gingerly took the box in his hands. It was familiar to him. The days he served as a Verger it was his task to make sure the paten had enough wafers on it. When the mass ended he would place the consecrated hosts in the box and store it in the Tabernacle. He always felt honored when he served.

Tears began to stream down Abner's face. He held the box. The others watched. They knew. He removed the lid of the box. Inside he found pristine consecrated communion hosts. He looked up. Through the tears he whispered, "Come. Come as you are. Come as we are."

One by one the remnant of Anglican Church in the Valley moved forward and received into their hands the Body of Christ. "Come," whispered Abner. "Come."

As Abner looked into the eyes of his brothers and sisters, he knew. "We are not alone," he began to whisper to each who came forward. "We are not alone. Jesus is with us. Our beloved Valley Church is alive. Jesus is with us."

Truly watched the scene unfold from his darkened vantage point at the back of the room. He watched until he could watch no longer. He moved forward. He could hardly be invisible with his long white beard. Being seen no longer mattered. What mattered was that he be a part of the Valley Church, and every church. That he be in with whomever understand it is their mission to rebuilt, restore and reignite the fire that burned in the hearts of all those who loved Saint John and loves it still.

After all had received the resurrected communion hosts Abner said, "Marshall Belyea, I hope you will forgive us for closing the meeting now. I know you have more to say to us. Could you come and be with us next week as we digest what has just happened in our midst. The Spirit has moved. We need to give the Spirit time to continue to move in our hearts and city."

Marshall Belyea knew. He saw what his findings had done for the people. He did have more to share but it could wait for another time. "It is my pleasure," he said, "to meet with you again."

Abner always had a small Book of Common Prayer with him. "My favorite service in our prayer book has always been The Service of Compline. I send us forth until we meet again with these beautiful words from that service. Let us pray. The Lord is with you."

VISIT, we beseech thee, O Lord, this place, and drive from it all the snares of the enemy; let thy holy angels dwell herein to preserve us in peace; and may thy blessing be upon us evermore; through Jesus Christ our Lord. Amen. LIGHTEN our darkness, we beseech thee, O Lord; and by thy great mercy defend us from all perils and dangers of this night; for the love of thy only Son, our Saviour Jesus Christ. Amen. [6]

---

[6] Book of Common Prayer, Anglican Church of Canada, 1962

BREAKFAST AT REGGIES

"Morning," said Reggie with a great big smile on his face. He often sat near the front door greeting locals and tourists. "You don't need to sign the visitor book," he chuckled as he greeted Truly. "You is a regular."

"Reggie's had become an institution in Saint John. It was like the city hall in miniature. It was one of the remaining landmarks on Germain Street. The patrons of Reggie's had seen many parts of the old city disappear right before their eyes. Reggie often commented to those coming in about that fact.

"Hey," said Reggie. "Did you know they took down that sign on the building up there?" He pointed uphill on Germain.

"You mean the big white Loyalist House up on the corner?" asked Truly.

"Nah," said Reggie. "The brick one on the corner. Said it is the oldest brick house in the city?"

"No way," said Truly. "Let me go check. I'll be right back. Hold the toast!" He shouted to Harriet.

In no time that Truly was back with a cloud of fog surrounding his head. Or maybe it was smoke coming out his ears."

"Told ya," said Reggie. "Told ya it was gone."

"Who took that down?" questioned Truly.

"How would I know," said Noll Huggard who was sitting in the corner by the front window.

"What?" said Truly.

"How would I know?" repeated Noll. "I just walk around here and notice things. Nothing to me what they do around here. I quit trying to figure out long time ago. Short as a whipstitch things change."

"What?" said Reggie. "What's that mean?" as he got up to clear off some dishes and straighten the newspapers people had left behind.

"Short as a whipstitch," repeated Noll. "How do I know? Just heard someone upcountry say it. Maybe it means people's memory around here is 'short as a whipstitch.' What is a whipstitch anyway?"

"Well, it's a wonder they didn't also tear down the Loyalist House across the street," commented Truly. "Next thing they'll be tearing down whole city blocks in the name of money. They call it urban renewal. I suppose they are trying to stop the businesses from moving out west of town." He paused. "So you tear 'em down and make them move. Ayah," he interjected as he breathed in. Truly had grown up in New Brunswick and he had the signature way of interjecting an 'ayuh' while breathing in. It was a way of agreeing. It was a way of creating space while listener and speaker thought about what was just said and what could be said next.

Noll concentrated on his oatmeal. The oatmeal gave him a cover for eavesdropping. He was a master at eavesdropping on and into conversations. Occasionally between spoonfuls, he would comment. "They got rid of that sign a long time ago," he said.

"You already said that," said Truly. "Why?"

"How would I know," replied Noll. "Just happened to notice it one day when I was headed up toward Old Stone Church. They get rid of a lot of things around here. None of my business. Just is."

"That's the kind of attitude," said Truly, "that gives people permission to do that."

"Do what?" said Noll.

"Do what I just said," replied Truly. He was starting to get a little aggravated with Noll. Noll could be cooperative or mysterious. He could be intuitive or oblivious. He could, sometimes, just be. "What's with you anyway," said Truly. "Your memory as short as a whipstitch?"

"You like that, don't ya?" said Noll.

"Like what?" said Truly.

"Short as a whipstitch," replied Noll.

"I give up, "replied Truly.

"Here's your toast," said Harriet. "Your bacon and eggs will be up shortly. Want anything else?"

"Some of those home fries." He replied. "Make the bacon crispy too."

"Yes sir!" she replied as she marched back to the griddle. The bacon was already getting on to crispy. She flipped the pancake she was making for Reggie. He had returned to the table and sat down with Truly.

"Give 'em a whack, will ya," said Reggie. "I like 'em flat."

"You got it Mayor!" she replied.

"Mayor?" said Truly.

"Yup," she yelled from behind the griddle. "He's the mayor of Saint John. Didn't you know?"

"Really?" said Truly. "Well he probably does see more that goes on in this town than some of the officials. After all who would have noticed that historic plaque gone? When you are so used to something being around, you begin to not notice it anymore. Kind of like half the people in this town have never visited the New Brunswick Museum or sat at Fort Howe. Our environment becomes invisible. People become apathetic until something is gone. Then they notice. Then it is too late. Just like this breakfast restaurant. Someday "Reggie's" will be gone. Reggie will want to retire. People think this is an institution that will be here forever. Tourists come here year after year. Just look at the guest book at the entrance. Once it's gone it's gone."

Reggie listened. He didn't quite understand so he ate his pancake in silence.

"Here's your bacon and eggs," said Harriet as she set them down in front of Truly. "Don't get any in your beard!" she quipped as she turned, laughed and went back to cooking.

"Hrumpf," sighed Truly. "So Reggie is the Mayor, you are the Health Inspector and I am the tax paying victim." He chuckled as he plopped the eggs on top of the home fries and dug in.

"That's right," said Reggie. "And Mayor Black knows it. I told him so."

"I bet he does," said Truly. "He better listen to you. He better listen period. I can't tell you how many times I've said to him, 'Please stop tearing down buildings in the city. You'll have nothing left.' He just looks and gives some lame excuse about renewal and putting the city on a financially stable course. He can't see beyond the windows of his office. Next thing you know they'll tear down all those buildings across the street. Manchester, Robertson and Allison will be gone. God knows what they'll build in its place."

"Eat your breakfast," said Harriet. "Ya can't solve all the problems in a breakfast."

"I can try," said Truly. "Some of these people couldn't organize a riot, no less set our beloved Saint John on a course that preserves, protects, defends and renews at the same time."

"Do you like the eggs?" asked Reggie. "I like the eggs here."

"Of course I do," replied Truly. Everyone likes breakfast here. It's an institution. It will be here forever."

Noll Huggard had heard enough. He had his own opinion of the place. "See ya," he whispered as plopped his woolen hat on and disappeared out into the morning fog that had descended on the city.

THE GATHERING

For once the clergy and shakers and movers in the city of Saint John had responded to a cry out to meet. The Reverends Wentworth and Hatfield had contacted others face to face. Their approach was to say, "The Anglican Church in the Valley is gone. This is our opportunity to become effective churches before we become redundant and the city is a goner." It didn't take much cajoling to convince the others to gather. All of their jobs were in jeopardy because their churches were in jeopardy. It didn't matter that they held court in some of the most beautiful and historic buildings in the city. City people had become blind to their surroundings until the surroundings were gone. Then they mourned. Hatfield and Wentworth had gathered their colleagues for a meeting at the back of Reggie's. The breakfast hour was almost over. It was a neutral, safe place for them to meet.

"It is better to avoid hospice care of our institutions and city" said Hatfield, "than to wait until it is too late and our history is just that, history! Then we all might as move."

"Or be buried," said Wentworth. "Once our beautiful buildings are gone, our history is gone, our reason for being is gone."

"I wouldn't go that far," said Monsignor Sweeney with a hint of an Irish brogue. He had been in New Brunswick long enough to pick up the lilt of 'ayah.' But there was no denying that he had come from Ireland, County Killenney, to be exact. The speech patterns of the 18th century Loyalists mixed with that of the 19th century Irish and created a distinctly 20th century Canadian New Brunswick sound.

"Aye," said Elder Laurence Colwell of the Germain Street Baptist Church. "We have dwindled down to a precious few. It may be the case that 'where two or three are gathered together,' but where there are only two or three, big historic buildings become an albatross. That may be the end to end all."

"It won't sink us," replied Sweeney. "We are THE Catholic Cathedral in the city. The bishop might shut down others around us but he won't shut us down. Our cathedral will survive. The Catholic Church survives no matter what!"

Monsignor Sweeney was a tall, handsome man with white hair. He had been a redhead in his youth. A redheaded Irish man with freckles sprinkled here and there. He wore his black robe with red buttons and piping as a badge of honor that he had endured many a crisis and blessing as priest. He was thoroughly Catholic but in regard to others in the city he was catholic with a little "c." He had been heard to say that it important that the people of Saint John stick together, honor their heritage and preserve their legacy of morals, faith and uniqueness. He wasn't a "Loyalist" in the sense of the group who had remained loyal to the Crown of England and fled north from the Colonies but he was a loyalist in that he supported preserving history, historical buildings and local heritage. "It's important that we keep what we have inherited," he had been heard to say. "That way we build on what has been and we create what is to be."

"If," said Sister Honora Collins, "what has been doesn't weigh us down and stifle our mission." Sister Honora proudly wore her black habit and whiffle in public even though some of the other sisters had adapted to a more contemporary dress. She had spent most of her life as a member of the Sisters of Charity of the Immaculate Conception. The order was attached to the Cathedral of the Immaculate Conception and loyal to Monsignor Sweeney of the same. "Sometimes," she continued, "buildings and history can be an asset. Sometimes they are not. If we sisters are going to continue our mission to the poor and needy in Saint John we must maintain our historic building. I think that our chapel should even be on the historic map and a stop off for tours."

"And our Cathedral" said Monsignor Sweeney.

"That's a fine idea," said Rev. Stuart Somerville, "but Centenary Church is sinking under its weight. And I don't just mean the weight of our big 1200 seat neo-gothic building. We may be custodians of a fabulous, historic building on the corner of Wentworth and Princess Street. We may have been designated as an historic structure of grand gothic design by John Welsh of New York City. We may represent the best of an example of rebuilding Saint John after the great fire of 1877. Even with all of that, we are now decaying into the ground. That history doesn't mean a twit to the congregation. Just imagine what it is like for 50 people to sit in a 1200 seat sanctuary on a Sunday Morning. Depressing."

"Yes," said Hatfield. "We are doing our best at Saint Luke's to keep up our membership while maintaining and preserving our historic building. We must do it, congregation or not. Our buildings may be obsolete in regard to our congregation but they are not in regard to our city's history and future." He paused. "We must do more than survive. We must find a way for these historic buildings to thrive."

"Agreed," said the Rev. John Bruce of the Church of Saint Andrew and Saint David, a United Church of Christ blend. "I moved here from Winnipeg out on the plains where everything old is old and everything new is celebrated. We don't have an unlimited inventory of historical buildings. We preserve what we have. We build new around the old. Saint John just seems to tear down, pave over, make a parking lot or build something new that has no architectural value. A hundred years from now, even twenty years from now, who will pay any heed or care about that god-awful Woolworth building at the head of King Street. It's been empty for years. No one wants it. The last time I was in there they had a lunch counter. Best pumpkin pie I ever ate. Now look at it. Maybe "we" ought to buy it and turn it into a shelter for the homeless. At least they wouldn't need to sleep in Kings Square."

"Exactly," said Sister Honora. "Remember the soup kitchen that used to be on Union Street? The city razed that to make a parking lot. I hear they are planning on tearing down the YMCA, no loss, and the old Library to make way for some no-descript government buildings. And this all happens right under our noses while the city sleeps. People don't pay attention to what is happening around them."

"We are still at it, doing church I mean," said Bruce, "because two churches joined together, denominations joined together and are preserving our church on Germain Street. At least we are part of the preservation and renewal that is happening on Germain. In fact, Germain is about the only street around where a tourist can see what Saint John looked like before they engaged in "urban" renewal with a wrecking ball."

"Well," said Wentworth of Old Stone Church, "they'll never tear our church down. Our parish hall might fall off the cliff one of these days but Old Stone Church, with or without a congregation, will survive. That ballast brought over on ships from the old world have us firmly planted on Carleton Street at the head of Germain. It's' not going anywhere." He got up and returned with the coffee pot. "Coffee anyone?"

"I grew up in the North End," said Colwell. "We lived on Victoria Street. I went to Alexandra School. Our family worshiped at Victoria Street Baptist. Just look at the North End now. When my parents moved into the city, the North End was a beautiful place. It was close to Indiantown. The Trolley came down Main and made a loop down there. Businesses thrived on Main. Children played in the street. The old houses, sure non-descript on the outside, were well-maintained and beautiful inside. Gorgeous woodwork, parlours, fireplaces, and the like. It was one of *the* places to raise a family in the city. Now look at it. Victoria Baptist is gone. Torn down. Houses are unkempt. The fog has done its job on paint and plaster. There are less than desirables hanging around. Even Main Street Baptist is teetering on the brink of extinction. I don't live there anymore, but the old streets, Metcalf, Victoria, Millidge, Main, are a special place in my heart. When I go there I see it as it was. I also see it as what it could be again."

Metcalf Street, North End

"Good point," said Hatfield. "Thankfully Saint Luke's still stands as a beacon for the city. Churches around Douglas Avenue are surviving. But, like has already been said, 'how can we help the city thrive and maintain its unique character, history and legacy? We lost The Anglican Church in the Valley several weeks ago. Fire took care of that piece of history."

"The remnant of the congregation is meeting at Old Stone Church," said Keirstead. "I don't know how long they will keep that up.

They are welcome as long as they need but I suspect Valley church is gone forever. Condemned to memory."

"By the way," said Monsignor Sweeney, "Where is the good Rev. Gwyn Davies from Valley Church? Did you contact him about this meeting?"

"We tried," said Hatfield, 'but no one seems to know where he is. I understand the Fire Marshall is still sifting through the ashes. So far it looks like no one died in the fire. Where he has disappeared to is a mystery. I'll keep trying to contact him. He's single so there's no wife or family that I know of to contact. Maybe their Senior Warden will know."

"Well, it's nearly noon." said Hatfield. "Thank you all for coming. Thank you for your interest and input. Can we agree to begin meeting regularly? Can we agree to feel out our congregations and contacts about this issue of historical preservation, survival and thriving?"

Everyone nodded their agreement.

"I suggest next time," said Hatfield, "that we meet at Saint Luke's. We can gather in our historic sanctuary. The beauty of such architecture and history ought to inspire and motivate us to make a difference in Saint John. Next week? Tuesday Morning? Ten?" Seeing that everyone agreed, Hatfield said, "Then let me close our time together with a brief prayer, a prayer for our city."

"Blessed is the Lord our God," said Hatfield, "who causes bread to come forth from the earth and who sustains and surrounds our City with love."

"That sounds rather Jewish," said Bruce, "We need to make sure the Rabbi attends our next meeting. I will contact him. And also let us continue to pray for Valley Church and their missing Priest Davies."

I REMEMBER

Truly Morrell often walked the city streets. He walked with a purpose. He walked with a sadness. Now that The Anglican Church in the Valley was gone he sensed the city was on the verge of a major shift. Urban renewal was nothing new in Saint John or anywhere else in the world. But urban renewal seemed to take little interest in preserving the old. Everything new was better. In many cities where areas had become derelict, historical preservationists, native sons and daughters and even urban renewal commissions were interested in saving the history of cities while creating new. Restoration, repurposing, renewing and building new were all part of urban renewal plans.

Truly walked along. He noticed what was, what had become and what is. The many shops and residences that lined Main Street on up to Saint Luke's church and beyond to Indiantown had been decimated, demolished or allowed to sink into the fog of decay. The Harbour Bridge that was built after much controversy had improved entrance and exit into the city while at the same time obliterating much of the city that made Saint John, the Loyalist City and a jewel of Victorian architecture.

He stopped. As he passed the spot that used to be occupied by Nairn's Lunch Counter he remembered. "There was nothing like a hot turkey sandwich smothered in gravy" he whispered to himself. "And," he continued, "Those pies Mrs. Nairn used to make. Umm Ummm." He whispered as he wistfully stood there imagining what used to be. "She made those pies from wild blueberries her kids had picked up at Rockwood Park." He paused. "Nothing like that pie topped with a big gob or Sussex vanilla ice cream."

"What did you say," said Evelyn Crandall who had been walking by.

"What?" said Truly. He hadn't noticed that he wasn't alone. He was alone with his thoughts but not alone.

"I said," repeated Evelyn, "What did you say?"

"Oh! Hello Evelyn," said Truly. "I hadn't noticed you there."

"I noticed" said Evelyn with her wry sense of observation and wit. "I noticed. You appeared to be in the middle of a daydream and having a good conversation with yourself. What did you say?"

"Oh, nothing," replied Truly. "I was just remembering. I am sure it is nothing you'd be interested in. The Commission on Urban Renewal definitely wouldn't be interested."

"Tell me," replied Evelyn. "I am interested since you bring up the Commission. I'm on the Commission. Mayor Black nominated me because I've been around for a long time. I've been around so long that people come to me to prove they've been born."

"What?" said Truly. "What?"

"People," replied Evelyn, "are always trying to get copies of their birth certificates for one reason or another. Travel. Pension, Passport. You know." She paused. "They seem to think that I've been around long enough and attended enough births to be able to corroborate that they were born." She laughed. "And" she continued, "the Mayor seems to think that also makes me eligible to be on the Commission on Urban Renewal. I do think there is a lot of renewal needed around this city but not in the way he and others on the Commission would like."

"What?" said Truly. "What are you talking about?"

"See that Harbour Bridge over there," she said as she pointed. "I wasn't for that one twit. I understand the need for it. It is difficult for traffic to negotiate the Reversing Falls Bridge and Douglas Avenue to get into city centre, but..."

"But what?" asked Truly.

"But," she continued, "I was against it from the start. I told the City Planning Board and the Commission on Urban Renewal that it would destroy the ambiance of our city while at the same time we would lose some of our most unique Victorian architecture. In addition some of our neighbourhoods might descend into dereliction. And they have. Look at the North End.

"That's where I'm headed," said Truly. "I lived on Metcalf Street for decades until moving over town. Now over town is even disappearing and sinking into the sediment of long ago. I walk over here pondering what can be done before there is another great fire or any more buildings are torn down. The Anglican Church in the Valley is gone. If we aren't vigilant, St. Luke's, Main Street Baptist and other architectural treasures of the area will be gone as well. Just look now how many of the old buildings are boarded up or being sucked up by the fog and sea air."

"Exactly," said Evelyn. "That's why I'm on the Commission. Every group needs a squirrel under the pews or a..."

"A devil's advocate?" asked Truly.

"Exactly," she replied. "Mayor Black thought he would have an allly in me being on the Commission. He never expected me, a little old lady, grandmother and Saint John advocate to throw a monkey wrench into their plans to demolish and rebuild. Just because you tear down something and build something new," she continued, "Doesn't mean that renewal will happen. People are often lured into moving totally out of an area to new places instead of finding creative ways to make the old new again."

"Like Manchester, Robertson and Allison?" said Truly.

"Exactly," she replied. "Businesses either go out of business, reinvent themselves or move out of town. You've probably heard the rumours about building shopping centres out of town. Walmart has made cities all over the United States think about their downtown areas and survival. Some cities have succeeded. Others have just succumbed to the Walmart effect and gone belly up leaving dead downtown areas that eventually are torn down or reinvented. Enough has been torn down already in Saint John. I want it stopped."

"I had no idea," said Truly, "that anyone on the Commission had the same feelings I had."

"I do," she replied. "I do."

"I wake each morning on the other side of dawn," he continued, "to find the city as it was the night before. In my mind it hasn't changed. I know better. When the fog moves in and I can't see my hand in front of my face, I stand at Fort Howe and "see" in my mind's eye, what the city was. I mourn. And I dream."

"Of urban renewal." She asked.

"Restoration and renewal." He replied. "Do you remember Nairn's Lunch Counter?" he asked.

"I do," she replied. "And Joyce's Food Market, Valley Cake shop." She paused. "Eddy Deep's Grocery and Lunch Counter survives but who knows for how long. The Dominion Store is on its last legs. Maybe another chain will raze and replace."

"Dykeman's Hardware," he said, "will probably go on forever. Places like that are needed, especially when people become interested in repair and restore."

"What are you looking at?" said Evelyn. She had just noticed that Noll Huggard had snuck up nearby and was leaning up against the front of Main Brace Naval Veteran's club."

"Nothin," replied Noll. "Just hanging around."

"Well," she replied, "don't you be sneaking around eavesdropping on conversations. It might get you in more trouble than you want."

"Nothin," he repeated. "Just killing time. Simms Brush Factory gave us the day off. Business has been on the decline. People being laid off. Rumours that they'll either go under or move out of Saint J. Nothin!" He repeated.

"Remember that," cautioned Truly to Noll. "I'll be moving along now. Evelyn, you take care. Keep me posted if you have any news about the Commission."

"Will do," she waved as she headed toward Centre City. Truly continued his daily circuit up around the North End and back home. Noll did what he always did. People wondered.

RELOCATION

"Look at that!" said Abner Short, Valley Church Senior Warden. "We haven't even finished grieving the loss of our beautiful church and they have installed that sign with their plans for demolition."

"They sure don't waste any time," said Truly. He had been out for his morning constitution and decided, like so many others, to swing down across the railroad tracks, the valley and pass by the church remains. "It's a sad sight indeed," he sighed. "I just don't know what is coming of our beautiful city. Just the other day I ran into Evelyn Crandall over on Main. All that's left over there is that Main Brace Naval Veteran's Club and I'd bet you a two dollar bill that will go belly up one of these days."

"The club? said Abner, "Or the two dollar bill?"

"Both probably," replied Truly. "We are becoming more and more like the states by the minute!" he quipped. "It makes me sad. What makes us different and interesting is disappearing into the ashes of time. Like your church."

Abner shook his head in agreement. They stood in silence surveying the scene. "Tears the heart right out of you," he whispered. "Our beautiful church is gone. Only God knows what will be in its place. One of those new industrial style buildings, I suppose." He looked toward the city. "Just look. Will you just look! Where is the beauty in that Harbour Bridge, a demolished Main Street and that god awful Lord Beaverbrook rink? Just look."

"And there seems to be no stopping the city's desperate attempt at urban renewal. Looks more like urban destruction to me."

The two had strolled up the street a bit and past the "do not cross" police tape surrounding Valley Church. The Commission on Urban Renewal had wasted no time installing a sign. The fire had afforded them an opportunity to act while others were busy grieving. Stunned, they silently stood and read the sign.

THE CITY OF SAINT JOHN REDEVELOPMENT NOTICE

"Existing tenants on" read Truly. **"EXISTING TENANTS!"** he repeated. **"Don't they give a twit about people's lives?"**

"Evidently not," said Abner. "There have been rumours swirling around for some time about the city demolishing whole blocks of houses to make way for urban renewal."

"Look at all the streets they are going to 'renew,'" he said with a sarcastic tone. "Doesn't anyone anymore have a say about their homes and future?"

"I guess not," said Abner. He continued to read the rest of the sign. "are being relocated." He paused. "ARE BEING RELOCATED!"

"Occupants," read Truly, "are being relocated and after the above date will not be assisted to relocate!"

From "The Lost Valley Blog"

"Sites will be cleared," continued Abner, "soon after. SOON AFTER. How very kind of them. Our church burns to the ground. We are left without our beloved church home. They move right in on it! SOON AFTER! We'll have to see about that!"

"You better move fast," said Truly. "Look at the bottom line. They mean what they say. They didn't waste any time clearing out Main Street to make way for urban renewal. And we know what happens after that demolition. They wait and wait and wait. They argue and plan. They moan about money. And still all of Main Street sits there vacant. What once was, is no more!"

"You betcha," said Abner. "And if they ever get around to making plans it'll be something that won't last as long as what they tore down. Nothing like only planning half way. And then half way ends up rebuilding half-fast and we know what that ends up being."

Truly chuckled. "Half – assed?" he said.

"Exactly," said Abner. "Before they act, we must act. I hear the clergy of the city have gotten together. Some of the rest of us need to do the same. But what?"

"I have some thoughts," said Truly. "Do you know Evelyn Crandall? She attends St. Luke's. A good woman."

"Yes, I do," replied Abner. "What are you thinking?"

"I ran into her on Main the other day." Continued Truly. "We stood and chatted for quite some time about this very subject. She appeared totally in love with our city. She grew up here, you know. She knows many people. For all I know she may have been at the birth of Mayor Black."

Abner's eyes bugged out as only he could make them when he was surprised. "No!" he said.

"Yes," said Truly. "She's one of those go-to people in the city. When you need a birth certificate, or need to know some other fact about the city, like where was Walter Pidgeon's father's store, you go to Evelyn. She knows everything. At least that's what people say. Anyway we chatted for quite some time about the demise of Main, the Harbour Bridge, and her beloved St. Luke's. Before we parted she told me Mayor Black had appointed her to the Commission on Urban Renewal."

"Really?" said Abner. "Why?"

"I'm not sure why," said Truly. "I suspect the Mayor thinks that he is doing the city a service by having someone so in love with the city on the board. A bigggg mistake on his part," said Truly as he rolled his eyes.

"Bigg!!!?" said Abner.

"Yes Big!" replied Truly, "because Evelyn will not only be an asset to the Commission, she will be a devil's advocate for the historicity of the city. She will advocate for what is left. I suspect she will do her best to throw a monkey wrench into the Commission's plans. We need to act before the bulldozers move in and people are thrown out." He paused. "Has the city contacted Valley Church about cleaning up these ashes yet?"

"Not yet," said Abner. "We still have to meet again with Fire Marshall Belyea. Then we will know more about the future of our property. I am sure the cleanup will be at our expense," he paused, "unless insurance comes through and covers it. If it doesn't, that will be the end of Valley Church AND I am sure the city won't help us relocate."

"Okay," said Truly. "Then since I have had a conversation already with Evelyn, how about I contact her and the three of us meet at Reggie's some morning soon?"

"Perfect," replied Abner. "But not Reggie's. It's too out in the open. People know people meet there to do business, legal or otherwise. Let's meet at Eddy Deep's Grocery and Lunch Counter on Elm Street. No one will ever suspect anything is going on by our meeting there. It will be a good opportunity to visit with Evelyn. Maybe she can be our secret agent on the Commission for Urban Renewal."

"Done!" said Truly. "I'm sure I'll bump into her again on my morning walk. We'll chat and make a date within the week. In the meantime, keep an eye on that sign and let me know if there is any activity. I will try to work undercover."

"A deal," said Abner, as he turned to walk back toward the ashen sight of Valley Church. Truly waved. He headed up Burpee Avenue to Mt. Pleasant Avenue toward Rockwood Park. It was one of his favorite routes. It took him past Holy Trinity Catholic Church a stone's throw on Rockland Road, a stone's throw from Burpee. History enveloped him as much as the overhanging trees. Nasturtiums were parading their last gasp of summer colour. There was a hint of autumn in the air and a sprinkle of red and orange in the trees. As he walked along he thought about the conversation with Abner and inserted it into the one he had previously with Evelyn Crandall on Main Street.

"We are all on the same page," he whispered, as he passed by one of the mansions owned by the Irving family. He appreciated their involvement in keeping the city financially running but he also wished they could do more to preserve than just ..." He was at a loss for words. Did the city need demolition and renewal or did it need a complete renaissance and rebirth bringing the old historical along with renew and renewal?

"Evelyn," he told himself, "will have some thoughts. And," he continued, "The clergy will also know how to be a catalyst for the city. They have expertise in hanging on to tradition while at the same time making the old new."

The dawn had turned the corner by the time he reached the path at Rockwood Park. People had already come and gone with their feed for the birds at the entrance to the path. The birds twittered in satisfaction and thanks for their morning nosh. Truly disappeared up the path allowing his thoughts to mingle with nature preserved in Rockwood Park.

"This park was designed by Olmstead a century ago," he whispered to the trees. "And just look at how it has been honoured and preserved. We must help the people of the city see the same value for our history as they see in this park." He walked on.

ASHES TO ASHES

"Ashes to ashes, dust to dust," said Abner to Maude as they sat and waited for Fire Marshall Belyea to arrive.

"And," said Maude.

"If you didn't have an ..." continued Abner.

"Stop it!" said Maude.

"Your belly would bust," laughed Abner. He did have a comical side to him.

"Stop it!" said Maude under her breath. "That's not funny!"

"I think it is," said Abner. "Every time I've been at the cemetery with Father Davies, I've just been waiting for him to slip and say that instead of the real words. He's the one who told me that joke."

"It's still not funny," said Maude.

"Oh Maude," he replied, "We've got to see a little humour in the ashes of our church. Maybe God wanted us to finally catch on fire!"

"That's not funny, either," said Maude, as she became even more annoyed with her husband's levity.

"Is too," he said.

"Is not," she replied.

"Is too. Is not, Is too," they repeated back and forth until neither could hear each other and each thought they had the last word.

"IS TOO!" shouted Abner.

"Is too what?" asked Nellie Summerville who was sitting two rows back.

"Never mind," said Maude as she turned around and glared past Nellie. She surveyed the rest of the crowd that had gathered. She knew to a person who would care enough to show up. She just wanted to make sure her assessment was right concerning who would be with each other on this ashen ride and who had already jumped ship for other churches with, as they would say, lless problems.

"What's he doing here," she said as she nudged Abner with her boney elbow. Maude may have been rotund from all the biscuits and molasses she was prone to eat, but her elbows stayed as sharp as the needle she found in that haystack she was always pawing through. She nudged him again. This time so hard that it caused a bruise that he would find after he stripped down for the night.

"Stop that!" he replied. "STOP THAT! I've got more bruises on my side than a …"

"Than a what?" she said.

"Oh never mind," he continued. "Who is here? And besides, no matter who it is, everyone is welcome here. Who is here?"

"That Huggard guy," she replied. "He seems to show up at the strangest times. Walking this city as if he owned it. Here, there and everywhere as creepy as the fog stealing in unannounced on a late summer night."

"So," he said. "Leave the guy alone. He's just interested. Maybe he knows something about the fire. Maybe he cares."

The crowd had swelled to about 67 people. Abner made note of the number and even mentioned "67." It always seemed odd that he could assess the size of a crowd. He was quite accurate. When the roll was taken he was correct.

"Humpf," he said, "67. Heinz has their '57,' we have our 67. Might be a good or a bad omen. Adds up to 13. "You know the tallest building in Saint John has no 13th floor."

"Silly you," said Maude. "Get over yourself and that superstition stuff. Soon you'll be saying Satan came down from heaven and lit this fire. Shhh. Here comes the Fire Marshall."

"Don't 'shh' me," said Abner. "Besides, Satan doesn't come down from Heaven. He comes up from Hell. And it's Hell that we are in right now."

"Whatever," said Maude as she breathed in with her characteristically New Brunswick way of giving or holding back ascent.

The nervous chatter in the room was filled with each person's opinion, solution and angst. It settled down to a quite hum as Abner stood to introduce Fire Marshall Belyea.

"Blessed is God, King of the Universe," he said, "and welcome Fire Marshall Belyea." The congregation didn't know what to make of that introduction, but they knew Abner and that he had a handy dandy imaginary pocket guide to quotes and quips. "Welcome," he said, as he sat down.

"Thank you for the welcome," said Belyea. "And thank you for your patience while we have done this investigation."

"Well our patience is wearing thin," shouted Levi Akerley from where he was standing along the side wall. Levi was an original. People never knew whether he was being serious or funny. Sometimes he came across as the original Loyalist who landed at the slip at the bottom of King Street. Other times he made it known that he had come in from the woods.

"Get on with it!" yelled Levi. "I haven't got all day. I left a rare chicken cooped up in a roll of wire back at the house. She's just waiting to get out to lay an egg." Levi did have chickens but not anything special. And as for one being cooped up in a roll of chicken wire, that might be the case or it might just be another one of his practical jokes. A way of saying he had something special and then knocking over the roll to say, "The joke's on you."

"Levi, Levi," shouted Abner as he rose and faced the crowd. "Let's keep some order here so that Mr. Belyea can finish and we can get on with whatever it is we are called to get on to."

Noll Huggard pressed tighter against the wall and slithered further away from Levi. He didn't want to be identified as being associated with him even if they were distant cousins. The more distant the better. He had enough of that "shirt-tail" relative business his brother was always talking about. No more relatives for him. Noll was happy to be left alone with his thoughts, opinions and purposes.

Abner stared the crowd into silence. "Please," he said, "Mr Belyea. Continue."

"Thank you," said Belyea. "We have concluded our investigation of the fire. As you know we found some interesting things. I showed you the communion ware, cross and cloths from the Altar. As you know the altar was not damaged."

"A miracle," said Nellie, loud enough for the people to hear that it sparked another uprising. "A MIRACLE," she said, more loudly this time.

"You can call it that if you wish," said Belyea. "But I can also tell you that fire does funny things. Sometimes it jumps over and saves, sometimes it consumes everything in its path. Think what you will. It's your faith and church. I'm just here to try to explain." He continued.

"The fire, we believe," he said, "was arson. Someone started this fire intentionally. I know you want to believe that it was an accident sparked by the workmen removing the old paint from the outside. It did look that way since they were using blow torches. But, …" he paused.

"But what?" said Maude Short.

"But the truth is," he continued, "The fire started from within. It may have looked like it burned from the outside in but it burned from the inside out. Someone set the fire. The hot spot where it started was somewhere around the pipe organ. Maybe someone didn't like organ music. Maybe someone didn't like this church. Maybe someone had a gripe to bear about Valley Church. That is left to your imagination. That I cannot answer. What I can say," he continued, "is that the fire was started and burned from the inside out. By the time it got to the steeple, the church was long gone. The workmen didn't even notice it was happening until they felt the heat coming through the exterior walls they were painting. Once the heat got there, the new paint fueled the fire. And of course," he paused, "once the fire got to the steeple, the church was gone. The steeple was a natural chimney to provide the whoosh of air needed to feed the flames."

Otty Thorne raised his hand.

"Yes," said Belyea.

"And," said Otty, "you didn't find any dead bodies?

"Not an ash!" said Belyea.

Maude jabbed her boney elbow into Abner's side.

"I said 'stop that," growled Abner in a whisper under his breath. "Besides," he said, "I'm not the only one who thinks "ash" is funny."

"That's why I jabbed you," she said. "Evidently you and Father Davies aren't the only ones who like to make an ash of themselves." She gave him the silly grin that only she could give. She knew she'd gotten him this time. The joke was on him. Several people sitting close to Abner and Maude over heard the exchange. They tried their best to stifle their laughter.

"I didn't mean to make a joke," said Belyea, "but sometimes a laugh now and then in difficult situations lightens the load we carry. As I said, Otty, we didn't find any remains of a person or any other living creature. If someone had died in the fire, we would have found something. But we found nothing. I was afraid that we might find Rev. Davies, but nothing. The investigation also has not revealed where he is. We have no idea. His whereabouts may be suspect. But we can't draw any conclusions as to who set this fire. As it stands now, it's an act of God. I'm not a religious man, but it is as if the fire of the Spirit singled out Valley church and decided to give your congregation an opportunity to rally around and be all that you might be. That's up to you."

"It's about time," said Levi, "that this congregation got lit up. And I don't mean by hitting the bottle."

"Be kind," said Nellie. "Be kind and we'll get through this. And by the way, don't make an ash of yourself." She had heard what Belyea said. She also heard the nuance. It was a rare pun that got by her. Usually she just groaned but this time she couldn't resist making a pun of her own. "Don't make an ash of yourself," she repeated loud enough for the rest to hear. Laughter.

"So what now?" said Abner, as he rose to take over the meeting. Levi had heard enough. His "what now" was to leave. Noll Huggard followed him in quick pursuit.

"What now," said Belyea, "is up to the congregation. We are done with sifting through the remains. I will leave up the yellow police tape but I'd suggest a more permanent barrier so people don't come prowling around for souvenirs. The site is basically safe for a few of you to carefully walk through. You might find something here and there that you can save. Other than that, you'll have to get a permit from the Commission on Urban Renewal to clean up the site. You'll have to decide plans if you are going to rebuild. You may have problems with the insurance company now that we have determined the fire was set. My work is done here but you are always welcome to call on me if there is any way I can help. I do have contacts with city hall, the city council and several other commissions. I'll be going. Thank you for coming and listening. Good night,"

"And also with you," said the gathering in unison, as if they had just heard Father say, "The Lord be with you."

"Good Anglicans," said Abner as he rose to adjourn the meeting. "Good Anglicans," he repeated with a chuckle as he also said, "And also with you." Some thought it funny. Others had no thought at all, merely sitting there waiting for the cue words so they could reply without thinking.

"I hope," said Abner, "that your "also with you," is more than a response. I hope, he continued, "you mean what you pray and pray what you mean. We are going to need everyone to pull together. When Father Davies returns, if he returns, he will be quick to remind us that the church is not a building. We are the church. Now is the time to prove it. We will adjourn for now. We will continue to partake of Stone Church's hospitality and worship there. In between times, we will meet here in our Parish Hall to pray and plan our next move. So, Let us pray: The Lord be with you."

This time the gathering was listening, if only for the word that they could leave. Their reply, "And also with you," was loud and determined.

"Let us," said Abner, "go out in peace to love and serve the Lord."

"Amen!" shouted Nellie. To that, someone in a most uncharacteristic Anglican form began to sing "Amen," and "When the Saints go Marching out." The singing continued out the door and into the foggy dark night of the city. It was one of the most memorable moments for Valley Church. That memory became their battle cry to be the saints of Valley Church marching throughout the city marching for renewal in whatever form, urban or otherwise, it might take.

WOOLWORTHS

Truly slipped into the swivel chair at the lunch counter. Woolworths at the head of King Street, along with Reggie's around the corner, was a favorite place for many folks to meet. Autumn was fast coming on. The trees were turning. "Frost is on the pumpkin," said Truly. It was time for some famous Woolworth's pumpkin pie.

"I'll have a hot dog first," said Truly, as Margaret Greene took his order. "And I'll follow up with a piece of that pumpkin pie before someone else gets it." He pointed to the thick slice that was ready for him on display in the pie case on the edge of the counter. "And pile on some of that real whipped cream you just made."

"You got it," she said. It only took her a moment to get the hot dog and return. "Mustard, Ketchup, relish and or sauerkraut?" she asked.

"Yes," he replied.

"Yes, what?" she asked.

"Yes," he repeated.

"You're funny," she said. "I already knew you wanted everything piled on top. Give it back to me and I'll fix it up Truly style." She grabbed the hot dog and off she went. She returned with the "yes" piled high.

"Now that's a hot dog," he said as he squished the bun together, tamped the "yes" down and opened wide."

Margaret watched. "Past the gums, look out stomach, here it comes," she said through laughter as Truly opened wide and stuffed one end of the dog into his mouth. "So what's new?" she asked.

"You tell me," he replied.

"Valley Church?" she questioned.

"Maybe. King Street?" he asked

"You tell me," she quipped.

They often played the "is too, is not game" with each other. Eventually they got down to the real subject, what each knew of rumours going around the city. Sometimes there was some good dirt. Sometimes there was sad news. Today there was a little of both.

"I hear," he said, "that business isn't what it used to be. Tourist trade is down along with customers. Too many businesses moving out west of the city."

"Ayuh," she sighed. "She took a deep breath and leaned closer over the counter. "I hear," she continued, "that this place is getting ready to fold. Folks are more interested in what those new stores have to offer. About the best we can do is all that tourist junk over there." She pointed to an aisle filled with flags, key chains and ephemera emblazoned with Maple leaves and the New Brunswick shield. "Just look at this store."

"Aye," he replied. "What about it?"

"Who shops in a Woolworths these days," she replied. "If you're looking for something like needle and thread, this place is okay. But as for anything else, you gotta go to one of those big stores. Canadian Tire, Zellers, even Simson and Sears. They have everything you want and some things you don't."

Evelyn Crandall had been wandering around the store when she espied Truly and Margaret. "Mind if I join you," she said, as she wedged her ample frame into the swivel chair next to Truly.

"Putting on a little heft, aren't ya?" said Truly. He winked. Margaret headed for the coffee pot so as to avoid the repercussions from that quip.

"That's the pot calling the kettle black, I'd say," said Evelyn. "You pregnant or just bulking up for your Santa gig?"

"Both," said Truly with a wink and pat of his paunch. "Both."

"You're funny," said Evelyn. Margaret had returned with the coffee. "Anything else," said Margaret.

"That piece of pumpkin pie," she said as she pointed to the last piece.

"No way," said Truly. "That's my piece. I already called dibs on it. Right Margaret?"

"Right!" said Margaret.

"Then split it with me," said Evelyn. "Neither of us need it. I just want it."

"No way," repeated Truly. "Besides that might be the last piece of pumpkin pie we get to have in this joint."

"What do you mean by that?" said Evelyn. "There'll always be pumpkin pie here."

"Don't count on it," said Margaret. "First off, Truly might beat everyone to it. But I don't think we can count on "always" for anything. Once Truly gets his fork into it that piece of pie it's not "always" anymore." She grabbed the pie out of the display case just in case anyone else had any more ideas.

"Give me that!" said Truly. "That's mine."

"We know," said Margaret and Evelyn in unison. "We know!"

"You know what?" said Noll Huggard. He had been lurking nearby in the men's underwear aisle. It was another one of his fetishes.

"Who said that?" asked Evelyn.

"Me!" said Noll as he stuffed the boxer shorts back into the package he had ripped open. "Me! You know what?" he repeated.

"Pumpkin pie," said Margaret. "Truly is about to archive it. Or should I say, Past the gums, look out stomach, here it comes," She laughed.

"You already said that," replied Truly with his fork poised to stab the pie. "You said that."

"So," continued Noll, "You know what?"

"That's what!" said Evelyn as she spun around to face the counter. She gave Truly a poke. "Past the gums, look out stomach, here it comes," she repeated what Margaret had said. "I'm a quick learner. Hadn't heard that quip in a long time. Past the gums!"

"Stop it," mumbled Truly through a mouthful of pie and whipped cream. He wiped the dollop of whipped cream that had landed in his white beard.

"Make sure you get it all," said Margaret. "No fair saving a dollop here or there for later." They laughed.

"So," said Truly through his pumpkin pie grin, "as I was saying. If they keep on with this urban renewal program we won't have a city. Margaret," he lowered his voice to a whisper and leaned close to Evelyn's ear. "Margaret seems to think the Woolworths's days are numbered."

Evelyn listened. She was a member of the Commission for Urban Renewal and as such was charged with being out and about in the city. The commission was interested in what she heard. "I'm on the Commission," she said. "Anything you have to say may be held against you."

"Thank heavens," said Truly. "I wouldn't want to be taken seriously and have no consequences. What will the consequences be?"

"Higher taxes," she replied. "Less tourists. Boring buildings. No businesses within easy walking distance. You name it."

"I will," he said.

Noll Huggard had inched his way to the end of the aisle closest to the lunch counter. He listened. He couldn't hear the entire conversation. But he heard more than enough. "I'll take these," he mumbled to himself as he held up a blue and white checkered pair of boxer shorts. "I'll take these."

Margaret had been watching him. Noll wasn't a thief in the usual sense. He didn't steal stuff. He just stole conversations and the one he had just overheard was of great interest to him. The city was his home. It was his purpose in life. He had been so distracted by the conversation that he stuffed the boxers in his pocket and started to head for the door.

"Don't forget to pay for those!" yelled Margaret. Noll stopped. "Oh yes," he whispered as he pulled the boxers out of his pocket. "Yes indeed."

"What was that all about?" asked Evelyn.

"Noll Huggard," said Margaret. "A harmless local with some odd behavior. Lurks around too much. Rumour is that he has the most extensive collection of boxer shorts in the city."

"No way!" said Evelyn. "How do you know that?"

"Just go down Metcalf Street on a Monday when everyone has their laundry hanging out. The line behind his house is festooned with boxers of every colour you can imagine. Quite the sight."

"Hmmm," commented Evelyn. "So," she continued, "as I was saying. I am on the Commission for Urban Renewal. The mayor appointed me because I'm an old timer. I know many people in the city. I often have my finger on the pulse of the city before anyone else."

"And how is the city's pulse these days?" asked Truly.

"Weak," replied Evelyn. "Erratic. Skips a beat now and then. Sometimes stops beating altogether. I want to see our beloved city survive and thrive. To me that means resurrection, renewal and restoration. Some of the others on the Commission can only see destruction. I'm listening to the city and bringing a perspective to the Commission that hopefully will slow them down and help them see ways to make the old new again."

"I hope you have some success," mumbled Truly through the last bite of pumpkin pie. Margaret reached for the plate. "Not yet," cautioned Truly. "I'll eat the crust too." Margaret backed off.

"I'll be out of a job," said Margaret. "This place will close. Then we'll see how serious the Commission is about renewal. I wouldn't put it past them to tear down this building AND the Old City Market. THEN we'll see what they have in mind. Probably another parking lot like the one over where the old Palace Theatre used to be. Just what we don't need is another parking lot. And for sure, Trinity Church doesn't need a parking lot. They can't fill the one they have now. People are running up country, shopping, or.."

"Or what?" asked Truly.

"I mean," she continued, "people don't seem interested in the old city or church. They'll be sorry once it's gone. There's no urban renewal once that happens!"

"I'm listening," said Evelyn. "You know how to reach me. If you see me on a walk about, stop anytime to chat. I'm all for urban renewal but not the kind so many people think of. I'm for restoration, repurposing and meaningful renewal. We're the Loyalist City. That doesn't need to mean we are stuck in the 18th century. Loyalists came here to create a new life and country. We can honor them, remember our heritage and build on it. Keep me in your loop of concerns and I'll make sure your concerns are heard at the Commission."

Margaret had gone back to wiping down the stainless counter around the coffee maker. Truly had licked the pumpkin pie plate clean.

"Gotta run," said Evelyn. "I have an appointment down at Manchester, Robertson and Allison. I'm trying to help them define how they can continue to do business on King Street. It's an uphill task."

Truly laughed. "That's for sure," he replied. "Shopping there is a challenge. Enter downhill and walk up hill through the store, one level at a time. One gets their exercise in there. It's one of the charms of the store. They built that place on the side of a steep hill. Today they would have leveled the site. Back then, they just built to the contour of King Street hill. And Whadda ya got? Manchester, Robertson and Allison's up-hill shopping experience. Or if you enter up hill, it's a downhill experience."

"Too funny," said Evelyn. "But you are right. If we lose that store we might as well lose the rest of King Street. So much for Urban Renewal. Catch you another time" she said as she swung her purse over her shoulder and headed out the door.

UNDER COVER

The grand Victorian homes have marched up and down both sides of Douglas Avenue for a century or more. The social class of the residents was determined by the location of their home. Captain Huggard's home perched on the edge of the promontory facing the harbour. From there his wife, Jenney could watch the schooners come and go. She spent early morning hours in the widow's walk watching for the return of her husband. Although he had sailed the harbour for thirty years, she still worried. The shoals hidden in the Bay of Fundy could do in the most experienced captain.

Haddon and Jenny had moved from Upcountry around 1910. They had a local shipbuilder construct their home. They left relatives behind. Hatfield Point on the Belleisle Bay provided an idyllic life but its distance from the city, harbour and conveniences made it difficult for the family. Even though the children protested the move, the city was more convenient. Haddon could sail and be home more often. The amenities of Saint John provided both education and entertainment for the children. Their little children mourned leaving the Belleisle and a Tom Sawyer like life. They adapted. Their son ran errands for neighbours. He delivered papers. He knew the city like the back of his hand. He played with Walter Pidgeon at Pidgeon's shoe store. Life was good.

And, the grand Victorian home on Douglas Avenue said to the city that they had arrived. Captain Huggard wasn't just a captain, he was a captain with status. He was the Captain of Douglas Avenue. He was a Loyalist and the Huggard patriarch.

Douglas Avenue was THE place to live. It was prime real estate. Anyone who was anyone with the means chose Douglas Avenue. The avenue said that one had arrived. The address was so prestigious that if one chose not to build there, one was questioned.

One autumn day Mrs. Jones was in conversation with a fellow choir member at Saint Luke's Anglican Church. She had just built a house on the outskirts of Saint John. She could have built on Douglas Avenue but chose a lesser site. The choir member said, "Mrs. Jones. You moved in from Rothesay. You could have built your house on Douglas Avenue but you chose to build out there where the houses are so common. Why did you do that?" Without having to think, Mrs. Jones replied, "I could have built on Douglas Avenue and been one of the "Jones" but I chose to build outside the city in a less prestigious area. I built a big house suitable for Douglas Avenue. Sure it looks out of place where I built it BUT, out there I am not "one of the Jones," I AM MRS. Jones."

Mrs. Jones effectively squelched the choir member's judgement of her. Or did she? From that time on she may have been MRS. JONES, but she was also, in the mind of the choir member, Mrs. HAUGHTY Jones. Nevertheless, her comment was indicative of the status that had prevailed on Douglas Avenue. Grand houses announced the presence of grand, successful and cultured residents. And the Avenue, as they called it, survived that way for many decades, until. Until the city began to decline. Until the economy began to relocate up river, over city, even to Monckton and beyond. The grand old houses were still grand but were quickly becoming grand shabby chic. And the chic was more shabby than chic.

The fog, the cold of winter, the wet of summer and the wind scrapped off the paint. Siding required continual maintenance. Families could no longer afford heating bills, taxes and upkeep. One by one the grand homes became multifamily residences. Home owners moved out to easier homes to maintain. Landlords lived off site. Renters cared less about where they lived than living itself.

It was on a night the fog had crept in while no one was looking. Or maybe that was just the point. Someone was looking and saw an opportunity. There had been a brilliant sunset the night before. Truly Morrell had seen it. He often lingered at Fort Howe to watch the cruise ships leave. The red sun reflected off their shiny funnels and windows, He worshiped the setting sun. He would wave. Many thought he was waving at the ships, the Bay and the setting sun. He was actually waving out to sea as he saw in his mind's eye, his father, a Captain, sailing off in the distance. His wave was a melancholy one. He waved good bye to father. It was also a goodbye to the city he had grown up with and loved. So much had been torn down that he could only revisit it in his mind's eye. Sometimes that was sufficient. Other times that egged him on to be proactive. He often sought solace from Evelyn Crandall. She brought him good and bad news from what was happening in the Commission for Urban Renewal. He would comment, "It's more urban destruction than renewal."

Truly waited. He knew the fog would roll in as soon as the sun had set. The air would chill, the warm water of the Bay of Fundy would let off some heat and the fog would gather. He watched as he saw the grand old family home on Douglas Avenue disappear in the mist. He remembered. He had visited there many times. His mother could make a meal or treat out of nothing. He had listened to the stories of the sea.

The fog crept in like a mama bear protecting her young. It hunted out every nook and cranny of the city. No one was immune to the fog. It seeped into every space. New paint applied that day experienced the pending ravages of time and weather. Long time natives of the city pulled their sweaters up tight around their necks and headed for home. The fog didn't deter them. Their knowledge of the streets of home was indelible. No amount of fog could obliterate what was. Truly knew. He may have been enveloped by the fog but the fog had not taken its toll on him. Instead, he relished the fog. It gave him a canvas on which to paint his memory of the city before urban renewal took over. Urban renewal could destroy the city. It could not destroy memory.

Truly watched. The city Centre disappeared. The harbour disappeared. Main Street below Fort Howe disappeared. There was nothing there to see anyway. It had been torn down.

Truly watched. The fog had done its duty. It rolled up Fort Howe so thick that even the SAINT JOHN sign so brilliantly lit and announcing the presence of the city disappeared. The plaintiff sound of the fog horn in the distance sounded its measured warning. Truly knew the three sisters light was also trying to peer through the thickness.

He stood alone. He had no thought of what the real warning was in the fog. He stood. Alone. With his thoughts. With the city as it was painted before him on the canvas of the fog. Alone. The fog and Truly. Only the fog knew. Only the fog knew what lurked in its cover and what would be revealed in the morning mist.

FIRE!

The sound of fire alarms screamed in Truly's head. Was he dreaming or was there actually sirens? He awoke from a restless night that had begun with fog and descended into comatose fog. The thought of the city, the scene he painted of what was and his sadness at what had become, had kept him tossing and turning. Awake but not awake. Alive but not alive. The Victorian city. Destruction. Hideous, non-descript buildings leaned into his nightmare and screamed. "Truly! Truly! You can't let this happen."

"What?" he said, sitting straight up in bed. It had been a chilly night. The fog had kept some of the late autumn warmth low to the ground. Still the hint of winter coming on crept into his second floor apartment on Germain Street. He had a choice apartment with a view. From there he could see the harbour, Market slip and beyond. But not this morning.

The fog was still so thick that he repeated the spoonerism he had heard on a radio blooper record when he was a boy. It made him laugh. It still made him laugh. "Damn!" he said. "As thick as sea poop! And that's no joke. That fog will either delight the tourists or degrade our city reputation. Damn!" he repeated as he pulled off his night shirt. He chuckled. His night shirt was red flannel with Santas emblazoned on it. People called him Santa because of his long white beard. They would never guess that Truly was "Santa." At least in his own mind he thought of himself as Santa bringing joy and cheer to a city that often descended into bi polar depression and sadness.

This was such a morning. "Some will see this," he whispered as he donned his boxers, red of course, and headed to the kitchen for some porridge. "Porridge with heavy cream," he continued. "Yes sir, people will either see this morning as something to relish, 'foggy morning in Saint John town,'" he hummed the tune, "or," he continued, "just another day in a city that is better hidden in fog than seen."

He heard the sirens again. "What the.." he said out loud. "What the devil is going on around here?" He pulled a matching red t-shirt on to cover up his Santa tattoo. His beard may have been long, but not long enough to make him decent for viewing in his window. He would never let "Santa" be seen in less than decent garb. "Need to keep up the reputation," he said.

The fog was thick. He didn't realize right then, but the fog had mingled with smoke. The smoke had hung at a level covering the entire city. "It's not enough," he said, "that we have to contend with fog, now we have to deal with smoke and fog." He tried to see through the fog. No use. He could just barely see down onto Princess Street below. "Fog." He repeated. "Smoke."

The phone rang just as he raised a spoonful of his porridge, brown sugar, butter and heavy cream. "Darn it all," he whispered. "I declare they must have a hidden camera in my place. Every time I have food heading for my mouth the phone rings!" He reached for the old black dial phone sitting nearby on the kitchen counter. He had resisted getting one of those new-fangled, powder blue princess phones. Old fashioned dial and black suited him just fine.

"Yes!" he said. "Make it quick. I've got porridge waiting to go over tongue and to the stomach, here it comes." He laughed.

"Funny," said the person on the other end. "Evelyn Crandall here," she continued. "Fire! Truly. Fire! Can you see it?"

"How can I see it," he said as he loaded up the porridge into his mouth.

"Whadda ya say?" she asked.

"How can I see it?" he repeated this time with a little less porridge mumble.

"Fire!" she repeated. "There's a fire across town. Put that spoon down for a minute while I tell you."

"Fire!" he shouted. "Fire! How would I know? The city is so socked in with fog. It is thicker than sea poop." He laughed.

"It's not funny, Truly," she repeated. "There's a fire over on the Avenue!"

"Douglas Avenue?" he asked.

"Yes! Douglas Avenue," she repeated. "I am all out of breath. I was out for my morning walk when the sirens went off. I'd just come out of Saint Luke's. I heard the siren. Then I saw the trucks racing around the corner and up the Avenue. I took chase as fast I could go."

"And?" he replied.

"And," she continued. "It's the Huggard house. You know the one with the widow's walk overlooking the harbour. Jenn Huggard used to hold court up there waiting for Captain Haddon. It's on fire."

"Fire!" he whispered. "I figured it would only be some time before there'd be more fires." He said to himself.

"What did you say," she replied.

"I said," he continued, "I figured that fire would strike again. The fire at The Anglican Church in the Valley is still suspect. The fire marshall may have concluded his inspection, but…"

"But what?" she asked.

"But," he continued. "Father Davies is still missing. The congregation is left in ashes, in more ways than one. And the church is gone forever. You probably know about the urban renewal sign that appeared shortly after the fire."

"Yes," she said. "The Commission on Urban Renewal takes every opportunity that comes along for an excuse to tear down, destroy, and sanitize what was once our beautiful Victorian architecture. They didn't so much as mourn the fire of Valley Church as they salivated at the opportunity to level that whole area. All they can see is opportunity to make money or to appear to the public as if they are trying to save our city from depression, degradation and doom."

"Really?" he said.

"Of course," she replied. "Not everyone in city government is interested in saving what was or rebuilding in such an architectural style that would beautify the city. Some are just in office or on commissions to see what they can get out of it. Kind of like Mrs. Jones building in an area beneath her self-imposed social status in order to be able to say she is Mrs. Jones, not just ONE of the Jones."

"You've heard that too?" he said.

"Sure!" she replied. "I know her from Anglican Church circles. She's a social climber. She's not interested in historical preservation. She just wants to see where she can climb to. I have news for her. She'll end up six feet under like the rest of us and leave behind in her wake, a city in ruins. Ashes to ashes, dust to dust is her motto. She may not realize it, but that's her end. Ours too."

Truly laughed. "So," he continued. "what about the fire?"

"Gone." She replied.

"Gone?" he asked.

"Yes," she continued. "Gone. I guess it started in the early morning hours under the cover of fog. The fog was so thick up there on the promontory that it took some time before anyone realized there was a fire. When it was discovered, it was too late. It was a goner. All the fire fighters could do was stop the flames from jumping over to the house next door, and the house next door. The whole avenue could have gone up in flames. I watched for a bit but had to finish my walk about and stop at the Dominion store that had opened by that time. There's a Commission meeting later this morning. I'm sure the fire will be on our agenda. Along with now what?"

"Now what?" he asked. "Now what do you mean?"

"Now what will the city do with another burned out building and an empty lot?"

"A parking lot," he replied. "Or one of those pre-fab, cookie cutter housing units."

"There goes the neighbourhood." She replied. "There goes our beautiful Victorian neighbourhood. Next thing you know, they'll start talking about tearing down The New Brunswick Museum."

"Never!" said Truly. "Never!"

"Oh yes," she replied. "All the commission can think about is how to displace. Heaven forbid they think of renew, rebuild, restore or replace! Sad."

"Indeed," said Truly. "My porridge is getting cold," he said as he scooped up some more. "Porridge, brown sugar, butter and heavy cream." He said.

"You're going to die of clogged veins," she said.

"Never!" quipped Truly through a mouthful. "Never! Santa never dies."

"It's your paunch," she needled him. "I've gotta go. Chat some more. I'll keep you posted. You keep me posted. Keep those ears unplugged and your eavesdropping senses honed. Maybe you'll hear something that will interest the fire marshal, commission and me!" Click. She was gone.

"Hmm," whispered Truly through the final spoonful of porridge. "Quite the woman. Rarely says goodbye. Doesn't give you a chance to say goodbye. She strikes while the iron is hot and then is gone. Leaves one to wonder. Leaves one to one's own conclusions. I guess I'll have to meander over town and check out the avenue. Maybe the fog will lift by the time I get there."

Truly combed his beard. He pulled on his jeans with red suspenders. He pulled a red sweater over his head and wrapped his Stuart plaid scarf around his neck. It was too early in the season for his Santa hat so he grabbed his red baseball cap. He'd had it made just for such occasions. He had his favorite slogan embroidered on it. "Santa wants to make Saint John great again!"

The heavy beveled glass door closed sturdily behind him as he stepped out on Germain Street.

Germain Street Beveled Glass Doorways

BREAKFAST AT REGGIE'S

It had been a fortnight since the clergy meeting at Reggie's. Valley Church had been declared a total loss. The Commission on Urban Renewal had posted that residents of the Valley were going to be relocated. Buildings were scheduled to be torn down. The fire on Douglas Avenue had set the city on edge. In addition, Father Davies still had not been seen since before the fire at Valley Church. "Where had he disappeared to leaving his congregation to fend for themselves?" That was the question everyone was asking. He wasn't found in the ashes of his church. But, as some were saying, "His absence was making an ash of him, no matter how beloved he was by the congregation and the city."

"Rabbi," said Rev. Wentworth, "I am glad you could make it. We have been waiting for your return. How was Montreal?"

"Same as usual," said Rabbi Rosenfeld. "I saw my few remaining relatives. The city has changed since I grew up there. But it's still home. I paid my respect at the graves. And I had several lovely evenings with cousins. Esther and Vern are getting on in years. I'm glad I had a chance to see them before they head to Florida for the winter."

"It is always good," said Wentworth, "to stay connected with our kin. We can create families wherever we settle but blood kin, even when we battle each other, is the best."

"Indeed," said the Rabbi. "I hear much has been happening here in Saint John over the past month. Fill me in."

"The City," said Wentworth, "is on edge. We have had two fires. The Commission on Urban Renewal is hell-bent on tearing down anything that doesn't look useful. They want to replace historic buildings with non-descript, meaningless architecture. The latest is that right after Valley Church burned, they announced that the people in the Valley would be relocated so that the buildings could be razed."

"What?" said the Rabbi. "Some of the most beautiful buildings in the city are there. Why not restore and repurpose."

"That's too much work," said Wentworth. "Besides, they say, where would the money come from?"

"Oil? Lumber?" said Palnick. "Creative financing. Tax incentives to encourage businesses to stay in the city."

WHILE THE CITY SLEPT

"Too much work," said Wentworth. "It's easier to tear down than it is to think creatively. Since they don't seem to have the motivation, we have decided . . ."

"Who is 'we'?" said the Rabbi. "By the way, call me Zeke. So who is 'we'?"

"The clergy in the city," said Wentworth. "Call me Jake. We are brothers in faith and this endeavour. We met two weeks ago to discuss the situation. We all agreed that we have historic buildings that are in jeopardy. Not only are our congregations declining, our buildings are in need of repair. We need to preserve what little we have left of congregational members AND the buildings we house. They are part of the city's treasure. They are the reason people come to see this city. IF the Commission on Urban Renewal keeps plowing forward..."

"There won't be a city to see," said Zeke. "I understand. We are even contemplating moving out of our historic synagogue on Carlton Street. But if we do, I assure you it will be to an historic house or building further across the South end. We'll restore whatever we move into."

"Perfect!" said Jake. "You are just the person we need to be with us. You have influence with the merchants in town. We have some influence with the City Councilors and the Commission. Do you know Evelyn Crandall? Do you know Truly Morrell?"

"I do," said Zeke. "They are solid native born citizens of the city and New Brunswick. They care."

"Indeed they do," said Jake. "Truly spends a lot of time observing the city. He always has his finger on the pulse of what is happening around him. He walks and talks."

"Good, good," said Zeke. "And Evelyn?"

"Evelyn," said Jake, "Is our insider spy."

"What?" said Zeke. "Dear Evelyn! A spy!"

"You got it," said Jake. "Evelyn knows many people in the city. She attends Saint Luke's Anglican. She has even been a member of their vestry. But most important, she has managed to get herself appointed a member of the Commission on Urban Renewal. The joke is on them!"

"How so?" said Zeke.

"The joke is" continued Jake, "that she isn't interested in Urban Renewal. She is interested in preservation and restoration. So she is like the proverbial squirrel under the pews ready to attack at any moment. She's our listening post. She's our insider. The Commission thinks they are safe planning what they are planning. They have no idea that kindly, gentle Evelyn is a plant. She reports to us after every meeting. Then we plan."

"Us?" said Zeke.

"Yes," said Jake. "The underground meetings of the Saint John Clergy. Truly, Evelyn, and sometimes Noll Huggard are our secret agents."

"Noll?" said Zeke. "Noll who rarely has anything to say?"

"Yes, Noll," replied Jake. "He may not have much to say but he has a knack for eavesdropping. Occasionally he drops a hint or two with one of us. Whenever we see him around the city, we make sure to meet, greet and secretly pump him for his thoughts. He wasn't happy at all when Valley Church burned but he did comment that the fire gave the commission "one less target for destruction.""

"Seriously?" said Zeke.

"Yes, seriously," replied Jake. "So our goal is to meet regularly. We want to keep an eye on the work of the Commission. Where we can, we want to throw a clinker in their mis-directed plan for urban renewal. We want to stop whatever we can being destroyed before it is too late. You say your congregation is planning to move out of your old synagogue. That's fine but even there, we want to make sure when you move that the building is preserved. It has witnessed years of Jewishness in Saint John. It is especially unique in that it is right across from Old Stone Church. It can easily find a new purpose. There's no need for another parking lot in that area, especially since businesses are moving out of town to shopping malls."

"I hear," said Zeke, "that Manchester, Robertson and Allison is on the verge of closing or moving. It's probably too late to avert that but just the same, perhaps we can have some influence on what replaces that structure if it is torn down."

"Rumour has it," said Jake, "That they want to put up one of those architecturally bland tall buildings. Their thinking is that a mall in the middle of King Street will save the city Centre. I think it is a pipedream. Evelyn is working her influence on the Commission."

"You know," said Zeke, "money talks. Where there is money involved, where people can see a profit for themselves, money wins out. Listen," he paused.

"Yes," said Jake.

"Listen," continued Zeke. "I have a cousin in Montreal. She is an architect. She is a graduate of the most prestigious architectural school in the colonies…"

Jake chuckled. "Colonies?"

"Yes, Colonies." Said Zeke. "I still think it was a mistake for them to divorce themselves from the Crown. They wouldn't be in such a political mess if they had the Queen to give them some stability."

"That's their problem," said Jake. "So what about your cousin?"

"Her name is Ella Osbourne. She goes by Elly." He continued. "What about her is that right now she is serving on the architectural preservation board of the Anglican Church of Canada. You know they have many, many historic structures across Canada. Congregations and Dioceses are always dealing with what to do with these historic buildings that congregations can no longer financially support. Elly is a consultant to the Anglican Church. She knows the ins and outs of preservation and political wrangling."

"Do you think,…" said Jake

"Do I think she might help us?" said Zeke. "I am sure of it. And since she is my cousin she might even come to Saint John and consult with our clergy group. I would even pay for her to come."

"Let's," said Jake. "Did you see her when you were in Montreal?"

"I did," replied Zeke, "And we even commiserated with the fact that much of our history is disappearing. She is as interested in preservation and restoration as we are."

"God moves in a mysterious way," said Jake. "Who knew?"

"Exactly," said Zeke. "I will contact her. I'll see if I can persuade her to come and consult."

"Perfect," said Jake. "We'll be meeting bi-weekly from now on. We must keep moving forward with this. We must not delay. Hello Truly," said Jake. Truly had just arrived for his morning coffee break.

"Hello Truly," said Zeke. "It's nice to see you. We're just about to leave so I am glad you came in. Rev. Wentworth mentioned earlier that you are a great observer of the city's activities. I appreciate that. I want to see the city preserved and restored as much as anyone else. Feel free to chat anytime."

"I am always up for a chat," said Truly as he found a seat near the counter. "I'll let you finish whatever it was you were chatting about. While you're at it, don't forget the fire that happened over on Douglas Avenue two nights ago. Add that to your topic."

"Anything," said Jake, "that adds to our ammunition stopping urban renewal and destruction is right for our agenda. Keep us posted, Truly. We're suspicious about anything suspicious."

"Me too," said Truly as he turned to place his daily order for oatmeal. "Me too. Catch you another time."

"I bet," said Jake, "there's something suspicious about that Douglas Avenue fire. If anyone knows anything, it's Truly. Let me know how you do with your architect cousin. I'll plan for our group to meet again in two weeks. This time we'll meet at Saint Luke's. Your cousin can see that magnificent building. That will inspire her to consult with us in saving Saint John. The city may be asleep but we aren't. We are wide awake and ready to pounce on that Commission on Urban Renewal. Evelyn Crandall will let us know when the time is right."

"You got it," said Zeke, "as he gathered up his briefcase and headed out the door. "Gotta get to the office. Blessings on you," he waved. "And," he whispered to himself, "save us from any more fires."

THE COMMISSION ON URBAN RENEWAL
"O Fortunati Quorum Jam Moenia Surgunt"[7]

"It's a happy day," said Chairman Israel McLennan as he called to order the Commission on Urban Renewal.

"I wouldn't call it that," replied Evelyn Crandall.

McLennan ignored Evelyn for the moment. He often ignored her. She had been appointed to the commission by Mayor Blake and McLennan was never quite sure why. Evelyn could be the kindly elderly lady, a woman about town, or she could be the needle just waiting to pierce a boil here and there. McLennan was never quite sure.

Mayor Joshua Blake had appointed McLennan chair of Urban Renewal for the city. He had expertise with infrastructure but that was about it. It was quite clear that he was not only chair for the benefit of the city, he was also there for his own reasons, not the least being political, financial and self-promotion. If one listened carefully to what he had to say, he could be heard mumbling under his breath, "We'll see where this position will get us." He had his eye on the Mayor's job. He really had his eye on being the Premier of New Brunswick. The longer, however, he rose and gained power, it was clear that he wasn't the brightest lightbulb on the chandelier. And when a dimwit rises to power, power is corrupted and pulls others down. Others jump on the bandwagon for the ride. McLennan was no exception.

"It's a happy day," Chairman McLennan repeated.

"I wouldn't call it that," repeated Evelyn.

"It's a happy day," repeated McLennan as he took note of those in attendance. He checked the names. There were twelve in all. Eight had been appointed by the Mayor. Four were of McLennan's choosing. The Mayor had selected people representative of the city. Each had their own expertise. McLennan had chosen those he thought would be supportive of his agenda, cronies, if one must say. If not cronies, at least prominent city individuals who would support the intended agenda of the Commission.

---

[7] Saint John city motto: Latin for, ("O Fortunate Ones Whose Walls Are Now Rising." or "O Happy They, Whose Promised Walls Already Rise")

The Commission had been established as one of the Mayor's promises: "To revitalize, renew and restore the city to its urban glory. To insure that the city lives up to its Loyalist founding and city motto. "O Fortunati Quorum Jam Moenia Surgunt" – "O fortunate one whose walls are now rising."

The city had fallen into unfortunate dole-drums. That happens with people who become blind to their surroundings. Buildings start to disintegrate. The scenery no longer holds a special interest for the residents. What was, has become has been. There is little or no interest in preservation. Except for people like Evelyn Crandall, Truly Morrell, Noll Huggard and now the clergy, there was little motivation to bring back what once was. It is easier to tear down than renew and restore.

"Let's get on with it," said Elijah Bentley. He had been appointed by the Mayor because he represented the city on legal matters as well as being a Crown Lawyer. Bentley liked to laud himself as being a lawyer of some distinction, even though he was from the British Virgin Islands. He saw himself as a real Canadian practicing in New Brunswick. No matter that times had changed. He liked to hang on to his contrived British accent and assumed status. People called him Bowtie Bentley behind his back because his signature was his flashy bow ties and his Bentley convertible. He was oblivious to the fact that he was often the butt of jokes.

"Right," said Evelyn. "It's not a happy day. We have work to do. Finish the attendance so we can get out of here and do something really productive. I'm scheduled to serve at the soup kitchen over on Union Street at noon. I suppose you have those buildings in your sights."

McLennan ignored Evelyn. He often ignored her. She was a thorn in his side. He looked past her as if she weren't there. On the slim occasion that he did listen to her, he discovered that she did have a relevant point. Now wasn't one of those times. "Shh," he said as he waved her off with his hand and continued with attendance.

"Albert Parlee," he said.

"Here," said Parlee

"Albert," continued McLennan, "I have you on the agenda to discuss the recent rash of fires. Be ready when I call upon you."

"Check," said Albert. He had some expertise in sleuthing out causes. He especially liked digging around in the proverbial ashes of mysteries. When he discovered a tidbit leading to a conclusion or a crime, he never hesitated to make it known. He was often quoted in the newspaper as having solved this, that or another mystery. Parlee had many friends in low and high places. He used them in a squirrely kind of way for his own benefit. Some had even found their way into his amateur attempts to write short murder stories. Truly Morrell was one whom Parlee liked to describe in his writings. "White beard. Bald head. Perpetual presence around the city." Albert would comment when he was researching this, that or another mystery. No one was innocent until Parlee proved them innocent.

"And," continued McLennan, "this time, let's keep your prejudices out of your report. You're the last one to be talking about short stature, grimacing looks and a waddle in a walk. Look at yourself before you call the kettle black."

Parlee slunk down in his chair. He knew when he had been chastised, put in his place was more like it. He was a valuable member of the Commission but McLennan wasn't going to let anyone leap over him and take all the applause for renewal or destruction of the city. McLennan could intimidate as much as ingratiate. He was as big and fat as Parlee was short and small. When McLennan stood up, which he often did while chairing a meeting, he towered over everyone else bringing a shadow over the proceedings. What McLennan wanted McLennan often got. But what McLennan wanted wasn't always to the benefit of the city, no less the Commission.

"Mary Jones," continued McLennan with the attendance.

"Here," replied Mary.

"Let it be recorded in the record," that Mary is here. Be sure to list her as THE Mrs. Jones." He laughed.

"That's not funny," said Mary. "I may be Mrs. Jones but you don't have to emphasize THE."

"You said it yourself," replied McLennan. "I'm just confirming what you said. Didn't you say when you built that grandiose, out of place house in the middle of such common housing that there you could be THE MRS. JONES instead of just one of the Joneses somewhere else, like up in Rothesay. Up there you could flaunt your wealth and just be one of the Joneses."

Mary took her hat off and set it on the chair beside her. She always wore a hat that properly matched her outfit. She shopped at Manchester, Robertson and Allison and Calps. That's where anyone who was anyone shopped. And Mary surely wanted to be "anyone" amongst the common ones. Mayor Blake had appointed her to the Commission for that very reason. She knew how to schmooze. She ran in any circle that came along that reeked of money and status. In fact, when the Queen came to visit some years before, Mary was the host for the afternoon tea. She had no clue that the Queen would much of preferred her favorite drink over some weak Red Rose Tea. "Dear," the Queen could be heard whispering, "a shot of Doubonet, a shot of gin, two ice cubes and a slice of lemon will do just fine." Mary didn't get the message. She served the Queen tea anyway out of her blue Periwinkle Royal Doulton service.

Mary adjusted her scarf and her face so as not to belie the fact that she was insulted. She much preferred to be in on the circle than to be on the fringe. She did know how to be appropriate rather than THE Mrs. Jones all the time. Appropriate is appropriate in appropriate situations. Adaptable is better when one wants something.

"Benjamin Northrup," continued McLennan.

"Here," replied Benjamin. "Ben is fine." He said. Northrup had moved into the city from upcountry. His family were originals. They traced their ancestry back to the first landing of Loyalists at Market Slip. As such they were originals. There was no in-breeding with them. They married Loyalists and behaved like Loyalists. Whenever "God Save the Queen" could be heard, Ben would stand at attention. The Northrups had been doing that since King George III had granted them 300 acres up on Bull Moose Hill in Springfield. They still owned the land. Their ancestors were buried up there. No matter that no one could find the graves. The wooden grave markers had long rotted and disappeared. Trees had grown up hiding any hint that the dead were buried there. Ben's great, great grandmother, Mary Northrup, had married James Huggard. Since it was the Huggard mansion on Douglas Avenue that was recently destroyed by fire, Ben had a connection and a keen interest in finding out the why of the fire. After all, whenever some of his kin were inflicted with disaster, Ben was ready, willing and sometimes able.

"Hurry it up," said Evelyn Crandall. "You may be happy, but I am not. You are wasting our time as usual. Do you have an agenda or are we going to ramble on again as before. It would be nice," she continued with her best proper and polite voice, "if we could come to some understanding of how we will preserve, restore and protect our beautiful Victorian city before any more of it goes up in flames."

"Protect," said McLennan, "is up to the RCMP. Beautify? Well perhaps some wealthy people can move into what's left of Germain,

Carlton, Victoria and other streets and renovate those decrepit buildings."

"Nice thought," said Bentley. "But that won't happen if we don't give them some incentive."

"You've got lots of money," said Mary Jones. "You buy some and restore." She moved her hat so as to see better instead of looking through the feathers.

"You're a good one to talk," said Bentley. "You could have done that very thing. Instead you chose to build that monstrosity out there with the pre-fab, double wide homes. It is so out of place it doesn't add a twit to that neighbourhood. It just makes everyone else feel small and insignificant."

"Exactly," said Mary. "I am THE Mrs. Jones, after all. Get on with it."

"I'm sorry I started this confrontation," said Evelyn. "Izzie, may I call you Izzie."

"Isreal, please," said McLennan.

"Okay, Israel," she continued. "I'm sorry I started us off on the wrong foot by saying it is not a happy day. I'm never happy when it comes to a fire that destroys one of our beautiful Victorian homes, or a church or whatever. It saddens me that our city is gradually disappearing on its own from neglect and…" she paused.

"And?" said Ben.

"And," she continued, "Sometimes it is disappearing at our own hands. How much have we torn down that could have been saved, restored and repurposed? Main Street, for instance. It is nothing but a wasteland. Not even the marigolds in summer marching down the middle are sufficient to give the impression of who we were and what we have become. They are a nice gesture on the part of city and the children but they don't replace what we once had."

"I agree," said Edna Boyle. Edna had been quiet long enough. She had been taking notes as well as making mental notes. Edna, with her thrift store clothes and perennial little black purse, had been sitting quietly listening and being a good secretary of the meeting. She often gave the appearance that she was neither smart nor listening. But she was a quiet presence. She could wield power when it was needed. It was that reason that the Mayor had appointed her to the commission. Edna had grown up on Metcalf Street during a time when that area was called Portland. Her family attended Victorian Street Baptist Church until it had met its end, closed and was torn down. She had witnessed the destruction of the beautiful stained glass windows. She knew how heavy the hearts of her parents were as they watched Portland, now called The North End, descend into tenements that had almost gone past their candidacy for restoration. The North End was approaching destruction.

"In a few years," she had commented to Mayor Blake, "There will be nothing left of a shell of what once was. Only memories. Then you might as well tear it down, level the place and let nature grow up. It is better to obliterate what once was than to let it stand there screaming decay, neglect, drugs, poverty and crime." Mayor Blake agreed. He put her on the Commission.

"I'm glad you agree, Edna," said McLennan. When McLennan wasn't blustering and bullying his way through a meeting, he could finesse the members into thinking his bluster was their agenda.

"Thank you," said Edna. "Now that we've spent an hour bantering and bickering, may we move on to something productive?"

"Let's" replied everyone present.

"Okay," said McLennan. "Then I retract my opening statement that "it's a happy day," and replace it with, "it's a day to remember. We've had two fires. Two of our historic buildings are gone. But now we have an opportunity."

"For what?" said Evelyn. "Hurry it up. I need to get over to Union Street for some meaningful people contact. People have needs while we are ..."

"Rambling," said Bentley. "I agree. What are you getting at?"

"Renewal," said McLennan. "Now we have an opportunity to tear down another section or two of the city in the name of Urban Renewal."

"What?" said Mary. "What?"

"We've already started," said McLennan, "to clear the way for beautifying the Valley now that The Valley Church is gone. Signs are up. People are going to be relocated. Some of those unsightly buildings will be torn down. And..."

"And?" said THE Mrs. Jones. "And?"

"And something new in their place," said McLennan.

"Just as I thought," said Evelyn Crandall. "Something new, bland and meaningless that will be torn in 40 years and add nothing to our city. I've heard enough of this 'happy talk' for today. I have people to feed, souls to feed and angst to be calmed down. Some of those people you are talking of displacing are the very ones we feed. I'll thank you to adjourn this meeting until next week. I think we all need to think about what we are doing and why we are doing it? What is the reason each of us is on this Commission? What do "we" want out of this? Just another bureaucracy that looks like it is doing something or a bureaucracy that actually does something AND something that is appropriate! I'm leaving now." She gathered up her huff and headed for the door. "Let me know when our meeting next is!"

"She means well," said McLennan as he smoothed out his ruffled feathers that had been disturbed by Evelyn's huffy exit. "She does have a point. Edna," he said. "Record that the meeting is adjourned as of 11:45 am this morning. Send notices out that we will meeting in a fortnight to continue this discussion. Let each of us consider what to do about the remains from the fires."

"Will do, chief," said Edna with a salute. She knew how to schmooze as well as THE Mrs. Jones or the next person.

"I'm going to take the opportunity," said McLennan, "since Evelyn brought up the subject, to go have lunch with the down and outers at the Soup Kitchen. Evelyn will be impressed. Maybe I'll learn something. Anyone else coming?" He looked around the circle. Seeing no takers he rose, adjourned the meeting and headed out the door. Ben heard him whisper, "Maybe this will get me somewhere in this city. Maybe the Mayor will be there."

MISSING

It was fortunate that no one had been burned up in the two fires. It was unfortunate, however, that the Rev. Gwyn Davies was still missing. He was prone to disappear now and then. The congregation didn't question his times away. They adored him as their priest. He was always attentive to the members. His story sermons and creativity touched their hearts. The city knew him as their story pastor. His disappearance was starting to ripple through the city.

Rev. Davies had been pastor of St. Paul's Valley Church for ten years upon emigrating from Wales. A number of members at Valley church were Welch. When it came time for a pastor search some years before, that segment of the congregation convinced the rest that a Welch pastor would be an asset. The Welch are known for their hymn singing. Valley Church loved to blend Anglican chant with Welch song. In addition to the church's traditional choir was the Valley Church Welch Men's Chorus. Rev. Davies had encouraged its founding. It had become a staple at many events around town. At Christmastime the Valley Church Welch Men's Chorus offered a widely attended concert at the church. Sometimes, weather permitting, an abbreviated version of the program was presented on the Edward VII Memorial Bandstand in Kings Square. All the church had to do was announce the event and people came out in droves. They were there to hear Rev. Davies as much as the men's chorus. His singing was legend. He was prone to break out in song. Sometimes just while he was out for his morning constitutional. He was always asked to give the blessing at the Annual Christmas Breakfast that the Sisters of Charity held each year. He never hesitated to sing it. It put people in the most thankful and Christmas mood.

Suo Gân
Huna blentyn ar fy mynwes
Clyd a chynnes ydyw hon;
Breichiau mam sy'n dynn amdanat,
Cariad mam sy dan fy mron;
Ni chaiff dim amharu'th gyntun,
Ni wna undyn â thi gam;
Huna'n dawel, annwyl blentyn,
Huna'n fwyn ar fron dy fam.

His voice and the Welch words always brought the gathering to silence. People didn't know what to say other than, "Thank you, Father. Would you please sing a little of it in English." He always obliged.

See the child that Mary bore
On her lap so softly sleeping
In a stable cold and poor
Ox and ass their vigil keeping
Flights of angels 'round His head
Sing Him joyful hymns of greeting
Peace on earth, goodwill to men
Each to each the song repeating

"What will we do?" said Evelyn Crandall to Truly. She had popped into Reggie's for a quick toast and coffee before heading over to the Soup Kitchen for her weekly volunteering.

"What do you mean?" said Truly. "What will we do about what?"

Noll Huggard leaned forward over his usual plate of two eggs over easy, bacon and home fries. He was seated at his corner by the window where he could watch the city pass. Reggie said the corner might as well be named "Huggard." Noll was bundled up in his usual wool sport coat and scarf. For a change he had removed his woolen driver's hat. He didn't drive. He'd never owned a car. But he liked the hat. It made him feel jaunty as if it was possible for Noll to be jaunty. He was more surreptitious than jaunty. He leaned further over his plate as if he were trying to disappear behind the food. "What do you mean?" he whispered to himself. Most people knew Noll as "that man who walked around the city." Some people called him the inspector. Others just called him. "What do you mean?" he whispered again.

"I'm not speaking to you," said Evelyn in her most officious tone. "I'm speaking with Truly. You just don't mind. Pay attention to the eggs. They have eyes that are supposed to see. And hear. Not you."

Noll hunkered down and acted as if he hadn't heard her quip.

"So," continued Evelyn, "What will we do?"

"Do what?" asked Truly.

"Since Reverend Davies is missing, what will we do for grace at the Christmas Breakfast?" she continued.

"Say it, I guess?" asked Truly. "Say it. As usual. Maybe he'll show up by then."

"That's what I mean," she replied. "It won't be usual if Rev. Davies doesn't show up. He's been missing now for a month. There's still no sign of him. No one seems to know where he's gone to. It's a good thing the Valley Church people love him so much. Any other congregation would be in full mutiny by now. They are so patient."

"And," said Truly, "They do have the Rev. Wentworth at Old Stone Church who is filling in. They are worshiping there while they try to regroup."

"That can't go on forever," she said.

"I know, I know," replied Truly. "But in the meantime…"

"In the meantime," she continued, "What are we going to do for grace at the Christmas Breakfast?"

"Sing it yourself," he replied.

"Ha!" she replied. "That will be the day. I tried singing in the choir at Saint Luke's. After a couple of weeks the director handed me a bucket and said, "Here. Stand out front and collect donations for the choir." Funny man, he. I was kind of insulted, but not too."

"That is too funny," said Truly. "Did you do as you were told? Did you find a tune in the bucket? Raise any money."

Noll almost spit his food out. He thought he was doing a good job of covering up his eavesdropping. But not so good. He nearly choked.

"I said," commented Evelyn to Noll, "pay attention to your own business. Our business will take care of itself."

"I surely hope so," said Truly. "It would be nice if Rev. Davies would call in. Appear. Do something. Surely he knows his church has burned to the ground. Or does he? Maybe that's why he's not around? Do you suppose?"

"Suppose what?" said Evelyn. "Suppose?"

"No," continued Truly. "Rev. Davies? Never. He's too kind. He's too, what would you call it?"

"Welch?" said Noll under his breath.

"What?" said Evelyn.

"Welch." This time Noll spoke up. "Welch. You know. Welch."

"Silly man," said Truly. "Don't pay any attention to him. He's the inspector. He comes up with the strangest observations." He paused. "Aye, Noll," he said. "You know anything about Rev. Davies disappearance. What about the fire?"

"Nothing I would share," replied Noll as he stuffed the last bit of home fries into his mouth. "Gotta go."

"Gotta go where?" said Evelyn. "To do some more of your sleuthing. Don't you think the city can run without your perpetual presence?"

"Don't know," said Noll as he walked out the door. He grabbed a handful of mints from the jar on the counter. "For later," he whispered.

"Strange fellow," said Truly. "Now what about Davies?"

"I hope he shows up soon," said Evelyn. "If he doesn't there's going to be more suspicion and rumours. There's already enough rumours swirling around about the Valley Church and the Huggard Mansion fires. The Fire Marshall told Valley Church that the fire was an accident. I don't believe him. I am suspicious since Rev. Davies is missing."

"No way," said Truly. "He would never."

"Never?" said Evelyn. "Still water runs deep. Sometimes a person can turn quick as a whipstitch."

"Ha!" he laughed.. "Where'd you hear that expression?"

"Up country," said Evelyn. "My cousin Carrol used it the other day as we were having tea. I didn't think to ask her what she meant but I suppose I can imagine."

"What?" asked Truly.

"Quick as a whipstitch?" said Evelyn. He nodded. "It's a quilting term. Loose. Fast. Kind of like basting."

"Basting," said Truly. "Now there's a term no one has used concerning this fire. While the mystery of the fire continues, it is as if everyone is being basted with hot butter."

"You're funny," said Evelyn.

"Funny," replied Truly, "but people listen to me. I often know before anyone else knows."

"Well," she said as she pulled here scarf around her neck, ready to confront the chilly morning fog, "Well," she continued, "if you find out what the devil is going on around this city, clue me in. Maybe I can convince the Commission on Urban Renewal to renew themselves and their thinking before they tear down anything else."

"Good luck on that one," replied Truly. "We all know most of the members are in it for themselves. "two for me, one for the city," or more appropriately, 'all for me and none for the city' is more like it. That chairman of yours, McLennan is his name?"

"Yes," she said.

"That chairman," continued Truly, "I think is just in it to see where it will get him. He has no more interest in urban renewal than a squirrel has planting acorns To grow trees. What a nut!"

"Okay," said Evelyn. "We're getting into unspoken territory. I've got to run. The Soup Kitchen is about to open and I'll have to say grace today. Or maybe we can get one of the down and outers to say it."

"Good luck on that one too," said Truly. "A little gratitude around here would be good, especially when it comes to what we had in this city, and what we are no longer going to have, thanks to the Urban Renewal Commission."

"Okay," she replied. "I'll keep that in mind. In the meantime, finish your oatmeal. It must be cold by now. Then again, maybe this conversation heated it up!" She laughed. "Gotta run. Catch you tomorrow if you're here. I'll expect a good report."

"Any report," said Truly. "Bye for now." She was right. His oatmeal was cold. "Here. Zap this," he said to Maude as he handed over the bowl of oatmeal.

"Another hot topic, Ayuh?" said Maude. "You ought to stay away from such heavy conversation. Eat your oatmeal first. Then I wouldn't have to zap it every morning."

Truly chuckled as he headed back to the table with his reheated oatmeal. "She probably knows as much as anyone else around here," he whispered to himself.

"Whatdaya say?" she said.

"Nothing," replied Truly. "Just nothing. After all this, Rev. Davies is still missing." He paused. "Just nothing."

THE COMMISSION

Another fortnight had gone by. Still no progress had been made concerning the fires, the disappearance of Rev. Davies or the plans for Urban Renewal.

"I spoke with the mayor," said Chairman McLennan as he called the meeting to order. "And…"

"And," said Bowtie Bentley, "and does he have anything important to add to our task?"

"Only that he wants us to speed up our work," said McLennan. "He's about to announce his candidacy for re-election and he wants to see some progress in the city."

"What kind of progress?" asked Evelyn Crandall. "More doom and gloom or something real we can celebrate?"

"Easy, easy," said Benjamin Northrup. "Rome wasn't built in a day."

"Nor torn down either," said Evelyn.

"Didn't take long to build my house," said Mary Jones. "Once I decided what and where it happened."

"Good for you THE Mrs. Jones," said Albert Parlee. "But that is just one house. And too boot, you weren't trying to repurpose an entire city. All you cared about was just one house in one neighbourhood. Did that spark any renewal out there in your neighbourhood, Mrs. Jones?" he said with some sarcasm in his voice.

"Hmpf," she said. "You ought to appreciate that I chose to build at all. Maybe I should have stayed out in Rothesay where all the women are strong, all the men are good looking, and all the children are above average."

"That's not funny," said Albert Parlee. "You've been listening to too much to A Prairie Home Companion."

"Just read all of Garrison Keillor's books," she chuckled. "This city is turning into a Lake Wobegone."

"Wouldn't have hurt my feelings any," said Evelyn, "If you'd stayed in Rothesay. I think I feel a bout of indigestion coming on."

"Ladies, Ladies!" growled McLennan. "I haven't even called the meeting to order yet and we've descended into the lowest of low."

"You started it," said Mary, "with that quip about the Mayor. What are we here for anyway? For our own benefit? Or are we here to see if we can remake this city."

"Remake!" said Parlee. "That's just the problem with everyone around this city. They either want to remake it or dissert it. People leaving in droves. Toronto, Winnipeg, Calgary. That's where they are all going. They see green grass and less fog."

McLennan banged his fist on the table. Edna Boyle followed that with her famous whistle. No one could whistle as loud as her. She had developed the ability when raising her children. All she had to do was hang out the window, put two fingers to her teeth, and give a whistle. ALL the kids in the neighbourhood came running.

"Ouch!" said Evelyn. "I'll never be able to hear the pitch in choir again."

"Pitch!" said Sam Greene. Sam had been quiet up until then, but when he heard anything to do with singing he had a comment. He was the other person in the city, besides Rev. Davies, known for his singing. The Mayor had appointed him to the commission because of his expertise in business. His family owned Greeneville on the Kingston Peninsula. He also owned several typical three story homes in the North End. His expertise, however, didn't show when it came to maintaining his real estate. The fog rolled in daily and Sam's attitude toward his real estate rolled out. In fact Sam was known, upon occasion, to take advantage of others for his own benefit. The Mayor had no clue. He just knew that Sam Greene was known about town and that Sam knew about the city. The Mayor was wrong. That didn't stop him from stacking the Commission for Urban Renewal.

"Shush," said Annalee Gaudet. She had been sitting proper. As the archivist from the New Brunswick Museum, it was her duty, said the Mayor, to preserve and protect. At most of these meetings she sat demurely taking notes. Her black hair pulled back in a bun, her black suit with white blouse and business pumps said that she was there for business. The only thing about her that gave a hint that she might be there with an ulterior purpose was the brilliant red lipstick. It was the only colour she ever wore. "Shush," she repeated as she put her finger up to her red lips. She had placed her number 2 pencil parallel to the yellow legal pad she carried for notes. She had a bit of OCD. That's a good thing when it comes to maintaining archives, not always such a good thing when relating to people. "Shush," she repeated. "Let's consider one another as we consider the city."

The group sat in silence. It wasn't often that Annalee spoke but when she did, people sat up straight in their reproduction Chippendale style chairs. Some looked out the window that overlooked the Old Loyalist house. Others seemed to think there was something on the floor. Sam Greene straightened his tie, piled up his papers in ready to make a dash for the door. Evelyn adjusted her hat. Mrs. Jones, THE Mrs. Jones, pursed her lips. She didn't appreciate being told but she knew when to shut up. Bowtie Bentley made note of the demeanor of those around the table just in case he saw an opportunity to bring a lawsuit against one or all. He could always use some cash in his pocket for gas in the Bentley.

"May we continue now?" asked McLennan. He paused. "Good! Then let us consider what progress we are making. The two fires…"

"What about the two fires?" said Benjamin Northrup? Our homestead up country on the Belleisle is no more. Burned to the ground. And all that is left is an empty space where it once stood. So what about the two fires here? Do you consider *that* urban renewal?"

"No," replied McLennan. "But," he continued, "It gives us an opportunity to continue to tear down and rebuild."

"Rebuild what?" said Evelyn. "We haven't rebuilt Main Street. In fact, I don't think we will ever rebuild it. It has just turned into a raceway for speeders. About the only good thing over there is the marigolds the children plant in spring and which the city tears up in the fall when they are dead. In between, Main is as dead as a communion wafer in the hands of a bigot."

"Now that's different," said Monsignor Rev. William Sweeney. He was the token clergy on the commission. The Mayor had insisted he join the commission because his church, The Cathedral of the Immaculate Conception, was such a visible presence over the city. Its spire reached to the sky. It could be seen far and wide. But the city surrounding it was decaying. The historic Sisters of Charity building next door was falling under the weight of declining membership in their order. They had found their purpose in being a way station for the homeless and down and out. Several churches on Waterloo Street had already closed. Someone had tried to turn one into a performing arts centre/theatre to no avail. There just wasn't the theater-going population in the city needed to support such a venture.

"Good one, Evelyn," said Sweeney. "I'll have to remember that next time I serve Mass. I hope I'm not the bigot who is holding the wafer of love. But you make a point. This commission sometimes seems more intent on its own purposes than serving the city. Are we really here for urban renewal? Or are we here for other reasons? Mrs. Jones?" he said as he gave her a sarcastic wink.

"Are you making a pass at me?" said Mrs. Jones.

"Hardly," said Rev. Sweeney. "And invalidate my vow of celibacy. That would be the day. There's no way I could ever come up to the level of THE Mrs. Jones." He had been listening all along. Nothing got passed him.

"I'm sorry," said Mrs. Jones. "I may be THE Mrs. Jones, but I am also a person of respect and intent."

"Really then," said Evelyn. "And what intent is that? Are you here to represent the city and residents or is there an ulterior motive for your being here?"

"Stop!" yelled McLennan. "You are all starting to sound like children. We have work to do and miles to go before we sleep."

"Or end up with no city at all," said Bentley.

"You too," said McLennan as he pointed his finger at Bentley and then let the finger point sweep the faces of those seated around the table. "You too! While we sit here dis-united the city rusts on into the ground. Now," he continued. "As I see it we have some major decisions to make. Let me list them." He turned to the chalkboard and began to list them.

1. The Central Railroad Station – what shall we do with it now that there are no trains.
2. Centennial Church – the congregation is about to fold and we'll be left with a 1200 seat historic building. It ought to come down.
3. Haymarket Square is nothing but a clogged, carbon monoxide disaster waiting to happen. No one gathers there anymore to sell their produce.
4. The Old Market has lost its patina, needs massive renovation, repurposing or destruction.

Evelyn reached for a tissue from her purse. She daubed her eyes.

"What's with you?" said Edna Boyle.

"It," sobbed Evelyn, "just breaks my heart to see our beloved Victorian city disintegrate before our eyes and to think we are partly responsible for it happening."

"Evelyn," said McLennan. "Evelyn. Stop. Let me continue so that we can be productive. I'm just making a list. We'll check it twice before we decide about any more urban renewal."

"What!" said Northrup. "Do you think you are Santa Claus? Are you a poet and don't know it."

The group laughed. They needed some levity now and then considering the job they are tasked to do.

"Thank you Ben," said McLennan. "I'm hardly Santa Claus. Truly Morrell with his long white beard is the city's real life Santa." He paused. "Let me finish this list. It will give us some things to think about between now and our next meeting. While we ponder what to do about these matters, work is proceeding to relocate the folks in the Valley and renew that area. We especially are interested in what to do about the burned out Valley Church property.

"They have to decide first," said Sweeney. "I am sure they will find a way forward when Rev. Davies shows up."

"Where is he anyway," said Annalee Gaudet.

"No one knows," said Evelyn. "We are all just praying he is safe and that his disappearance has a good explanation."

"Continuing on, with the list," said McLennan.

5. The North End – how can we encourage property maintenance and restoration?
6. The buildings around King Square: the Woolworths, Calps, The Palace Theater.
7. Queen's Square. It is surrounded by some of the most beautiful buildings in the city. How can we encourage restoration?

"Can we agree?" he said, "that between now and our next meeting each of us takes time to observe these areas of the city. Can each of us come with some ideas of how to proceed?"

Seeing agreement, or at least a desire that the meeting be over, McLennan added, "Good. Then for next time let us come prepared. And if you can think of any other areas of the city we might consider for renewal, bring those ideas too. We want to make Saint John the best, most productive and beautiful city in the Maritimes."

"Agreed? Good!" before anyone could say any more, McLennan announced, "The Meeting is adjourned!"

DARKNESS

The evening fog had rolled in. It lingered. Waiting. It wasn't always clear what it was waiting for. Many assumed it was waiting for the sun to rise, warm air to hit and blue skies to appear. That was always the case. But what was going on under the fog?

The fog obliterated the specter of a city in renewal. Truly Morrell liked the fog. It comforted him. It helped him mourn. There are many ways to grieve. With the city under wraps, the fog provided a comforting fluff for his thoughts. He could rebuild the city from his memory. He could dream. He could imagine the day when old historic buildings would be honoured and restored. He even visualized the day when new buildings would fit in rather than intrude. Then he would find a pillow to lay down his head next to his beloved wife. She had passed the winter before. He needed the fog for comfort. She needed the fog for warmth where she lay overlooking the Bay of Fundy in Cedar Hill Cemetery out on Manawagonish Rd. His wife had loved the sea. The movement of the tide in the Bay of Fundy had always comforted her. So Truly chose Cedar Hill where they could both lie in eternity next to the sea they loved.

Truly didn't need to make frequent visits to Cedar Hill. He knew the view. It was indelibly etched in his mind and heart. The fog helped him see clearer. It provided a canvas on which he mindfully painted what had been and what could be. "It's strange," he said to himself, "how fog surrounded grief can help clear the mind." The fog.

In daylight hours the Saint John fog brought a strange whiteness to the city. It covered everything in a fine mist that looked benign. But the fog was never benign. Hidden in its droplets was damage and destruction. No amount of oil paint on old wooden buildings built after the Great Fire of 1877 could resist the fog. The paint welcomed the fog. The buildings attracted the fog. The fog wrapped itself tight as a ladies glove worn for an evening out. But this was no evening out. This was daily. Sometimes the fog was so thick that there was nothing to see.

"It's us," said Evelyn Crandall as she walked along Main. Truly had suddenly appeared from the midst of the fog. "Where are you going at this hour?" she said. She wasn't surprised to see him out so early. She was a little startled. The fog had made her think she was alone. Suddenly he appeared.

"I'm headed to Fort Howe." He said. "And where are you going at this socked-in hour?

"Saint Luke's" she said. "I'll be late." As she continued on up the slight incline toward the church. "You have a good look from Fort Howe if you can through this soup." She waved. He couldn't see. She had disappeared into the shroud.

Life was like that when the fog was in. It was the bane of existence for many people. For some the fog provided opportunities. Looking out the window some mornings, the most unmotivated of people could be heard saying, "Fog's in. No point in getting up today." They would go back to bed, turn up the heat and pull the fog up over them for some more sleep.

Then there was always those people who took advantage of the fog. But it was dangerous to do that. The city slowed to a rowboat's pace. What had ground to a halt the night before tried its best to get back up and running. The screech of railroad cars through the night. It gave some hint that life was still happening. But it was never clear. How could it ever be clear when there was fog?

Fog. London Fog. If one lost their bearings or mind, one could imagine they were in London or San Francisco. "I don't know why," whispered Truly, "Saint John isn't hailed as the fog capital of Canada. We ought to have a reputation. We ought to benefit from the fog. Instead," he whispered to himself, "people seem to remember a Reversing Falls that isn't reversing. They need to see it at the right time of day. People," he continued, "seem to remember driving through here and not seeing anything. They can't wait to get through and head to PEI or Nova Scotia. Not much we can do about the fog. There's lots we can do about what used to be. I sure hope that Commission on Urban Renewal doesn't get any ideas about the Old City Market. If they save nothing else, it ought to be the City Market."

Fort Howe was deserted at this foggy hour of the morning. There was the occasional car creeping up through the fog. It was a convenient place for the idle to sip their morning Tim Horton's coffee or... "Don't go there," he whispered. Truly wished he had gotten a cuppa, but less to carry was more convenient. In addition he didn't need another maple crème donut. He had just the right paunch for his Santa role. He swung his leg over the top of the split rail fence and sat looking out to sea. The Saint John sign had switched itself off. The only glow of the early morning was just that, early morning. The sun unsuccessfully trying to sneak its way through. He was alone. He thought.

The clock in the steeple chimed the hour. Truly counted even though he already knew. "One, Two, Three," he whispered. He could hear the clock in Trinity Church over time answer. "Four, five, six, Six O'clock and all's well." Sometimes he felt like the city watchman sitting on the hill watching, waiting. He hummed the tune to one of his favorite Advent hymns. The words had always haunted him.

> *Watchman, tell us of the night,*
> *What its signs of promise are.*
> *Traveler, o'er yon mountain's height,*
> *See that glory-beaming star.*
> *Watchman, doth its beauteous ray*
> *Aught of joy or hope foretell?*
> *Traveler, yes; it brings the day,*
> *Promised day of Israel.*[8]

"Watchman tell us of the night," he spoke out loud, "Watchman, tell us of the night," he paused trying to remember the rest of the verse. "For the morning seems to dawn," he continued. "Traveler, darkness takes its flight; Doubt and terror are withdrawn."

"Ha!" he laughed. "The morning is trying for dawn but all we have is thick fog. Very thick fog. But," he continued, "That's just fine with me. This way I don't have to look at the destruction the Commission on Urban Renewal has brought on the city."

"What?" came a voice through the fog.

"What what?" said Truly having been startled by the voice out of the fog. He looked around but could see no one. "What?" he repeated.

"That's what?" said the voice.

"What?" shouted Truly.

"I said, 'that's what!'" answered the voice.

"Who's there?" asked Truly.

"Just me," came the reply. "Just me."

Truly sat quietly. Had he heard? Where was that voice coming from? Was it the fog itself speaking?

"I'm here," said the voice.

"Where?" said Truly.

---

[8] John Bowring, 1792-1872

"Over here," replied the voice. "Been here all along. I felt the fence shift when you sat down. Disturbed my silence for a bit."

"I'm sorry," said Truly, "But ..."

"Noll Huggard," replied the voice. "I like it up here just as much as you. I come up here often. The fog clears my mind of cobwebs, especially since our place burned on Douglas Avenue."

Truly didn't reply. He sat there letting the intruder destroy the view he was constructing in his mind.

"You there?" said Noll.

"No!" replied Truly. "No. I'm not here. I am somewhere else long ago. Long, long ago."

Silence.

Truly wasn't sure if Noll was there, if he was still there. Truly thought Noll a harmless, lost soul. But Noll could also be creepy. He wandered the city. He seemed to have no purpose in life. Work and walk, that's what he did day in, day out. People knew him. But they never really knew him. Nor did Noll know anything but himself and the city.

"You there?" asked Truly. He could hear breathing. Noll had moved closer but not close enough to be seen through the fog.

"It'll be a lovely morning," said Noll. "I like these kinds of mornings. The fog brings the cover of darkness. And then, like right now, a red glow begins to appear. Look over there."

Truly couldn't see Noll nor could he see in what direction Noll indicated to be 'over there.' He assumed Noll was indicating a hint of sunrise. Truly looked. Toward Cenrtre city he could see a red glow rising. "The sun," he whispered, "is going to take care of this fog." What he didn't anticipate was that the rising sun wasn't the only red glow in the sky.

"Red sky at night, sailor's delight. Red sky in morning, sailor's warning" whispered Truly. "It may be that kind of day."

THE PEW

Evelyn Crandall entered Saint Luke's and found her favorite pew. She had sat there so many years that no one would dare sit there. Her butt had worn a space that no longer needed any Murphy's oil soap. The sextant didn't bother with her pew.

It was another typical morning. She was always happy to start the day with morning prayers. Her encounter with Truly on the way through the fog had only confirmed that she needed more than ever to pray. The Commission on Urban Renewal meeting had disturbed her. It also motivated her.

There was something about St. Luke's that assured her all was right with the world even when it wasn't. St. Luke's on the outside appeared to be just another bland church perched on a hill overlooking the Bay. There was nothing unusual about its architecture. Tourists passed by. It was just another church. Saint John natives had even become so accustomed to St. Luke's presence that they no longer noticed. Many had never been inside.

Evelyn cozied herself into her familiar and worn pew space. She was alone. The building embraced her. She knew she was in the presence of the divine. She always felt the presence of the divine. The morning fog was just confirmation of a God. It soaked into her clothing down to her white skin. It touched her like no person could. If there ever was a hint of regret or mean spirit, the fog, St. Luke's and the divine took care of it.

She looked around. No matter how many times Evelyn sat in St. Luke's, she was always filled with awe. God was there. When she felt the most rejected, alone and lost, she could always find God and herself in St. Luke's. The meetings of the Commission on Urban Renewal brought her down. St. Luke's made her spirit soar. She tried to keep a positive frame of mind but the ulterior motives of McLennan and others disturbed her. They had even suggested that St. Luke's might be a target for their urban renewal. "If St. Luke's could be torn down, it would open up the entire corner for better traffic flow," said McLennan at one meeting. Evelyn was horrified.

"How can they think such a thing," she said to herself. "This church has stood on this spot for a century or more. It is called the "Sentinel on Main Street. If they ever tear down this holy place, I'm done. They can bury me over there on Cedar Hill where there's a view of the Bay of Fundy. At least the Bay will be there for eternity."

The Victorian beams soared overhead as Evelyn bowed her head in prayer. They embraced and comforted her. Shipbuilders had pieced them together in such a way that if, turned upside down, the church would float. Now, with the less than honourable motives of the Commission, St. Luke's was in danger of sinking.

"This church," whispered Evelyn, "has been a beehive of activity for decades. Sure, it's not packed with people every Sunday but it stands as a beacon of goodness in a neighbourhood that is descending into despair. If they ever have such nerve to tear down St. Luke's they will be aiding and abetting the rack and ruin of what is left of the North End. There will be no North End anymore."

Evelyn felt a droplet of water. "The roof can't be leaking," she whispered as part of her prayer. "Maybe" she continued, "the fog is creeping into this building." Just then another droplet landed on the prayer book she had opened to one of her favorites. "The church is crying," she thought to herself. "Crying," she repeated out loud.

Although the sun was trying to dispense with the fog outside, it wasn't enough to light the sanctuary. Still the sun crept through the brilliant stained glass window over the altar. The window didn't need much light for it to influence the ambiance. The colours spread down over the altar and around onto the floor. They mingled with what seemed to be tears dripping from the ceiling.

She was alone. "I must be imaging this," said Evelyn louder than before. "Imagine," she continued, "The building is crying. It mourns all those who had worshiped here. It mourns, like so many of us, for the city we knew. Main Street is gone. Victoria Street Baptist is torn down. Buildings are boarded up. Beautiful homes with their Victorian woodwork and gingerbread have turned into tenements."

Evelyn began to cry. Her tears mingled with those of St. Luke's. Imagined or not, she would testify as long as the day is that she felt and heard the old building cry.

"Shipbuilders raised those beams so that we might," she whispered, "be transported to eternity. Look at that! Overhead cries. Shipbuilders," she whispered. "Their intent, as much as that of the congregation, was that St. Luke's would stand here as long as time, a sentinel to Main Street, the North End and a city in need of grace."

Evelyn smoothed out the damp page of the prayer book. Tears had mingled with the words. She prayed.

ALMIGHTY God, Father of our Lord Jesus Christ, Maker of all things, Judge of all men: We acknowledge and bewail our manifold sins and wickedness, Which we from time to time most grievously have committed, By thought, word, and deed, Against thy Divine Majesty, Provoking most justly thy wrath and indignation against us. We do earnestly repent, And are heartily sorry for these our misdoings; The remembrance of them is grievous unto us; The burden of them is intolerable.

Evelyn paused. "What," she said, "am I confessing? I didn't do anything. I am trying to stop others from doing what they ought not to be doing. If 'they' keep tearing down this city there will be hell to pay." Evelyn considered for a moment what she had just said. It wasn't in her nature to judge others unless they deserved to be judged. When she did judge others, she was quick to confess her own sin.

She could hear a siren off in the distance. That wasn't so unusual in a city the size of Saint John. It was unusual that the sound seemed to be coming from all directions. "Now what," she thought. "Lord help us," she continued as she finished the prayer. The page of her prayer book was now quite soggy from the mingling of the tears. She prayed:

"Have mercy upon us, Have mercy upon us, most merciful Father; For thy Son our Lord Jesus Christ's sake, Forgive us all that is past; And grant that we may ever hereafter Serve and please thee In newness of life, To the honour and glory of thy Name; Through Jesus Christ our Lord." [9]

"Amen," she heard whispered from the back of the sanctuary. Rev. Hatfield had quietly entered. He had been sitting in the back pew for quite a while. He prayed daily for the city, St. Luke's and whomever might be in the sanctuary"

"Have you been here long, Father?" she asked.

"Long enough," he replied. "Long enough to...

"To hear my prayers and see my tears?" she asked.

"Aye," he replied. "Aye. And they are heart felt." He had walked forward and sat down alongside her. That pew was also familiar to him. Rev. Hatfield had been Rector of St. Luke's long enough to know the names of people who had gone before and people who had passed since his arrival. He never sat in a pew without remembering who had sat

---

[9] Prayer of Confession from the Order for Holy Communion, The Anglican Church of Canada Book of Common Prayer, 1918.

there. To him, the church was never empty. It was filled with the presence of the faithful who had been there over the decades.

"It's beautiful," he said. "Isn't it? I never come in here without sensing the presence of the divine. It gives me purpose for a new day."

"Beautiful," she whispered. "I feel the same." She paused. "I must be going."

"I understand," he said. "But would you like to come with me next door to Welsford Drugs. We can have a cup of coffee and commiserate. I suspect you need someone to listen."

As they left the church to its sentinel duties, they passed Noll Huggard on the way in.

"Hello Noll," said Rev. Hatfield. "Out for your morning constitutional?" he asked.

Noll shrugged as he slipped into the very back corner pew.

"Hold down the fort," said Rev. Hatfield as they left.

"Odd fellow, that Noll," said Evelyn. "When you least expect it, there he is."

"Harmless, I suspect," said Rev. Hatfield. "A shame about his family home burned to the ground on Douglas."

"They'll do okay," commented Evelyn. "They're members of Main Street Baptist. They take care of their own."

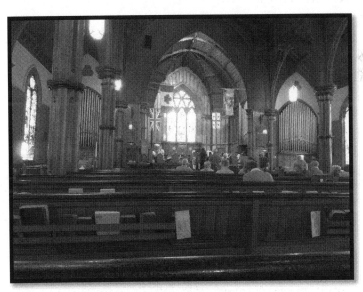

St. Luke's Anglican Church - Interior

FIRE

It wasn't a glow of dawn that Truly had noticed through the fog. "You there, Noll," said Truly.

No answer.

"Hey, fella," he repeated. "You there?" Again no answer. "Guess he crept off into the fog. Funny fellow he."

It had been some time since Evelyn had passed by on her way to St. Luke's. Truly thought about all that she had said about the Commission on Urban Renewal. He was as disturbed as she about all the tearing down of venerable old buildings. "Those buildings," he whispered, "have stood here for ages." He paused as he looked out through the fog. The red glow of the morning seemed to brighten.

"Those buildings," he continued, "have stood the time. Of course they need some renewal and restoration, but, ..."

He paused. Off in the distance he heard the scream of sirens.

"They're headed somewhere," he said. "Somewhere." He squinted to see if that would help him peer through the fog. The red glow seemed to brighten. For the moment he considered it to be just the beginning of another day. The sun would dispel the fog and the city would return to normal. "Normal," he thought. "What's normal these days is the razing of buildings with nothing to replace them. Sad." He whispered as he shook his head.

The sirens came closer. He couldn't see Main Street. The fog had lifted down below Fort Howe. But he could see a flashing of lights racing along from the North End to over city. The warmth of early autumn began to roll in. The fog started its descent into dew on the grass. The city began to emerge. As the fog descended Truly could pick out a steeple here and there piercing up through the gloom.

"Trinity," he whispered as he began to count them as their spires poked through the descending murk. "Old Stone Church. Holy Cross Cathedral..." he paused. "Saint Andrew and Saint David on Germain Street," he whispered. "The Admiral Beatty."

He repeated. "The Admiral Beatty. Something's going on," he whispered. "The Admiral Beatty appeared to have a halo of red and orange flickering behind it."

The gloom descended further into the ground. He imagined how the flowers on Kings Square were celebrating its arrival. It was their mourning drink that allowed them to bring cheer. The Centre city had been dying for years. King Square refused to die. "At least," he thought, "the city keeps up its appearance with flowers."

"Flowers," he thought. "Flowers. That glow isn't coming from happy flowers." The reds and oranges flickering behind the Admiral Beatty intensified. Horror struck him.

"Fire!" he yelled. "There's a fire over near Queen's Square. Fire! Another fire. And right where the Great Fire of 1877 happened. It must be contained," he shouted as he ran down the hill to Main Street. Truly wasn't one of those fire chasers. He was someone who cared deeply about the city. He was attuned to anything that happened to the city that would destroy. He knew that once buildings were destroyed, the city was loathe to rebuild. If they did rebuild, it was usually some inane structure with no intrinsic value other than to house some more indigents or indigent commissions and agencies.

"Fire!" he yelled loud enough that Evelyn Crandall and Rev. Hatfield could hear as they walked to Welford's drugs.

"FIRE!" he yelled louder. Noll Huggard even heard. Noll, of course would be interested in anything that brought excitement to his life. With the fire at his parent's mansion on Douglas Avenue, Noll found himself living in a two room, cold water flat on Metcalf Street. That was okay with him. He didn't entertain. He paid few attention to relatives. He spent much of his time walking the streets of the old city or listening to the radio in his room. People often wondered about Noll. They figured he was a harmless bloke who had just lost his purpose in life. "Maybe," some thought, "he might be running for office or surveying the city so that it will be in his memory." They paid little attention to Noll.

"Fire!" yelled Truly as he ran faster. If the city had any forethought to its needs, it might have preserved the old Main Trolley line that ran from Indiantown to Centre city along Main Street. Truly could have hopped on board. But there was none. Public transportation was non-existent. He could do no better than run as fast he could.

WELSFORD DRUGS

"Good early morning," said Mr. Welsford as Evelyn and Rev. Hatfield found a booth away from the door and the chill rolling in with the fog. "It's another Saint John chilly morning out there," he continued. "Something warm this morning?"

"I'll have a cup of coca," said Evelyn, "with just one marshmallow on top."

"Hot tea," said Rev. Hatfield. "As hot as you can make it, with just a tad of milk."

"Coming up," said Mr. Welsford.

"The fogs of times," mused Rev. Hatfield, "eventually catches up with us."

"Catches up?" asked Evelyn as she arranged herself on the hard wooden booth that had welcomed many a local over the years. She took off her hat and placed it beside her. "Catches up?" she repeated.

"Yes," said Rev. Hatfield. "Sooner or later the times catches up with us while we are least ready to deal. Just take for instance, how the buildings along Main Street were all torn down. We had been doing business with those merchants for decades. More than once, I walked along that street on my way to a meeting over town. I used to take the trolley but that is history."

Evelyn nodded. She knew exactly what Rev. Hatfield was talking about. She had come up against members of the Commission on Urban Renewal who had exactly the attitude he was describing. Of all the persons on the Commission, she seemed to be the only one who was interested in preservation and restoration instead of what they called renewal.

"They are bent on destruction," replied Evelyn. "You're from a good Loyalist family. Many of our parishioners at St. Luke's go back to the 18th century. The Dykeman's for instance descend from Garret Dykeman and Eunice Hatfield. Their eldest son was Gilbert who married Dorcas Manzer. They were child loyalists."

"Indeed," said Rev. Hatfield. "They are in my ancestral line. In fact, I am related to the Dykeman's of Dykeman Hardware. It's just around the corner and down on Adelaide Street. They're distant kin. Shirt-tail kin, but kin just the same. Gilbert and Eunice must be rolling over in their graves. Sometimes I think I can hear a rumble when I walk by the Old Loyalist Burial ground over city."

Evelyn chuckled. But it was a chuckle that betrayed what she was really thinking. Sometimes a chuckle is helpful in the right situation. It covered up mourning. Evelyn often used it at Commission meetings to distract the members from what she was really thinking about the Commission's work and the member's participation. Her chuckle this time was tearful.

"You're crying again," said Rev. Hatfield.

"Yes," replied Evelyn. "The memories of what our beautiful city was like before all this renewal and destruction just..."

"Just grieves you?" he replied.

"Grieves me," she continued. "And allows my sinister side to rise. I work at keeping it under wraps. But, everyone has a little bit of evil in them. I'm no different. I just emphasize the positive."

"And downplay the negative?" said Rev. Hatfield.

"Exactly," continued Evelyn. "I think it is better to think the best of others, hope the best and when opportunity arises, work like the devil to make sure the best happens." This time she laughed. "Well," she continued, "I don't mean 'devil.' You know what I mean."

"I do," said Rev. Hatfield. Mr. Welsford had delivered the tea and cocoa and sensing that there was more to this coffee klatch than small talk, he lingered a moment.

"Important business this morning?" he asked. "I don't mean anything that can't be shared. Don't mean to barge into some heavy counseling session. Just seems..."

"That we are disturbed?" said Evelyn.

"Yes," he replied.

"We are," she said. "This business of Urban Renewal is close to the surface of doing good or boiling over into destruction."

"Hasn't done much for my business," said Welsford. "If they tear down many more buildings in this neighbourhood," he paused, "and if many more businesses and churches go out, I'll be going out of business too. You can't keep a business going when the neighbourhood declines and disappears."

Evelyn and Rev. Hatfield nodded. They watched Welsford return to his position behind the lunch counter.

"You know," continued Evelyn, "that fire at the Anglican Church in the Valley may have been an accident, they haven't concluded yet, but for some it was an opportunity."

"Opportunity?" asked Rev. Hatfield.

"Yes," continued Evelyn. "It was an opportunity for the Commission on Urban Renewal to really move in and destroy. That church was one of the last strongholds of that historic district in a city that has gone sour. Once the steeple came crashing down the morale of the congregation took a dive while the Commission saw opportunities. The Commission seized the opportunity. The congregation continues to mourn, search for Father Davies and meet in lesser and lesser numbers at Old Stone Church. They will never rebuild. If and when Rev. Davies is found, that will further determine their future. His disappearance is fueling the flames of rumours. Rumours are hard to stop. You know," she paused, "there's been rumours for years about St. Luke's closing and being torn down. If that ever happens…"

"That!" said Hatfield, "will be the end of this neighbourhood."

Mr. Welsford rushed by. The door slammed behind him as he focused all his attention on what seemed to be happening over city. The fog had lifted. He could hear fire sirens in the distance. And he saw the glow in the sky over Centre city down behind the Admiral Beatty Hotel. "Fire," he whispered. "The city is on fire again."

Evelyn and Rev. Hatfield left their tea and cocoa behind. They had also heard sirens off in the distance. They joined Welsford just when a ladder fire truck passed by with its sirens screaming.

"There goes another historic building, I suspect," cried Evelyn. "You know five years ago the Canadian Inventory of Historic Buildings project recorded what the bulldozers had missed. In two weeks the students had located 250 historic buildings. They even noted that almost everyone who lived in Indiantown, the North End, could tell you what building Walter Pidgeon had lived in! That's how extensive their questionnaire was."

"If," said Rev. Hatfield, "they came back today, sadly they would have an easier building inventory job. Looks like another one is going down in ashes. I just hope it's not something really historic."

The fog had lifted but their mood had not. The three stood in silence as they listened to the wail of sirens off in the distance. Welsford could hear the incessant ringing of the payphone in the old wooden booth inside. He didn't have the heart to break their silence to answer it. The phone rarely rang. When it did it usually was for no good. He knew.

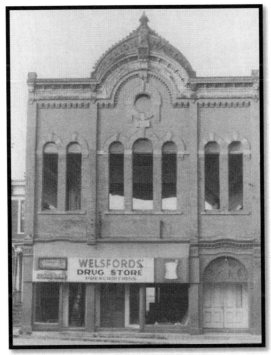

Welsford's Drug Store [10]

THE COMMISSION MEETING

With the sound of sirens off in the distance, McLennan called the meeting to order. Evelyn had hailed a taxi since her Welsford Drugstore interlude had made her late.

"Well," said McLennan. "It's another happy day in Saint John."

"Is not!" said Evelyn with just barely disguised annoyance with McLennan's continual happy attitude.

"Why Evelyn," said McLennan. "Every day is a happy day in Saint John. The fog has come and gone. The flowers on King Square are celebrating the dew. And there's another fire to our advantage."

Evelyn snarled. She didn't often snarl but this time a snarl was appropriate. She had placed her bright hat with a red flower smack dab in the middle of the table. "The flowers on King Square," she said, "are a poor excuse for historical preservation and urban renewal. They neither toil nor spin while we weave a web of deceit and doom."

"Evelyn," said Father Sweeney, "Evelyn. Let's give the man a chance for us to make some progress." Father Sweeney could wield an iron fist when it came to the cathedral but in other places around town he was seen as the peacemaker. "A kind man" could often be heard said about him.

"I'll give him a chance," said Evelyn, "when I see that he has the city's best interest in mind. So far all we have accomplished on this commission is crash and burn. And when the burning seems to happen on its own, he celebrates it." The sounds of sirens filtering in through the window slightly interrupted her thought. "Another fire, I suppose," she continued. "At the rate this city is going we might as well have another Great Fire. Perhaps then people might awaken to what they have."

McLennan sat down at the chairman's seat. This didn't seem to be a time to lord it over the group by towering over them. The mayor had given him a job to do until the Bay of Fundy stopped its rhythm of rise and fall, fall and rise. At the moment the commission seemed to be caught up in the swirling waters of the Reversing Falls and there didn't seem to be any way through them without encountering danger. In fact, he knew, that there was no going through the Reversing Falls as long as the waters were muddied with rising and falling tides. Somehow he had to get the work of the commission under control. He had reasons and they weren't always the most honourable.

Mary Jones was a little miffed with all this banter. "I've been doing my part," she said, hoping to change the subject. Instead her comment made matters worse.

"Sure," said Albert Parlee, "you've been doing your part. The only thing is, your part is all about yourself and nothing to do with the city. Go ahead," he continued, "build a big mansion in a rundown neighbourhood and then think others will follow suit."

"Some have," said Mary.

"Some have what?" asked Annalee Gaudet.

"Some have followed suit," said Mary as she adjusted her posh woolen scarf she had bought at Manchester, Roberts and Allison.

"That's right," said Benjamin Northrup. "Some have followed the rest of the rats right out of the city all the way to Moncton, Toronto and even Calgary. The ship is sinking and what has your big house done to keep people here and renew and preserve our city? Nothing!"

Mary pulled the scarf tighter around her neck as if to choke out the criticism. "I guess I've been told," she muttered. "Get on with it."

Mary might have been told but had she gotten what they had told her? "Unfortunately," said Edna Boyle, "no amount of telling you seems to get through to you. Why are you on this commission anyway? Is it to just flaunt your big house, your wealth and status as THE Mrs. Jones or are you genuinely interested in our city?"

"Of course I am," said Mary. "I love this city."

"Then," said Evelyn Crandall, "get off your hobby horse or find another and better steed to ride out of town on. Either be of some benefit to this commission or get out! Either stop seeing what you can get out of this or make a contribution." Evelyn was mad. It wasn't like her to speak so sharply to others but the conversation with Rev. Hatfield earlier that morning, the tears dropping on her prayer book and the thought that St. Luke's might be in the line of demolition fire caused her to be angry, sad and grieving all at the same time.

"I agree," said Annalee Gaudet. "As the archivist in this group, I am most concerned about preservation even in the wake of renovation, renewal and destruction. It concerns me that what urban renewal has spared, St Paul's Anglican Church in the Valley for instance, careless workmen, finished off."

"Do you know something we don't know?" asked McLennan.

"No," she replied. "I do know that the fire there was suspicious. Why would a wonderful church like that suddenly catch on fire when it was just about to celebrate its 150th anniversary? The congregation was deeply indebted to this commission for spurring them on to restore their beautiful church. Now what do they have. Ashes and a missing Priest."

"Hasn't Father Gwyn Davies shown up yet?" asked Edna Boyle.

"Do you think," said Evelyn, "we'd be discussing this if he had? Wherever he is, I hope he's safe." She paused. "Or at least asking for forgiveness for whatever he's doing or has done."

"Has done?" said Benjamin Northrup.

"Yes," she said, "Has done. For all we know he may have planned for those painters to set that church on fire. Maybe he was covering up something he didn't want known. Maybe he's off on a toot. Maybe...."

"Maybe," said Northrup, "he set that fire."

"Speaking of fire," said Father Sweeney. "Those sirens off in the distance are making me nervous. We've had two fires in the past month. Valley Church and the Huggard Mansion over on Douglas Avenue. I sure hope," he continued, "this isn't becoming a trend."

"Do you think," asked McLennan, "that someone is trying to help us along with this urban renewal work?"

"Well," said Northrup, "something is going on in this city. While we sit here and argue amongst ourselves shops are closing on Kings Street. They either close for good or move out of the city. I suppose the next to go will be Manchester, Roberts and Allison, Scovil Brothers, Calp and the Old Market."

The entire commission gasped in unison. The thought of the Old Market being closed and torn down was abhorrent to everyone. The mayor had tried some years before to get rid of that eye sore. Fortunately the citizens of the city rose up and protested. The Old City Market had been propped up with tax dollars and somewhat restored. It was seen as possibly the catalyst for the renewal of the Centre city. If local residents no longer relied on getting their fresh produce and meats, at least the market could serve as a place where tourists would come and see what the city once looked like, before urban renewal.

"The Old City Market," said Evelyn, "will never be closed or torn down. If anyone ever tries, it will be over my dead body."

"And," said McLennan, "quite a body it is!" He lowered his voice and whispered to himself, "Soon perhaps!"

They all laughed. They weren't sure if McLennan was trying to inject some levity into the meeting or distract them away from his real reason for chairing the commission.

The phone rang. Edna Boyle ran to the desk over in the corner to answer it. The others strained to hear as they watched her face turn from rose red to slate gray. "I'll tell them," she said.

"Tell them what?" asked Evelyn. The sirens had gotten louder. The sound coming through the closed window was even more disturbing. Each suspected.

"Tell them," said Edna with some hesitation, "That, that, ..."

"That what?" said Northrup.

"That the magnificent Greene mansion on Princess Street was in flames." She sobbed.

"And Old Centenary Methodist Church next door?" asked Parlee.

"They're pouring water on it right now," said Edna. "I hope they save that magnificent historic building."

"It's about time that congregation caught on fire," said McLennan.

"That's not funny," said Evelyn as she grabbed her hat and headed for the door. The rest didn't bother to comment about McLennan's lame excuse for humor. They were too stricken by the prospect of the city once gain going up in flames that they all left en mass. What they thought they might accomplish by heading over toward the fire was only conjecture. "Perhaps," they thought, "there might be some gory details to see or a cause to be sleuthed out."

CRASH AND BURN

By the time the Commission on Urban Renewal arrived on the scene, there wasn't much left to see. The gray stone walls were still standing. The roof had collapsed into the middle in a crash and burn way. Truly Morrell had run as fast as he could and was standing some distance away from the fire. Noll Huggard had somehow managed to be in the area on his daily walkabout. He silently stood in the shadows. The fire of the Greene mansion brought tears to his eyes. One more beloved historical building was gone. Its ashes joined those of the Valley Church and his own home, the Huggard Mansion on Douglas Avenue.

"How did it start?" said Albert Parlee who had gotten there ahead of the rest of the Commission.

"How should I know?" said Truly. "Looks intentional to me but then again, these old buildings need their electric rewired. Might have just been a mouse, rat or squirrel having their noonday meal on some insulation. Could be anything."

Noll shrugged his shoulders. He pulled his woolen peak cap down as far as he could. It didn't do much for his appearance nor did it protect from the chill that the fog left behind. "Might be the fog would have helped stop this fire." He commented.

"That's a stupid thing to say," said Parlee. He was as stunned by another fire as the rest of the Commission. For once, even McLennan was speechless. How would he interpret this loss? Would it just be another jewel in his urban renewal crown or would it be a wakeup call to take urban renewal seriously?

"I suspect," said Evelyn, "that now you will be happy again. Here is one less building you have to deal with. The Greene mansion might have needed some restoration. It certainly didn't need destruction. If you took urban renewal seriously, you'd find some way to offer owners of these decaying buildings some funds to restore them to the original glory."

"Humpf," said McLennan. "That will be the day. Try to find a benefactor to do that. All big business and government wants to do is tear down. They don't even want to replace. The mayor would rather have a vacant lot or a parking lot than some boarded up hovel."

"I suppose," said Truly, "if you thought you could make some money out of this renewal business, you'd find a way. Why are you so resistant to …"

"to saving the historical part of our beautiful Victorian city?" said Evelyn completing Truly's sentence.

"Exactly," said Truly.

"I agree," said Noll.

"I'm glad you agree about something," said Parlee. "You spend more time walking around this town than anything else. Why don't you be useful?"

"I am," said Noll. "I'm writing a book. I want to remember before everything is gone."

"Well," said Edna who had been silently watching the Greene turn to ashes, "leave this chapter out and get on with helping us."

"I'm helping," muttered Noll, as he sauntered off toward Queen's Square. He knew when he'd been beaten at his own game. No use standing around watching another building turn to ashes. Fire had already broken his heart. He didn't need to be broken by the commission's insensitivity to him and the citizens of Saint John.

"He's helping, alright," whispered Truly to Evelyn. "He's helping just like the rest of you progressive people on that Commission who think they are helping save our city."

"Don't include me in that group," said Evelyn. "I'm trying to stop them from doing any more urban renewal damage. In fact, I am beginning to think that this Commission on Urban Renewal, at least some of them on the commission, have no mind for UR at all. McLennan, for instance, is always making comments about being happy. I don't think there's anything to be happy about. The more beautiful Victorian buildings we lose, the more people we lose, the more generic and bland our city becomes. We might as well stop calling it the Loyalist city. It can just be another cruise port on the tourist trap itinerary of a cruise line. What are these tourists taking pictures of?"

"The fog," laughed Truly. "You wouldn't believe how many times I have been up at Fort Howe when a cruise ship is in port. Those money grubbing cab drivers often bring up a boat load of tourists in the thickest fog of the season. They get out. They stand along the fence staring out into the fog. Then, of all things, they take photographs."

"Of what?" she said.

"The fog, I guess," answered Truly. "Evidently they have never seen fog." He shook his head.

"And that's what I mean!" said Evelyn. "There's at least one of us on that Commission who is trying to keep them in check. Some of the others are just plain lazy and going along for the ride to see what *they* can get out of it. In the meantime the city is crashing and burning."

"GET BACK! GET BACK!" yelled a fire fighter as he rushed toward the crowd standing around. "The front is about to fall. GET BACK!"

The crowd obeyed just in time to turn and see the façade of the Greene Mansion crumble inward.

"It's gone," said Evelyn.

"Gone!" said Truly. "Another one is gone. Fortunately it looks like Centenary Queens Square church is going to survive this one. It'll only be a matter of time. That congregation has dwindled down to a few. No point of them worshiping in a thousand seat sanctuary that has historic significance. It'll go down one of these days. Not just today."

They stood there in silence. Many in the crowd couldn't believe what they were seeing. Some were mourning. This fire just added to their grief. Others were just curious. They had lived so long with their Saint John surroundings they no longer "saw" what they had, no less appreciate it. Buildings had just become buildings.

"You know," said Truly, "it is sad that the people in this city have become so apathetic toward what we have. And their apathy has spawned a Commission on Urban Renewal which they think will solve everything. And while our citizens slumber into apathy, others go into action."

"I know," said Evelyn. "I know."

"These progressive people," continued Truly, "have become regressive to the point of absurdity. They all should be run out of town. Never to be permitted any freedom ever again within our culturally significant city. Every single historical building should be preserved and kept in the manner in which they were intended."

"Truly," said Evelyn, "I didn't know you were so protective of our city."

"I am," he said. "We as a community should be mindful of our ancestor's plans for our great city. For those who think they are progressive, I have a few suggestions. If they wish to build any new structures, do so in the manner of our forefathers. My ancestors, you know, started this city. Some of them are buried over in the Loyalist Burial ground. I am a member of the United Empire Loyalists!"

"Well," said Evelyn, "that's nice but does the UEL do anything but gloat on their heritage?"

"Yes, yes, they do more than that," continued Truly. "I at least speak from a heart that is filled with admiration, love and concern for our Loyalist beginnings. We preservationists can be progressive too. We just don't think everything needs to be torn down to bring about renewal."

"That's true," said Evelyn.

"All those who appear progressive," he continued, "appear to be a blight on our city. May our souls and the souls of our off spring be damned to burn for eternity. We are not prepared to follow and live in the ways of our founding fathers and build accordingly. Take the high road and may we only see the dust trail of our final leaving or ending. Whichever comes first." [11]

"You ought to be a preacher," said Evelyn.

"No, No," said Truly. "I would make too many people uncomfortable. Some of them ought to be. There are better places for me than in the pulpit. That would spell the demise of Centenary Church for sure if I were to preach there!"

"Well then," said Evelyn. "Keep on doing what you are doing. Wherever you can, speak the truth that is in your heart about our city. I'll back you up. I'll make sure the Commission knows there are others in the city who don't approve of their renewal work."

"It appears there's nothing more to do here," said Truly. "I'll catch you later. Maybe at Woolworths. I'm about ready for another piece of that pumpkin pie."

---

[11] Vern M. Garnett of Saint John offered this commentary on the present state of the city in 2017. He has given me permission to use this quote.

THE CLERGY MEETING

It seemed appropriate for the city clergy to hold their next meeting right next door to the Greene Mansion at Centenary Church. The ashes of the fire had taken several days to turn cold. Centenary Church had survived. Holding their meeting right in the heart of what appeared to be another push for urban renewal would spur others on. If they came out of curiosity to see the remains of the fire, that was enough. If they came out of genuine concern for the city, that was better. At least, it would be good for them to gather together to assess their thinking since the first meeting and to commiserate with each other. Rev. Somerville at Centenary Church could definitely use support and encouragement.

"I made some tea," said Rev. Summerville. He had arranged the chairs around a large table set with a lace cloth and his collection of English bone china teacups. "I thought some hot tea and scones might calm us into a productive discussion."

"Will this be in the paper that you poured," chuckled Rev. Bruce from Saint Andrew and Saint David. Bruce did have an uncanny ability with his brogue to lighten the mood. But one ought not to be deceived. Although he would readily jest, he was always up front with how to proceed. His jest was just an interlude to his thought process.

"Funny," said Sister Honora Collins. "Funny, but not. While the city is burning, people are starving and we are gathered for crumpets and tea."

"Scones," reminded Rev. Summerville. "Scones and tea. I don't mean to distract. Just offering hospitality to you all. I have thought for years that if enemies would sit down and eat together, the world would be a far different place." Rev. Summerville was the eternal optimist when it came to solving the world's problems. "You know," he continued, "I do believe that the solution to the world's problems, and probably to St. John's problem is love. But," he paused, "has it ever really be tried?"

"We try every day," said Sister Honora. "We feed anyone who come. It does make a difference. So, Rev. Summerville, your point is well taken. I apologize for making such a rude remark about your serving us tea and crumpets."

"Scones," he corrected, as he poured her some tea.

"Correction heard," she said. "Now," as she sipped her tea, "let us get on with it!"

"Indeed," said Rev. Hatfield. He had become the chair of the gathering by default. Since his church, Saint Luke's perched on a hill overlooking Main Street, he was in the middle of urban destruction. His church stood as a sentinel to all who viewed the city from many angles. "Let us," he continued, "check in."

"Here," said Rev. Jacob Wentworth of Old Stone Church. "I'm here and happy to see the rest of you." He looked around the table and acknowledged the presence of each. "Father Sweeney," he greeted. "I hope you are well and your parishioners flourishing." Sweeney nodded. "Wentworth, Bruce, Colwell, Somerville, Collins. It is good to see you all. I am, however, sad to note that we are still missing Rev. Gwyn Davies from St. Paul's in the Valley."

"He's still missing," said Hatfield. "No one seems to know where he is or what he's up to."

"And," continued Wentworth, "his congregation from St. Paul's continues to worship at Old Stone Church. But they are getting tired of the stress, lack of leadership and confusion. They are as concerned about the loss of their church and neighbourhood as many are."

"All except," said Sister Collins, "The Commission on Urban Renewal."

"Do you know something we don't know?" asked Hatfield.

"Not much more," she answered. "I do listen to the people who come to the soup kitchen every day. Evelyn Crandall comes quite often to volunteer. She has dropped a comment here and there about the intransigence of the Commission on Urban Renewal. She seems to think that several on the Commission are not that interested in urban renewal."

"What?" said Somerville. "We could sure use some urban renewal around here, especially since the Greene Mansion next door to us is gone. God spared this historic church building. I'm not sure for what, but we were spared. We could have gone down in a blaze just as quickly as the mansion, the Huggard house and St. Paul's. Thank the Lord we survived."

"Yes," said Hatfield, "But what have you survived for? Your congregation is dwindling. This church, beautiful as it is, is pretty outdated for your little congregation. You've dwindled down to a "precious few," as they say, and now what?"

"We can," said Somerville, "be an historic relic or we'll find a new way forward. I am sure that the Commission on Urban Renewal has their eyes on our historic church just as much as they have their eyes on the New Brunswick Museum, St. Luke's and some of the other precious historic buildings of our city."

"St. Luke's? NEVER!" commented Hatfield. "Evelyn Crandall will see to that. She came by the morning of the Greene fire. We sat in our historic sanctuary and cried. She spoke briefly about the attitudes on the Commission on Urban Renewal. We agreed, 'over our dead bodies' will St. Luke's ever be torn down. We feel the same about much of the rest of our Victorian city."

"Did she give you any insight as to what is happening?" asked Rev. Sweeney.

"Only that McLennan, the chair of UR, kept commenting how happy he is all the time," said Hatfield.

"Happy about what?" said Rev. Bruce.

"Happy, I think," continued Hatfield, "that all of these fires made their work of UR easier. The fire at St. Paul's Valley church made it easier for them to tear down an entire neighbourhood in the name of urban renewal. Urban destruction, in my estimation. And the congregation there is at a loss as to how to continue to exist."

"There's corruption on the Commission on Urban Renewal?" asked Rev. Wentworth.

"Isn't that always the way," commented Elder Colwell of Germain Street Baptist. "If it weren't for Germain Street being so well preserved, they'd be coming after that entire street as a target for destruction. And then what would we have? Some non-descript apartments in a city that is losing population and businesses by the day. Who will want to live in those ugly buildings..." he paused, " or have the means to?"

"I'm guarding St. Andrew and St. David, with my life," said Rev. Bruce. "We are an anchor for real urban renewal and restoration. If our church, and yours Colwell, were ever torn down, there goes the entire neighbourhood on Germain."

"I think," said Rev. Somerville, "we ought to pause for a moment of silence, take a deep breath and sip our tea, before we continue."

As they sat there in silence, Sister Honora began to hum one of her favorite morning songs. She sang in Latin. Many considered the language dead but in Sister Honora's gentle voice, many heard the presence of the Holy Spirit descend and dwell among them. Her voice soothed the conversation away from despair to hope and expectation.

"I think," said Rev. Wentworth, "that since St. Paul's meets at our church, we might take a moment to remember them in silent prayer. He watched as each in their own way prayed.

"Amen," said Rev. Hatfield. "Now," he continued. "I do have some good news. Evelyn Crandall has agreed to be our secret agent on the Commission on Urban Renewal. She said she would fill me in after each meeting. She already is a devil's advocate for the commission. Whenever," she said, "McLennan makes comments like being happy about the state of a fire," she questions him about his motivation. In her kind, but sometime snarky way, she is ready to question anyone on the commission who seems not to have Saint John in their best interest."

"Wonderful," said Rev. Wentworth. "And I have been in touch with Rabbi Zeke Rosenfeld. He couldn't be with us today but he has agreed to bring his architect friend from Montreal to meet with us. She is on the United Church Commission on Historic Preservation. She is well known across Canada and will bring her expertise, gratis, to help us save what is worth saving in Saint John."

"When can this happen?" asked Rev. Somerville. "We have to be ready with some kind of plan for our historic buildings. Sooner or later the Centenary congregation will either move to a store-front or close. THEN the Commission will be ready to pounce. I suspect they would rather tear down this wonderful gothic building than restore and repurpose it."

"Exactly," said Rev. Hatfield. "And you do know that Old Centenary Methodist church was designated a local historic place for its architecture and its association with the Great Saint John Fire of 1877. The wooden church was destroyed in the fire. Your church was built out of stone as an example of buildings that would be resistant to fire. In addition, Old Centenary Church is recognized for its grand Gothic Revival architecture. It was designed by John Welsh of New York. The church seats 1600, which is far more than any of our churches today need."

"And I am sure McLennan," commented Bruce, "would take note of that and use as his justification for its loss of usefulness in a city with a declining population."

"According to what Evelyn Crandall has shared with me," said Hatfield, "McLennan doesn't care much for history, beauty or architecture. She thinks he might have an ulterior motive for his so-called urban renewal projects."

"Graft," whispered Sister Collins.

"What?" asked Wentworth.

"Graft," she continued. "Too often these people in political power only have their own interests at heart. It is a cold day in January that one finds a politician who is genuinely interested in the position for the purpose of society, people and the city."

"That's rather harsh," cautioned Rev. Colwell. He paused. "But too often true."

"The hour is getting on to noon." Said Hatfield. "I think we've accomplished much in our discussion this morning. Specifically, let us meet with the Rabbi and architect in two weeks. In the meantime, can each of us be particularly attentive to conversations we hear around us in our congregations and our being about town?"

"Agreed," said the group in unison.

"Then," said Hatfield, "Let us depart in peace. And let us keep our congregations and our historic buildings close to our hearts and prayer. One never knows when the good Lord will speak to one of us with a way forward."

PUMPKIN PIE

"What's your last name, anyway," asked Truly to Margaret as she came away from the grill to wait on him at the Woolworths.

"Who wants to know?" she quipped. "If you don't know by now, I'm not telling."

"No, seriously," said Truly. "We've know each other for a long time. As long as there's been pumpkin pie here we've know each other. But I never bothered to ask your last name. What is it?"

"Why do you want to know?" she asked. "Besides, I thought you knew everyone in this city. Have you got something in mind?."

"I might," he said. "What's your last name? For all I know, we might be related."

"You're related to everyone in this city," she replied. "It wouldn't surprise me if we were, but I hope not."

"Come now," said Truly, "that wouldn't be so bad. It's good to have kin. What's your last name?"

"Promise you won't tell?" she asked.

"Promise," he replied. "What is it?"

Margaret leaned over the counter. She looked around to see if anyone might be within earshot. Most people knew her last name but she didn't like it broadcast. She wasn't the black sheep of the family but she didn't want to be identified with some of them. She leaned closer. She was quite a buxom girl. Her boobs brushed against the top of the counter. Truly leaned in.

"Here's my ear," he said. "What's your last name?"

Margaret cupped her hand to Truly's ear and whispered. "Greene. I am Margaret Greene."

"What!" exclaimed Truly.

"Shhh!" cautioned Margaret.

"Greene," he repeated, "of the Greene Mansion fame. Greene of the fire?

"That Greene," said Margaret. "My father was Sam, the singer and businessman. I have no idea where he is now. He skipped town on some shady business deal never to be seen again. Our family has struggled ever since with that mansion on Princess Street. Kind of a blessing that's it nothing but ashes now. One less thing for our mother to deal with."

"So what now?" he said. "What about the mansion now?"

"Nothing," she replied. "I haven't been in it in years. The first chance I got, I left. The rest of the clan can deal with the fallout. I want nothing to do with them. I have this job. I have my apartment. I have a few friends. I have my reputation."

"Reputation?" asked Truly. "Want to…

"Want to what?" she said.

"Oh, I was just thinking," continued Truly, "that maybe sometime you'd like to go out with me. A movie. Dinner, or something."

Margaret didn't have a chance to answer. Anyway, she was stunned that someone like Truly who knew everyone would want to date her, a lowly lunch counter worker. She straightened up, adjusted her bosoms and smoothed down the Woolworths apron. She wanted to make a quick getaway but while they had been talking, several customers had perched on the red stools and needed attention. One of them was Noll Huggard.

"Noll," said Truly, "what are you doing sneaking around here? Where'd you come from?"

"Dunno," said Noll. "You wouldn't care anyway. Just around."

"Just around," said Margaret. "That's your problem. You're just around. Perhaps if you'd been around at the right time, your parent's home on Douglas Avenue wouldn't have caught fire."

"Dunno," said Noll. "Don't much matter anyways. I don't live there. Have myself a flat over on Metcalf Street."

"That's a come down for a Huggard," said Truly. "I mean, Metcalf Street is a nice place but houses are falling into disrepair, people are moving out and some are even boarded up. Next thing you know, urban renewal will move in and flatten the area."

"Cheap," said Noll. "Cheap."

"You are cheap," said Margaret. "You come in here wanting coffee and…"

"And pumpkin pie please," he demanded.

"And you never even leave a tip," she continued. "I have to keep an eye on you to make sure you pay the check."

"I pay," said Noll. "I pay."

Margaret had retrieved the next to last piece of pumpkin pie. Noll had his head buried in it. He shoveled in forkful after forkful .

"Margaret," said Truly, "Please get me that last piece of pumpkin pie before someone else grabs it. Best pie in town."

"Whadda ya talking about," asked Noll through a mouthful of pumpkin.

"None of your business?" said Truly. "If you're writing a book, leave that chapter out."

"Not writing a book," said Noll. "Just want to know. Might come in handy someday to know."

"Know what?" asked Margaret.

"Whatever it is you're talking about," said Noll. "I saw youse over at the Greene Mansion fire. Curious. Just curious."

"Yes, curious," said Truly. "And another loss to our beautiful Victorian City. If urban renewal and fires keep happening, we'll have nothing to urban renew."

"True," said Noll. "But sometimes…"

"Sometimes what?" said Margaret.

"Sometimes things are what they are," replied Noll.

"Now that's the most profound thing I've heard you say," said Truly. "When you're finished with that pie, why don't you disappear into the fog from whence you came?"

"Be nice," said Margaret. "He can't help himself."

"Well it's true," said Truly. "He is always lurking around. Especially when there's a thick fog. I can't for the life of me figure out what is so fascinating to him about walking the streets of this city day in and day out. Odd fellow he is."

Noll had already finished, left his money on the counter and headed for the door. The fog had rolled back in so he had pulled his peak wool cap down to his ears and wrapped his scarf tight. People knew Noll. They thought he was harmless. The Huggards were an upstanding family. Every family seems to have at least one member who is different from the rest. Noll was that one. He'd been raised with good morals. His father, the patriarch, ruled the household with an iron hand and a heavy Bible. His mother was the epitome of motherhood. She was loved by all in the community. She loved Noll as much, if not more than she loved the other children. Even so, Noll ended up walking the streets, keeping to himself and observing life in the city pass by.

Margaret and Truly watched as Noll pushed the heavy door opening onto King Square. He disappeared into the fog.

"So what about it?" said Truly.

"What about what?" asked Margaret.

"Want to?" asked Truly.

"Want to what?" replied Margaret.

"What is this, a Laurel and Hardy conversation, "Who's on first. What's on second? When's on third?" replied Truly. "I said, What about it? Want to go out with me sometime?"

"Oh that," she whispered. "I'll think about it. Maybe. Finish your pumpkin pie."

"While you're thinking," said Truly, "let me know if you hear any dirt about that fire at the Greene mansion, since you're kin. I'll be back for more pie."

THE RABBI

"We are planning on moving," said Rabbi Rosenfeld as he greeted the clergy at the door of Synagogue Beth Torah on the corner of Carlton Street and Wellington Row. "We've been across the street from Old Stone Church for decades but our congregation has dwindled. We think we can have a more useful building over near Leinster and Wentworth Streets. Parking is better there. There's an old mansion we hope to purchase. When we restore it, our place will be an example to the city of how these old buildings can find new life."

"I know where you mean," said Rev. Hatfield as he led the rest into the parlour of the Synagogue. "Thank you for inviting us to meet here. I've also asked Evelyn Crandall to attend. She's on the Commission on Urban Renewal. She's agreed to be our sleuth on that Commission. "Evelyn, this is Rabbi Rosenfeld."

"Good Morning," said Evelyn. "We have met before but not formally. I applaud your congregation for persevering in the wake of so much controversy over the centuries. Your people have made important contributions to the city of Saint John."

"Welcome to our house, said the spider to the fly," quipped Rabbi Rosenfeld. He had an uncanny ability to find humour in all situations. "I don't mean to say that you're the "fly" coming in. Just making a funny. Perhaps you can help us entrap those in our city who seem to be working for urban destructive renewal."

Evelyn laughed. "I saw the humour in your comment," she said. "It is good to inject some levity into everyday life. If we didn't laugh, we'd be such sour people no one would want to come to our beautiful city. And if we stop being curious and observant, we might as well die."

"Agreed," said Rev. Hatfield. "Where will we meet?"

"Follow me," said the Rabbi. "Our parlour is comfortable. Some of the ladies of our local chapter of Jewish Women of Canada have been so kind to prepare some challah, jams and tea."

The room on the first floor of the synagogue was pleasantly decorated for small meetings. Chippendale style side chairs were evenly spaced in a circle in the centre of the room around a rug that one of the members had brought back from Jerusalem. . A mahogany table was set with Shabbat candles ready for the Sabbath. The women had brought out their finest silver embossed with the Star of David.

"The lace cloth on the table," said Rabbi Rosenfeld, "was made by my great-grandmother. It was one of the things my mother rescued as she escaped from Poland. Thank God, blessed be He, that she escaped in time. I treasure this cloth and only use it for special occasions. You all are special colleagues and friends."

"It is a blessing to be here," said Sister Honora. "And a special blessing for you to share such important things with us."

All the clergy and Evelyn Crandall had arrived for the meeting. Some had never been inside the synagogue so they were especially interested in seeing another of Saint John's historic buildings.

"Have you ever noticed," said the Rabbi, "that way up high on the front of our building facing Old Stone Church has a window with a Star of David and a cross in it? We treasure the fact that we share the same space in the city with Old Stone Church. Although we will be moving to a new, restored building on Wellington Row, we won't forget the importance of being brothers and sisters with you all."

Rabbi Rosenfeld had a long history of having warm relationships with people of many different walks of life. He knew what it was like to live under prejudice and he knew what it is like to live a life of love and acceptance. He had been instrumental in forming the Inter-Religious Council of Montreal. When he attended the Hebrew Union Rabbinical Seminary in Cincinnati he was known as a peace maker and civil rights activist. Some of his best friends across North America were clergy of other religions. In addition, he had graduated from Mount Allison College where he was exposed to many faiths. It was there that he heard the divine call.

"I am glad that you all could come today," said the Rabbi. "Before we begin, I would like you to meet my friend, Ella Osbourne. Ella was first in her class at the School of Architecture at McGill. We first met at McGill before I transferred to Mount Allison. We became good friends. Ella has been the architect for many important projects across Canada. She is also an authority on historical preservation. I am so happy that she agreed to come meet with us."

Ella wasn't at all what they expected an architect to look like. Her flaming red hair had turned to grey. Her freckles remained. She was dressed in a blue skirt and white blouse, the uniform for many Ivy League type colleges. She was kind of frumpy. Her appearance betrayed her reputation.

"I'm happy to be with you," said Ella in a formal, stilted accent. Her speech sounded as if she had practiced for decades what she thought an architect ought to sound like, slightly haughty but approachable.

"Ella," continued Rosenfeld, "has roots in New Brunswick. One side of her family can be traced back to the Loyalist Burial Ground. She even has relatives buried up-country at Big Cove. Her ancestry credentials are as impeccable as her architecture."

The three women, Ella, Evelyn and Honora, sat together in the circle. The others found their seats.

"Before we break bread and meet," said Rosenfeld, "I would like to light the Shabbat candles. I know it's not the Sabbath but I see nothing wrong with bending the ancient rules a little. I am reform, you know. And it is always good to call the light of the divine into our presence."

Rabbi Rosenfeld stepped to the table and lit the candles. "I know this is rather untraditional, but," he said, "I just love this prayer from Fiddler on the Roof. If you know it, sing, or hum along with me. I'll make the words fit our gathering." He began to sing.

May the Lord protect and defend us.
May He always shield us from shame.
May we come to be
In Saint John a shining name.

May we be like Ruth and like Esther.
May we be deserving of praise.
Strengthen us, Oh Lord,
And keep us from the strangers' ways.

May the Lord protect and defend us.
May the Lord preserve us from pain.
Favor us, Oh Lord, with happiness and peace.
Oh, hear our Sabbath prayer. Amen. [12]

It was obvious to all that the divine had descended into the room. They continued to hum the tune as Rosenfeld said: *"Blessed are you, O Lord God of the Universe, who brings forth bread from the earth."*

---

[12] Jerry Bock, Sabbath Prayer Lyrics, Fiddler on the Roof.

Rosenfeld gestured toward the table. "Come," he said, "Come share in bread from the earth, tea, and friendship. Come. While we eat, Rev. Hatfield, would you start our meeting?"

"My pleasure," said Hatfield. "Ella, we welcome you to our city. I know you have family roots here. It is a pleasure to have you visit. I hope you can help us focus our work at preserving and restoring what is left of our beloved city."

"It is my pleasure," she said, "to be with you. It has been many years since I visited here. I remember the city. It has changed so much over the years. My first observation is that the city looks sad. Perhaps it, is mourning the loss of so many beautiful and historic buildings. I know that grief is driving all who wish to preserve what is left. Sometimes urban renewal is carried out in haste and panic. When a city is declining, governments will try anything to stop the exodus of businesses and residents. Too often decisions made in haste make things worse. Buildings that could be saved, restored and repurposed are only seen as problems instead of solutions. Rabbi," she said, "your congregation, it appears, has carefully assessed your building needs. It is determined to be a solution rather than a problem. I understand, that as you move to a new location, you have carefully assessed a new purpose for this building."

"That's right," said Rosenfeld. "We won't leave this building until we know the buyer and what purpose the building will have. This historic building could be a museum, library or even some condominiums. If it were carefully converted to unique and desirable housing, it would bring in residents to the area who might become members of Old Stone Church, Trinity or any of the other churches on Germain Street. We are being careful with this building before we move."

"Excellent," said all those gathered.

"And," continued Ella, "that is how urban renewal ought to happen. This crash and burn attitude that so many cities have results in substandard buildings that have no intrinsic value. Fifty or a hundred years after they are built, they are torn down for something even less worthy of saving."

"That's the very point," said Evelyn Crandall, "I have been making at the Commission on Urban Renewal meetings. Unfortunately many on the commission want to take the easy way out." She paused, "Or any way out that will line their pockets with cash. Sometimes I think the chairman, McLennan is just interested in adding to his wealth and seeing where this job will get him."

Sister Honora leaned over and whispered in Evelyn's ear. "Be careful you don't say that at a meeting. They'll throw you out on your ear, or find some other way to shut you up."

"Ella," said Rosenfeld, "has agreed to consult with us about the parts of our city that are important to save. She has agreed to spend a week with me. If the rest of you approve, we will do some walkabouts in all sections of the city this week. If we can meet next week, she will report her impressions and a few recommendations. I know that is a short time but we don't have any time to lose the way the Commission is progressing with its destructive urban renewal. Look how they moved in right after the Saint Paul in the Valley fire and leveled that neighbourhood without any plans to speak of."

"Next," said Somerville, "will be the burned Greene Mansion. I bet they have their sights on our church. God forbid Centenary falls to the wrecking ball!"

"Once they find out," said Rosenfeld, "that Beth Torah synagogue is going to move over there and restore that magnificent mansion on the corner, they might begin to see some light through their imagined fog. It is our hope that Beth Torah will be the catalyst for others to move in and restore. Once people see what can be done with a beautiful Victorian building, others will follow. I hope."

"That's an excellent plan," said Somerville. "I would be happy to take a day to walk with you both."

"And I as well," said Evelyn Crandall.

"And I," said Sister Honora.

The willingness of Somerville, Crandall and Honora caught the imagination of all the rest gathered. Each agreed to take a day with the Rabbi and Ella on a walkabout.

"Now I am excited," said Evelyn. "And, as we walk, we can chat with persons we meet. It can be a good publicity stunt as well as a fact finding mission. I won't say anything to the Commission unless they ask. I don't want to mess up their plans, whatever they may be. That can come later!"

"Then," said Hatfield, "it's a plan. Each of us will take a day with The Rabbi and Ella. We will meet back here in a week. Is that good Rabbi, or should we meet at one of our other churches?"

"Let's meet at St. Andrew and Saint David on Germain," said Rev. Bruce. "I'll take a turn. It will also give us an opportunity to be reminded of what the city looked like before all this renewal destruction. Germain Street is beautiful. Our church is anchoring down that neighbourhood along with Germain Street Baptist."

"Done!" said Hatfield. "Thank you, Rabbi, for bringing Ella to Saint John. And thank you for this blessed space and welcome. Before we leave, sign up for a day to walkabout. I've made a chart of the days and the areas we can cover."

THE REV. GWYN DAVIES

The congregation of Saint Paul's Anglican Church in the Valley continued to meet at Old Stone Church. Their Vestry Hall had survived the fire but no one seemed to have the courage or willingness to meet there. Without Rev. Davies, they were leaderless. The loss of their building, and watching other parts of the city burn, was a concern to them. But of more concern was the developing mystery of where had Rev. Davies disappeared to. And why?

Rev. Davie's disappearance was a topic of discussion throughout the city. Rumours abounded. Even before word was out that he was missing, people were talking about the cause of the fire. Some thought it might have been an accident. Others imagined that the Commission on Urban Renewal had something to do with it. There were even those who thought the congregation had done it to get insurance money. The rumour that Rev. Davies might have set the fire ran rampant through the city once it was revealed that he was nowhere to be found. People couldn't imagine another reason for his disappearance. No amount of denial on the part of the congregation that loved him would stifle that rumour.

"Any news?" yelled Harriet from behind the high top counter that hid the grill.

"Any news what?" said Abner Short as he found a seat near the plate glass window at Reggie's.

It had been a chilly morning. Autumn was marching on to winter. Frost had tried to form on the outside of the plate glass facing Germain Street. Instead the cold formed a drippy mess on the inside. Patchy frost and patchy fog had once again visited the city. Reggie had placed some bar towels along the sill to avoid the water dripping onto the floor.

"I don't want to get an old lady down," mumbled Reggie. He really meant he didn't want to have an accident. Reggie's age didn't stop him from making funny. People enjoyed Reggie's sense of humour.

The morning sun hadn't been enough to dispel the fog and frost. Patchy frost was at her best this time of the morning. "She" was enough to do in the brilliant flowers a couple of blocks away on King Square. They dropped their heads as summer colour faded. Soon the city maintenance crew would come and make some attempt to extend summer by planting hardy fall flowers.

"What are you up for this morning?" yelled Harriet.

"Coffee and," yelled Abner. "Back at ya. Do you always have to yell?"

"Ayah, I do," replied Harriet. "It's the only way I can manage this grill and you transients. What are you up for this morning?" she yelled again.

"Coffee and Oatmeal," he replied. "And make sure the oatmeal is totally cooked. I'll have some butter, brown sugar and heavy cream to go with it."

"That'll put it on," she chuckled. "Comin' right up. You can get your own coffee."

Abner headed toward the coffee urn. Just as he was drawing his coffee into the heavy mug, Rev. Wentworth of Old Stone Church came in for his morning chug-a-lug as he used to call it.

"Best coffee in town," he said to Abner. "Mind if I join you?"

"My pleasure," said Abner. "I'm expecting Maude any minute. And a couple of others on our vestry might come in too. We can push a couple of tables together."

"Here's your oatmeal," said Harriet as she set it up on the high top counter. "You can get your own heavy cream out of the cooler over there. Hello Father," she said to Rev. Wentworth. "In for your morning meditation? Are you going to associate with…"

"With me?" replied Abner. "Of course he is. He's so kind to let us meet at Old Stone Church, the least I can do is let him park his with us whenever, wherever."

"What's that mean?" asked Harriet.

"It means," replied Abner, "there are more who are going to join us this morning. I'm gonna push these two tables together just in case."

"Just in case Rev. Davies shows up?" she asked.

"That's not funny," said Abner. "He's been missing too long. We have no leader. We don't know what our future holds."

"Probably some more urban renewal," quipped Harriet.

"What do you know about that?" said Wentworth.

"Enough," she replied. "Enough."

"Don't be coy," said Wentworth. "What do you know?"

"I know there's a lot of meeting going on in here," she said. "Almost daily someone from that urban renewal group comes in and whispers over in the corner. They're a surreptitious bunch."

"What do you mean by that?" asked Abner.

"I mean," she continued, "they are always whispering about something and then laughing. That McLennan has a little bunch of groupies that follow him around. I don't trust them one twit. Who knows what they are up to? For all I know they are casing out this joint to see if they can tear us down. Or perhaps do some urban renewing."

"Well," replied Abner, "you could do some redecorating or renovation. This place hasn't changed since you opened it."

"That's the beauty of the place," replied Harriet. "The sameness comforts Reggie. If we were to change anything Reggie wouldn't approve. If we were to think about changing this place, we would have to consult with Reggie first. It's his joint. We always include him in all decisions."

Reggie had been listening to this as he cleared a table and straightened up newspapers left behind. Harriet could see he was becoming agitated by the conversation.

"Don't worry, Reggie," she said, "nothing is going to change here. You're the boss. As long as you want us, we'll be here for you and Reggie's will be the place to be, meet and be seen."

Reggie sat down. Harriet's words had calmed him down.

Abner and Wentworth sat across from each other at the now longer table in the window. The dew on the inside of the plate glass had dried enough that they could watch the passersby on their way to somewhere or nowhere. Noll Huggard had ambled by on his way to whatever.

"Odd fellow, that Noll Huggard," said Wentworth. "Odd."

"Odd," said Abner, "But harmless, I suspect. He's just about town. Always wears that wool peak cap and suit dressed up as if he's on his way to some important meeting. Doesn't say much."

"Harmless," said Wentworth. "A lost soul, I suspect."

"Anyone else gonna fill up that table," yelled Harriet. "Or are you going to take up space that some paying customers could use?"

"Harriet," whispered Wentworth. "Harriet," he repeated. "She can ..."

"Can what?" yelled Harriet. She had ears like an elephant and could hear just about anything, especially when anything had nothing to do with her or when anything was said that wasn't for her to hear.

"Nothing," replied Abner. "Go tend to your grill."

"I'm expecting," continued Abner, "at least our Junior Warden and a couple of others from our vestry. I doubt if we will solve any problems this morning. At least we can commiserate over the loss of our church and the disappearance of Davies."

No sooner had Abner commented, Elisabeth and Gordon Spragg entered followed by Levi Akerley. Abner saw Truly Morrell pass by so he waved him to come on in and join the gathering.

"Quite a gaggle you've got gathered now," quipped Harriet. "I suppose you all are just going to take up space. Get your coffee and get at it."

Levi laughed. Gordon and Elisabeth ignored the quip and retrieved some tea. Truly sat and watched.

"So," said Abner. "What do you suppose about Davies?"

"I suppose," said Levi, "that he is missing." He laughed.

"Funny," said Elisabeth, "but not funny."

Levi was always the one to add some laughter, or a jab when needed. Now was the time.

"I suppose," said Levi.

"You suppose what?" asked Elisabeth.

"I suppose," Levi continued, "that our good Rev. Davies got chased by a bear right out of town."

"Don't be silly," said Elisabeth.

"And," continued Levi, "when the bear got close to him, he ran up a tree."

"Silly," said Elisabeth.

"But," continued Levi, "when he got up the tree, he probably realized bears can climb trees."

"So," said Elisabeth.

"So," continued Levi, "Rev. Davies probably reached down and pulled the tree up by the roots so the bear couldn't climb up after him."

Abner laughed. Elisabeth pursed her lips. Harriet had been listening for the punchline that she knew would come. She bent down behind the high top counter in a fit of laughter. Truly stifled.

"That's a nice story," said Abner, "but we still don't know where Davies has gone, if he'll be back, and what he's up to?"

"Gone but not forgotten," said Levi. "I suppose we'll just have to surmise and wait. If he ever comes down from that tree, maybe the bear will chase him right back to us." He laughed.

"Seriously" said Abner, "There must be some way of finding him. The Fire Marshall Belyea wants to find him. So does the RCMP. Davies might have something to say about the fire.

"Eat your oatmeal," said Maude. "It's getting cold. All this conflab is doing is confusing and comforting. Typical church. Solving problems without solutions."

"I suggest," said Rev. Wentworth, "that you continue to gather as Saint Paul's. That you continue prayer. And, that you continue to use Old Stone Church. Your path forward will become clear. There are options. If Rev. Davies never shows up, you can continue to be your church. One solution might be to merge with us. Until that time…"

"Until the path becomes clear," said Abner, "We ought to go forward in faith. God knows. We don't. But…"

"But," interrupted Truly, "urban destruction continues. You all can put a stop to it. Perhaps that is the reason Davies is gone and Saint Paul Church is in ashes."

Truly's comment had stunned the gathering. They had not thought that Urban Renewal could have a part in their fire and future.

"I think," said Abner, "Truly is correct. There is a plan we don't know. It is ours to remain strong, faithful and a church community. Let's depart with that in mind. I'll call a vestry meeting in a week. In the time, let us rest in silent meditation. Let us listen to the heartbeat of the city and the still small voice of the divine."

"And watch out for bears," yelled Harriet from the grill. "About time you people freed up that table. The tourists from the cruise ship that just docked will be swarming in. Give 'em some space."

A WALKABOUT

It was a perfect day for a walkabout. The temperature for late October had moderated just enough to allow a hint of fog that provided the proper atmosphere for one seeking to experience the Saint John effect. There were a number of things the city was famous for, not the least being the fog. The famous Reversing Falls drew tourists to the area but like the fog, they could be a disappointment. Many people have visited the city and commented, "Nothing to see." Locals would always respond, "When were you here: low tide, high tide or slack tide? If you were here during slack tide, there *was* nothing to see. The Falls are only spectacular during the changing of the tides."

"Still not much to see," would be their response. Unfortunately the rampant crash and burn described as urban renewal had in many areas of the city, confirmed their comment. What once was, was no more. Whole sections of the city, Haymarket Square, Union Station, Saint Paul's Anglican Church in the Valley, Lansdowne Avenue, Wellington Row, Union Street, Carlton Street and Magazine Street had all been transformed or "renewed" by the Commission on Urban Renewal.

Truly Morrell could name, one by one, the magnificent buildings that had peopled the city Centre and side streets of his beloved Victorian City. But Truly wasn't the only person who could do that. Noll Huggard walked the streets day in and day out. He observed the city from many angles from the loss of his parent's mansion on Douglas Avenue to the transformation, or desiccation as he put it, of Market Slip where the Loyalists had landed. The Slip was also the place from which his grandfather had sailed three mast schooners to around the world. Noll saw the old city through the fog as he walked. He mourned.

Truly also mourned. He even mourned the loss of the most mundane buildings such as St. Peter's and Duffrin schools on Magazine Street. Their architecture had become invisible to the natives, just another boil on the sore of a city in decline. They were demolished with the excuse that students needed modern facilities. "How ironic," thought Truly one day as he walked by. "They have torn down those beautiful schools and replaced them with a building that is a "quote" of the original. The architect tried to mimic the architecture of the old school. And to add insult to insult, they have built wooden toothpick duplexes where the hundred year old cemetery used to be. Those duplexes someday will be razed and replaced with something more inane. They should have left the dead alone!"

Rev. Hatfield, Evelyn Crandall, Rabbi Rosenfeld and Ella Osbourne had gathered at Saint Luke's for their turn at a walkabout.

"I walk these streets all the time," said Hatfield. "Many of my elderly parishioners still live in the area. The one good thing about some of the urban renewal is the parking lots nearby. They have provided a lifeline for Saint Luke's. Many of our members have moved out of the area. But they have left their hearts at Saint Luke's. The parking is easier for them to continue to be with us."

"The rest of us walk," said Evelyn. "I walk from over town." She held the door open so that they could enter Saint Luke's for a moment out of the chill. "Wait till you see this," said Evelyn to architect Osbourne. "You will be stunned!"

The silence of the empty sanctuary with its vaulted Victorian ceiling enveloped the little group. Osbourne stood. As Evelyn had warned, she was appropriately stunned. She did not expect such architecture. Awe overcame her. "The thought," said Osbourne, "that anyone would even consider tearing down this building is a mortal sin! It's worse than a mortal sin. It's would be a crime if this church was ever lost."

"Agreed," whispered Hatfield. "I am awed into silence every time I come in here. The architecture speaks for itself. I don't have to say much, or say anything at all in a sermon. The people sit in the middle of a sermon. This building screams love, forgiveness, culture, steadfastness, beauty and more because some shipbuilders toiled night and day to create this!"

"Stunning," said Osbourne.

"I'll say," said Evelyn. "It is more than stunning. It is home. I don't know what I would do or where I would go if I lost this home."

Rabbi Rosenfeld was equally silenced by the architecture. "I too don't know how anyone could even think about…"

"About tearing this done," finished Hatfield.

"Exactly." Said Rosenfeld. "The temple was torn down in Jerusalem. I know it is important to worship the divine. Buildings can become the divine. But they can also represent the relationship people have with the divine. The same holds true for this city. The buildings, the few left standing, and the ones torn down, represent the people. When they are gone, the people might as well pack up and leave."

"I had never thought of it that way," said Hatfield. "What we are about to see as we walk, is not just buildings. It is people. And when the Commission on Urban Renewal tears down buildings without regard for the people..." he paused. "That is not urban renewal. That is destruction of lives. That is dishonoring the people who built this great city. That is dishonoring who live here now. Once something is gone, it only exists in minds and hearts. Eventually that is gone too. History fades, memory fades, and the culture of a great city dies."

They stood in silence. The din of the city could barely be heard through the thick walls. The screech of trains lumbering through what once was, belied the fact that there was still life before death.

"No amount of urban renewal, McDonalds, benign office buildings or low-income housing can replace this magnificent building and what it represents," said Osbourne. "I suspect this is one of the last places people in this neighbourhood can come to find solace."

"And," said Evelyn, "many have never even seen the inside of St. Luke's. It is no wonder, then, that so many have such little regard for a building that just looks bland and plain. Once this sentinel of Main Street is gone, God forbid, the city will be gone."

"I'm making a list," said Osbourne. "Shall we continue our walkabout?"

The fog had disappeared. A brilliant autumn sun had replaced it making the neighbourhood look better than most. The little group stepped out into the sunlight.

"We'll head further into the North End down Main Street." Said Hatfield. "This area used to be called Portland before it was incorporated into the city. I think our next stop ought to be Main Street Baptist. But," he continued, "along the way let us be sure to make note of some of the buildings that used to house vibrant businesses. Welsford Drugs is one of the last remaining businesses. Some buildings are still architecturally important."

LOVELY PARKING LOT

Commissioner Israel McLennan stood at the corner of Wellington Row and Union Street. Jelly bean houses, as the locals called them, marched up one side of Wellington Row. Their colours, painted to accentuate their architecture belied what some thought of their presence. Doors with elegant beveled glass had been allowed to deteriorate. Only the glass sparkled in the mid-morning sunlight. The Loyalist House, a revered landmark, reflected the sun's rays. Its fresh white paint announced to the city that it was important, one of the last remnants of Loyalist living.

Many who visited The Loyalist House rarely noticed that across Wellington Row on the other corner stands a non-descript brick building.

"I bet," said Noll Huggard to McLennan, "that …

"That what?" asked McLennan as his thought about the area was interrupted.

"That many never notice that house over there," Noll pointed, indicating the brick building on the corner. "That house is the oldest brick building in the city."

"Who says?" asked McLennan.

"That little blue plaque on the wall says," replied Noll. He pointed toward the building. "See that little blue plaque? That says."

McLennan squinted. "I've never noticed that before," he replied.

"That's the problem with this city," said Noll. "Too many people don't notice our beautiful city." He paused. "Or at least they don't notice, or have never noticed the city we once had and is no more. If it weren't for that Loyalist House, it would also fall into that big hole they are digging behind it."

"Urban Renewal," said McLennan.

"Hrumpf," shrugged Noll. "What are you going to do about Douglas Avenue and the hole left where our burned down mansion used to stand?"

"Urban Renewal, perhaps," replied McLennan. "It's on our list along with the New Brunswick Museum. We'll deal with Douglas Avenue when we get to it."

"I bet," shrugged Noll. "And…?"

"And what?" said McLennan.

"And… just and," said Noll.

"Lovely parking lot," said McLennan as he pointed to the big open space across the street from the jelly bean houses.

"Maybe," said Noll. "Was that your plan?"

"Maybe," said McLennan. "The houses there were derelict. Not worth much. So…"

"So," said Noll, "a parking lot was more important and beautiful? What happened to the people who lived there? Displaced like me to a hovel in some other part of the city that you have slated for demolition?"

Silence.

McLennan didn't know what to say. He was especially surprised at the conversation since Noll had been known as a man of little words. When he did have something to say, it was usually caustic or important. McLennan sensed that this conversation was a little of both.

"Lovely parking lot," repeated Noll. "Was that the only solution you could come up with? Does that parking lot enhance the history of our city?"

Silence.

"Are you going to tear down," continued Noll, "where I live? The North End is sinking under its own weight. I'm just camping there in a building that once was glorious with its hardwood trim, floors and vista of the harbour. Huh? What have you got to say about that?"

McLennan didn't know what to say. He sensed the conversation had turned the corner. Noll could be a wisp in the fog or a thorn in his side. He could be both at once.

Silence

"What do you say?" asked Noll.

"I'm thinking," replied McLennan.

"Don't think too hard," said Noll. "You might come up with some more ways to destroy my city."

Silence.

McLennan circled the area with his eyes. He looked from the Loyalist house to the Brick house to the jelly bean houses to the parking lot and back again.

Noll waited. "Well?" he asked.

"I have to admit," said McLennan, "that you have a point. I'm not sure what we were thinking when we razed a whole block of buildings in the centre of the city in order to build a parking lot. Many of the businesses have already moved. Some, such as Manchester,

Robertson and Allison, Scovil Brothers and the Woolworths are on the verge of moving or folding. Don't need parking for non-existent customers. The cruise ship tourists certainly don't need parking."

"Exactly," said Noll. "You've torn down my beloved city. And you keep tearing it down. That Commission doesn't seem to be working."

"It has been difficult," said McLennan. "Evelyn Crandall continually calls me on the carpet. Mary Jones thinks she's done good by building a big mansion in a derelict neighbourhood and then calls it urban renewal. All Annalee Gaudet can think about is her precious archives."

Silence

McLennan hadn't heard Noll talk so much in all the years he had observed him. He thought he was just a harmless transient from a respected family. He never suspected that Noll might be useful to him. "Perhaps..." his mind wandered off to places unknown.

Silence

"What say you?" asked Noll.

"You don't want to know," said McLennan.

"Try me," replied Noll.

"Perhaps," answered McLennan.

THE NORTH END WALKABOUT

"I say," suggested Rev. Hatfield, "that we make a circle. Let us walk down Main Street to the bottom and Robinson Square. That's called Indiantown. Then we'll swing around up Victoria Street, circle Victoria Square and head up Metcalf Street toward Saint Luke's. By that time it ought to be lunch. We can stop at Welsford Drugs. Fred can make us a sandwich. We can compare impressions."

"And," said Evelyn Crandall, "I'll have one of his famous ice cream sodas. Pineapple Orange ice cream with vanilla soda would be great."

"So," said Rabbi Rosenfeld, "the first thing I would like you to notice is how Main Street is in transformation. It is actually in decline. Many of the businesses, Nairn, Welsford, Dykeman, are on the verge of closing. Many people have moved out. Houses have become derelict and places for more unfortunate citizens of Saint John. At the turn of the century, I am told, this area was a beehive of activity. Children safely played in the streets. Homes that look rather mundane on the outside were, still are, places of warmth. Perhaps we can see inside one of these three story places." [13]

"Notice," said Evelyn as they walked past Main Street Baptist, "this church is right on the street. It takes up such a big space and is so much like a fortress that people rarely notice its architecture."

"It's a typical church of the late 19th century," said Osbourne. "Not particularly unique but still a sturdy building that could be restored and repurposed. Think about it as a church and an upscale series of lofts."

"Nice idea," said Hatfield, "but the rest of the neighbourhood will have to change along with it if anyone upscale is going to want to move in."

The little group continued walking down Main Street passing one empty store after another.

"Now," said Osbourne, "this is rather interesting. Just look at these magnificent Victorian houses perched on the rock cliff above Main

---

[13] See Appendix for a partial list of businesses that used to exist in Saint John.

Street. They must have a view of the Saint John River, Reversing Falls and maybe even the Harbour. Beautiful."

"Beautiful indeed," said Evelyn, "But…"

"But," said Hatfield, "difficult to maintain. The fog, wind, rain, dampness and winter takes its toll on these buildings. The upkeep is far beyond the ability of today's residents. That's why so many have been broken up into apartments or torn down."

"Sad," said Osbourne. "With the proper care and restoration, these would be prime properties for renewal of this area. People would want to live here. And look at all these little storefront shops. This could be the artsy part of the city."

As the group turned the corner Robertson Square and the river came into view.

"And just look at that view," said Osbourne. "This little square is one of the city's gems. I bet many citizens don't even know it is here? In the spring after a winter of heavy snow, the freshet comes in and floods this park, but that also is part of its charm."

"When I was a girl," said Evelyn, "my father and I used to walk down here. The old river boats were stored down here. This is Indiantown. It was a picture to see. Sadly, those boats are all gone. Those times have changed."

"But," said Osbourne, "what if someone with the resources and imagination brought back a river boat or two. They could ply the Saint John River three seasons of the year, dock down here, and create the perfect vista for artists."

"Beautiful," said Rosenfeld. "I like the way you think. Costs tons of money, but I like the way you think."

The little group turned the corner and climbed the hill up Victoria Street into Victoria Square.

"Another square!" exclaimed Osbourne. "And a square with more beautiful houses and a school."

"And," said Hatfield, "someone had the wherewithal to save Alexandra School. They converted it into apartments. Nice apartments. Shall we turn down Metcalf Street and head back to Saint Luke's? Metcalf Street will give you a good impression of what the North End looked like before so many buildings were abandoned or torn down."

The little group continued their inventory of significant and mundane buildings. As they approached 31 Metcalf Street they noticed Noll Huggard was sitting on the stoop.

"Hello Noll," said Evelyn. "What are you doing out here?"

"Stoop sitting," said Noll. "Taking a break from walking."

"Do you," said Evelyn, "live here now since your family mansion burned?"

"You got it?" said Noll. "This is where we first lived before the mansion. Had to find someplace to live. My siblings didn't want me hanging around with them. So here I am."

"You lived here long ago?" asked Hatfield.

Noll nodded as if that was enough to express his distaste for what he thought the little group might be up to.

"Urban renewal?" he asked.

"No," said Hatfield. "This is Ella Osbourne from Montreal. She's an architect. Her specialty is historic preservation. The clergy of the city asked her to come and assess what we have left to preserve or restore."

"Hrumpf," sighed Noll. "Not much."

"Oh yes," said Osbourne. "There is much to be preserved here. Even this old house where you live is worth preserving."

"Used to be," said Noll. "Since the woodshed out back burned off, all that's left is the front flat. Cold water at that."

"I bet," said Osbourne. "Even so, it is a remnant of beautiful Victorian architecture. Would you let us see?"

"Maybe," said Noll.

"Humour him," whispered Evelyn to Hatfield.

"Noll," said Evelyn, "I bet you might be the richest resource the city has for remembering what this city was like before urban renewal."

"Might be," said Noll.

"Well," continued Evelyn, "I bet more than might be. Who else has walked every street in this city for the last 70 years? I bet you can tell us every building that was torn down. I bet you can even tell us what business was where."

"Could be," said Noll as he appeared to get a little interested.

"And," said Osbourne, "these old buildings on Metcalf Street that are disappearing into the ground and which few people even notice, hold memories beyond measure. Imagine all the children who have played in this street. Imagine the history that these buildings have seen."

Noll stood up as if to disappear inside. Instead he looked up and down the street.

"What do you see, Noll?" asked Rosenfeld.

"My grandfather," he replied. "My grandfather walking up from the harbour after he moored his schooner."

"See," said Osbourne. "You do remember. You are an unknown historian."

"I mourn what has been lost," he replied.

"But," said Evelyn, "Here you sit on the stoop of a building that is part of your family history. It has changed. The street has changed, but I bet we could still see remnants of the glory days when this building was built. May we see?"

"Maybe," said Noll as he looked up toward the second floor window. "Grandmother used to sit in that window and watch for Grandfather."

"Is that the front parlour?" asked Osbourne.

"Yes," said Noll. "Two parlours."

"Let us see, please," said Osbourne. Noll had reached to open the door to the stairs leading to his flat.

"Come on," he gestured.

Noll led the way. The others followed up the stairs that curved to the right as it approached the second floor flat door.

"Smells," said Noll.

"Smells," said Osbourne, "like history. That old linoleum smell that comes from stair treads and paint. Makes my tingle all over. I can't wait to see."

The door to the flat opened into the second parlour.

"Second parlour," said Noll. "Front one is over there. And to the left, a formal dining room with push-through from the kitchen. Bedrooms all along the side, pantry, and cold water bathroom. Quite brisk in the winter."

"Magnificent," said Osbourne. "Look at the Victorian woodwork. The fireplaces. Two of them! And the windows. This is beautiful."

"Old," said Noll. "but…"

"But home," said Hatfield. "Similar to the house I live in down the end of Main. Handsome woodwork, hardwood floors, and a prime location if,…"

"If" said Rosenfeld, "we can get some funding to restore these places and encourage this to become an "in" neighbourhood like Germain Street."

"If," said Osbourne, "is always the response. Let's think positive. I'll add this and other homes to our list of houses worthy of historic restoration. When I write up my impressions I will slant it as "When" the city begins restoration instead of renewal."

Noll appeared pleased that for once a place that he loved was also loved by others. He had been mourning so many losses from his family mansion to St. Paul Anglican Church in the Valley. One of the reasons he did so much walking was to remember instead of wallowing in reality.

"I'd make you tea," said Noll, "but all I have is a hot plate and cold water. I get my eats at Nairns, the Woolworths, the Riviera or Welsford's. Might as well give them some business. I encourage them to stay in business.

"I think," said Osbourne, "that I have a good feel for this part of the city. It's almost noon so let us head to Welsford and wrap up today's walkabout. I believe that Rev. Somerville is scheduled to walk me around the South End and Queen's Square tomorrow.

COMMISSION

"I'm happy to see you all," said McLennan, as he called the meeting to order.

"I'm getting mighty tired of you being happy," said Evelyn. "Instead of being happy, how about being responsible about real urban renewal instead of your crash, burn and celebrate technique."

It wasn't often that Evelyn turned from charm to disarm. This was one such occasion. After spending time with the walkabout group, she was more determined than ever to block anything McLennan tried to do.

McLellan ignored her. Most of the Commission had arrived for their regularly scheduled meeting. Mary Jones brought her haughty attitude. Annalee Gaudet had her number 2 pencil stuck in her hair ready to archive anything worth archiving.

Barrister Bentley had arrived in his Rolls. He was, as usual, decked out in his powder blue shirt and pink bowtie. He didn't know it, but locals disparagingly called him "Bowtie Bentley," because he drove a Rolls and wore a bowtie. That didn't make much senses, other than his name was Bentley. His membership on the Commission on Urban Renewal was rather odd in that his expertise was in criminal law. His ability to solve crimes *and* get criminals off was well known. The Commission was almost a waste of time and money for him but his curiosity, in addition to his owning some landmarks in the city, got the better of him.

Father Sweeney had just come from a meeting with the Bishop. They had met on numerous occasions about the need for restoration of the cathedral. There was never a thought the cathedral would be torn down but buildings around it had been slated for urban renewal. The Bishop saw urban renewal as an opportunity for the cathedral to re-assert its presence in the neighbourhood. There was a possibility that its historic neighbourhood could be spared. Sister Honora had also been known to promote the saving and restoration of neighbourhood buildings as a way of revitalizing that part of the city.

"So," said Evelyn.

"So what?" asked McLennan.

"So," continued Evelyn, "What do you have to say for yourself. What's your plans now for our beloved city?"

"Urban renewal," replied McLennan. "We need to address the issue of vacant spaces left after the recent fires."

"And that is?" asked Evelyn.

"That is," replied McLennan, "Do we let those pieces of property create another hovel in the city or do we use them as an opportunity…"

"For more crash and burn?" finished Evelyn.

"No," said McLennan. "an opportunity for urban renewal."

"That ends up," replied Evelyn, "as ugly as what you've already created. You've just replaced one eyesore with another eyesore. There's nothing "renewal" about what you've been up to. Just look at that parking lot on Wellington Row. What good is that?"

"It brings business into town," replied McLennan. "People need a place to park."

"Park for what?" replied Evelyn. "Park so that they can do a walkabout and see what isn't to be seen?"

"Evelyn," whispered Father Sweeney, "careful. We don't want him to get any ideas."

"I heard that," said Mary Jones.

"I did too," said McLennan. "Ideas about what?"

"Nothing," said Evelyn. "Just nothing. You'll see."

"See what?" said McLennan. He was getting agitated realizing that he was losing control of the commission as well as the meeting.

"See what?" he repeated with emphasis.

"If," she replied, "you did a walkabout like we did," she paused, "you might see."

"Walkabout?" asked McLennan.

"Yes, walkabout," said Evelyn. "We have done one walkabout. We intend to do more. Then you'll find out."

"Who is doing these walkabouts?" asked McLennan.

"We are," replied Father Sweeney.

McLennan was rather non-plused to find out that there was an undercurrent running through the city that might threaten his position. His best laid plans might not materialize. McLennan felt as if he had suddenly been t-boned in an accident that wasn't supposed to happen.

"We?" he repeated.

"Yes, we." Said Father Sweeney. "When St. Paul's Anglican burned to the ground, we saw how you immediately went into action to erase that neighbourhood off the face of the Saint John map. There were many historic buildings there. In addition, people lived there. The Commission under your leadership and without any discussion on our part, moved right in, displaced the residents and began bulldozing one of the most genteel and beautiful sections of the city. All that remains over there is Mt. Pleasant Avenue on top of that hill. You left the mansions at the expense of the more common housing and residents. It's a wonder you didn't also raze Holy Trinity Church. You destroyed the neighbourhood. Many of the parishioners from there used to walk to church. Now they are gone. That puts Holy Trinity in jeopardy."

"And who is this "we" you refer to?" asked McLennan.

"The clergy of the city," replied Sweeney. "We have also been meeting. We started out by wanting to assist St. Paul's. Our meeting quickly transformed into how to save what historical buildings we have left. Many of our congregations are in those buildings. Some of our congregations are in steep decline. We can see that if any of our churches close, such as Centenary, you'll have your hooks out to crash and burn."

"I'd never," said McLennan.

"You have already," said Evelyn. "And I am suspecting your swift action has more to do with what you can get out of this than what will benefit our beloved city." She paused. "There! Now I've said it."

Her comment about McLennan sucked the air right out of all those seated around the table. Some had thought the very thing. None had the nerve to express the thought. Some had even heard rumours about McLennan's hush-hush relationships with big business and contractors in the city. Several on the commission assumed that McLennan was profiting from his leadership of Urban Renewal.

Evelyn knew. And she had told of her suspicions to the "we" Sweeny was referring to.

"We?" repeated McLennan. "Who is this 'we?'"

"I told you," said Sweeney, "The clergy of the city. If you are going to lead a Commission on Urban Renewal that is bent on destruction, we are going to lead a group of clergy and citizens who are determined to save our beautiful city from disappearing."

"That's right," said Evelyn. "And we are in the process of doing walkabouts. We'll have a report for you. And it will be made public. Rabbi Rosenfeld has brought an architect friend of his from Montreal. She is an authority on historical preservation. She's walking about with us and making a list. We are identifying…"

"You don't need to say anymore," shouted McLennan. "I'll do the identifying. I'll be the judge of what stays or goes. I'll...." McLennan was more than miffed that some others would hurdle over his responsibilities.

"I'll?" said Evelyn. "Perhaps you ought to say, "I'll be in jail if I don't put the city above profit."

McLennan was furious. Sweeney tried to calm him down. Mary Jones couldn't care less. She just wanted her house that proclaimed her THE MRS. JONES protected. Annalee Gaudet was furiously writing.

"This is one for the books," said Annalee. "Archives." She repeated.

"Don't," said McLennan. He continued to yell.

"I will," said Annalee as she replaced her number 2 pencil into her hair.

Barrister Bentley was quite amused by the whole scene. He suspected that eventually he would be called upon by the city to sort out this mess. From the tone of McLennan and Evelyn's spat, he suspected there might even be a murder, or at least arson involved.

"I'm leaving," said Annalee.

"Me too," said Evelyn. "I don't need any more of your abuse. Furthermore, we're doing another walkabout tomorrow."

"We'll see," said McLennan. "Next meeting as usual," he replied. He had gathered up his papers, stuffed them into a worn leather brief, and headed for the door.

"Don't let the door hit you on the way out," said Evelyn.

Albert Parlee laughed.

Father Sweeney patted Evelyn on the arm in an attempt to confine her frustration and anger.

"I'll join you and Somerville tomorrow," said Sweeney to Evelyn. "Come with me. We'll go eat with the needy at the soup kitchen over on Union Street. We need to support them. I hear McLennan is thinking of razing that block of buildings."

"For what?" said Evelyn.

"Only God knows," replied Sweeney. "I'm sure we'll find out. Hopefully before it's too late."

WALKING CITY CENTRE

Pockets of gentility remained in the south end and flowed over into the city centre. King's and Queen's Squares provided a burst of colour that the city fathers, (and mothers) made sure was protected. The thought had always been that King's Square, Queen's Square and the Loyalist Burial grounds would be the hallmark of the city. Mayor Blake had been heard saying that he would protect them at all costs. That wasn't saying much, because he was willing to allow the Commission on Urban Renewal to work their havoc in areas around the squares and burial grounds.

Only a few years were needed for the landscape of the area to significantly change. The Admiral Beatty, the go-to hotel in the city, had been downgraded into apartments for the elderly. The Palace and Strand theatres had been torn down. The Riviera restaurant, one of the few real restaurants where the tourists could find a place for a sit-down had been closed. Tourists could no longer find a serving of hot turkey sandwich dinners smothered in gravy and topped with peas, mashed potatoes and cranberry sauce. Hot turkey sandwiches had been a New Brunswick gourmet delight.

Tourists were consigned to a converted stall in the Old Market for a sandwich or something unique like a DLT, a dulce, lettuce and tomato sandwich. The one or two remaining authentic merchant stalls of fish and produce gave a hint of what the Old Market was when it teemed with housewives and errand boys doing their daily shopping for their evening meal. Woolworths was still open and serving its famous pumpkin pie but, as Margaret Greene had said, "soon it will be history…just another empty building vacant and an eyesore in contrast to the beauty of King's square."

Many other businesses had folded. Goldstein's Music Store disappeared along with its sheet music, pianos and booths for patrons to listen to music before buying. Pidgeon Haberdashery had closed long before its illustrious actor Walter Pidgeon died. Calps Department Store had disappeared. Manchester, Robertson and Allison and Scovil Brothers were talking about closing or relocating. There was even a rumour that the Red Rose Tea sign was going to be painted over. It, along with the familiar odor of the pulp mill teetering on the edge of the Saint John River and The Reversing Falls announced gave the city its unique atmosphere. The pulp mill odor, viewed by tourists as a nasty stink mingled with what Commissioner McLennan called "urban renewal."

Rev. Somerville had suggested that the group doing the Centre City/South End walkabout meet at Centenary Church on the corner of Wentworth and Princess Streets. "We are centrally located between King's and Queen's Squares," said Somerville. "It will be perfect starting spot for our walkabout. Additionally," he continued, "we are in close proximity to the burned out Greene Mansion and other sites in the Centre City that have suffered from urban renewal."

Evelyn Crandall walked over from her restored Victorian home on Queen's Square. Rabbi Rosenfeld, Architect Ella Osbourne and Father Sweeney arrived by car. Ella was spending her time in Saint John with her old friend, the Rabbi. Since he and Father Sweeney lived near to each other, they came by car. Rev. Hatfield had decided to forego this walkabout commenting, "You have more than enough qualified persons without me throwing in my two cents."

"Welcome to my neighbourhood," said Rev. Somerville as the car pool arrived. "Evelyn and I have been admiring this starting point, Centenary Church."

"And mourning its condition," said Evelyn. "I live over on Queen's Square. Welcome to my neigbourhood, where all the women are strong, all the men are good-looking, and all the children are above average." She chuckled. "And where too much of the neighbourhood is going to rack, ruin or renewal."

"You've been listening too much to A Prairie Home Companion on the radio," laughed Rabbi Rosenfeld. "That guy can make comments about any neighbourhood that gets to the heart of the matter, I suspect. Satire is often the truth."

"Indeed," said Evelyn. "Sometimes you just gotta laugh. No matter how sad the situation, laugh! Then again, you gotta cry. Once a building is torn down its history is gone forever."

"And," commented Rev. Somerville, "once a building is degraded under its own weight or neglect, it becomes a target for demolition. Sometimes it doesn't even take neglect for a building to lose its worth. Look at that burned out hulk of Greene Mansion next door. The fire fighters did a mighty good job of saving Centenary Church but.."

"But," finished Evelyn, "Now the Commission on Urban Renewal has its sights on Centenary. They don't give a twit that it is on the Canadian Register of Historic Places."

Ella Osbourne leaned back as if to make an architectural drawing in her mind.

"Standing right here close to the building," said Somerville, "isn't the best place to observe this church. Let's walk across the street. Over there," he pointed toward the Hayward home on the opposing corner of Wentworth and Princess Streets.

There was no traffic in either direction so they took their time to look up and down both of the wide streets. Wentworth went downhill toward the Bay of Fundy. Except for an occasional brick Victorian home, the street was lined with three-story wooden homes erected in haste after the Great Fire of 1877. Princess Street in both directions dipped down to the Harbour on one side and to the Dry Dock side of the Bay on the other..

"It's a glorious sight," commented Osbourne. "This vantage point on top of this hill is prime."

"Indeed," said Evelyn. "After the Great Fire residents were anxious to rebuild and restore their Centre City community. Not everyone could afford grand homes. The ones who could built grand and sturdy. Wait till you see Queen's Square. This house," she pointed to the Hayward Mansion," is the residence of the owners of Hayward and Warwick. They have been the premier importers of bone china in Saint John for a century. Their establishment, a business institution of the city, is located off King's Square on the lower end of Princess Street toward the Harbour. The Hayward family is the salt of the earth," she paused, "or should I say 'this rock pile" we love and call Saint John."

The group turned to face Centenary Church on the opposing corner. "I see what you mean," said Osbourne. "That building, from this vantage point, is stunning."

Evelyn was still on her "promote Saint John" thinking. "Have you ever been to our Provincial Capital, Fredericton?" she asked Osbourne.

"Never," replied Osbourne.

"Well, if you ever go there you'll notice how different it is from Saint John. That city is on the flat along the Saint John River. It is as flat as the plains of Manitoba. It is such a contrast from Saint John."

"Really?' said Osbourne.

"Ayah," continued Evelyn, "And you know what?"

"What?" said Osbourne.

"The people in Fredericton," continued Evelyn, "say that they can spot the people from Saint John."

"Really?" replied Osbourne. "And how is that?"

"The people from Saint John," continued Evelyn, "when they are in Fredericton walk as if they have one leg shorter than the other."

"Evelyn!" commented Sweeney.

"It's true," said Evelyn. "Saint John is so up and down one hill to the next that we walk as if we are always walking up or down a hill."

They laughed. The laughter broke the tension of the sadness that had descended as a result of the state of disrepair of Centenary Church.

"This church," said Rev. Somerville, 'Old Centenary Methodist Church is one of our designated local historic places. Its architecture is associated with the Great Saint John Fire of 1877. It is a good example of the architecture used in rebuilding the city. You'll see more of this kind of architecture as we walk down Wentworth to Queen's Square and back around up Germain Street."

"It's magnificent," said Osbourne. "But I can imagine the difficulty it presents to your congregation."

"Indeed," said Somerville, "the church seats 1400 people and we are down to about 100 on a good Sunday. We can no longer maintain this structure. We either sell it, move or disband. It breaks my heart. This building was dedicated in 1882. One year later the church celebrated the 100th anniversary of the landing of the United Empire Loyalists. The wooden church was destroyed in 1877. Locals suffered greatly after the fire. I'm sure their building such a fortress of a church was a consequence of the fire. Wooden buildings went up like matchsticks."

"Do you know who the architect was?" asked Osbourne.

"Yes," replied Somerville. "John Welsh of New York City. It has been recognized for its Gothic Revival architecture. Notice the beautiful array of lancet windows and trefoil and quatrefoil patterns that grace the exterior of the building. They are continued on the inside. The steeply-pitched roof is made of hammer-beam construction. It was built to seat 1600 but can accommodate 2000 in total."

Rabbi Rosenfeld gasped. "I had no idea," he commented, "that it could seat that many people. Was the congregation ever that large?"

"Never," replied Somerville. "The church was built as a monument to those who lost everything in the Great Fire. It was also intended to serve as one of "THE" possible gathering places for important events in the city. And grand it has been. So many people, of late, have never seen the inside. Grand city wide events are better held at Harbour Station. That holds many more people in its architecture designed to accommodate rather than impress."

"Where is that?" asked Osbourne.

"Harbour Station arena is over town, tucked below the Centre City cliff. It's on the site of the old Union Railroad Station. The city," said Somerville, "didn't think ahead that Union Station could have been restored and transformed into a magnificent venue for all sorts of events."

"Instead," said Evelyn, "the Commission's willingness, in fact aggressiveness to crash and burn down so much of our historic Victorian city, has resulted in..."

"Bland, bland, bland," replied the Rabbi.

"Well," said Somerville as he headed back across the street. "Come with me. Let's take a quick look inside before we head downhill toward Queen's Square."

Somerville led the group through the back door, down darkened corridors into the sanctuary. The main doors to the church had been sealed years ago. Except for Easter Sunday's it was not necessary to have such a grand entrance. As they entered the sanctuary their eyes were drawn upward.

"I told you," said Somerville. "The colours of the stained glass windows, made in Montreal, the lancet windows, the hammered beams," he paused. "It always creates a sense of awe. What a shame that the awe of this building can't be implanted in the minds and hearts of our members and the citizens of Saint John."

"That's what's wrong with the Commission on Urban Renewal," commented Evelyn. "They lack a sense of awe. They have no sense of spirit, history, heart."

"And I've said it before," commented Sweeney. "Our citizens have become numb to the awesome location, architecture and scenery of this city. Too bad we can't transport them all to netherland somewhere else where they might have their eyes opened."

"Let us continue," said Rosenfeld as he headed toward the door. The others followed.

"I think," said Somerville, "the best route for this morning is to go south on Wentworth Street to Queen's Square. Then across Queen Street to Germain to Princess Street. We'll end back at Centenary."

"Sounds good to me," said Evelyn. "I'll point out some of the homes of our most prominent citizens."

"And once we are on Germain," said Rosenfeld, "you can look down Duke and Princess Streets toward the Harbour. You'll be able to see what is left of Canterbury and Prince William Streets. Many of the buildings that served the harbour are gone. Just a few, an old Custom House or two remain."

"And," said Rabbi Rosenfeld, "if you look up Wentworth while standing here at Centenary Church, you can see the old Scovil Mansion on the corner of Leinster and Wentworth. It's been vacant for some time. My congregation is in the process of purchasing it. That's where we intend to move after we restore it to its former grandeur."

"And?" asked Architect Osbourne.

"And," he continued, "Our current synagogue building across from Old Stone Church will be sold to someone interested in historic preservation. It will find a new purpose to be an anchor for that neighbourhood."

As the group headed down Wentworth toward Queen's Square they passed Noll Huggard. He had been leaning against a lamppost as if to be making a mental inventory of the city and the situation.

"Hello Noll," said Evelyn. "What are you up to this morning?"

"Fog and pulp mill," replied Noll.

"Fog and pulp mill?" she said

"Fog and pulp mill," he replied. "Wouldn't be Saint John without fog and pulp."

Noll was his typical mysterious self. Walking the streets. Observing when there was nothing to observe. Taking in the city as it once was, especially when the fog and smell of pulp was heavy in the air. This morning the fog had burned off, not so the smell of pulp.

"Well," said Evelyn, "We've got to be about our business. Make sure that lamp post doesn't fall over under your weight."

"Pay him no mind," said Somerville to Osbourne. "He hangs around a lot. I suspect he knows more about this city than the city itself."

"And then there's Truly," said Evelyn.

Truly Morrell had been passing by. He was on his way over town to the Old Market but since the "tour" group looked interesting he decided to tag along for a bit.

"It's all good," said Rosenfeld. "Truly is one of us."

The walkabout continued on its planned route. Architect Osbourne made note of the beautiful restored Victorian homes around Queen's Square and along Germain Street. "Now," she said, "this is what I call urban renewal. The residents of these homes definitely care about the city and their neighbourhood. Just look at the beautifully restored beveled glass doorways, crenelated roofs and lovely plantings in window boxes. THIS is what we want to see a Commission on Urban Renewal participate in. Thankfully there's no crash and burn here."

When the group turned up Princess Street from Germain to head back to Centenary church, Truly peeled off.

"I'm on my way to the Old Market," said Truly. "Need some fresh salmon for dinner. Thanks for letting me tag along. If you need a voice, I'm here."

"There's a Commission meeting in a week," said Evelyn. "I'm ready to bring some conclusions to them. Ella," she continued, "Do you think you might attend with me?"

"I think," said Ella, "that my best plan is to write up recommendations to present to your clergy group. Let them decide how to proceed."

"Good idea," said Somerville. "I'm sure the Commission is already on notice that grumblings are traveling around the city about their destructive renewal. We'll meet next before you head back to Montreal. Next week?" he asked.

"Agreed," said Ella. "That will give me sufficient time to write up a report and have a final meeting with you."

Noll had moved across the street from where he had been holding up the lamp post.

"Still there?" yelled Evelyn.

"Still!" replied Noll.

"Man of few words," said Evelyn to the gathering as she headed down the street to home.

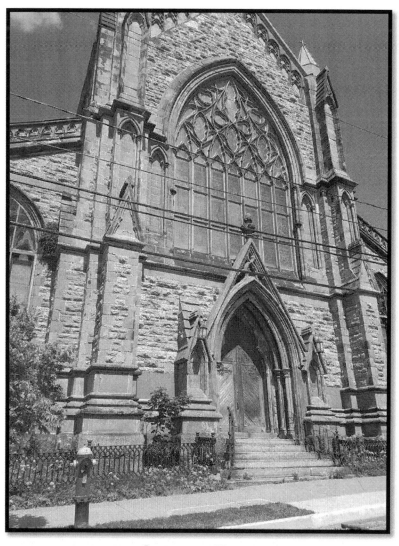

Centenary Church
Photograph taken in summer of 2017

WHILE THE CITY SLEEPS

Things happen while we sleep. People die. Burglars steal. Arsonists light fires. Murderers plot and kill. Cities slowly change. Saint John is no different than any other city, except for its unique history, geography and genealogy that could only be found there.

The steep outcrops of rock, the highest tide in the world, the fury of the Reversing Falls, that and more, have made Saint John what it was and is. A legendary heroic figure Glooscap of the Wabanaki peoples, is said to have been responsible for the creation of the Saint John area and the Reversing Falls. Long before the arrival of the Loyalists fleeing from the wrath and fury of the American Revolutionary War, and long before Saint John was even imagined, the harbour and its surrounding land outcrops waited for those who would come and build upon its shores.

The marigolds march up and down the center of Main Street in summer. Signs along the way declare them to be part of the Marigold Project envisioned by some gentle soul, an "Evelyn Crandall" perhaps, who mourned the destruction of Main Street. They saw the possibility of a marigold memorial.

Decades have passed. Beloveds who built the city lie deep under snow up-country, over Manawganish Road, or flow with the tide of the Bay of Fundy. Loved ones have thrown their ashes to the wind and the sea. A generation or two dearly connected to those early city fathers and mothers lived on in houses built with sweat, tears and labour. The sea was home and livelihood. But, slowly, little by little, the city changed, while the city slept.

Cities change intentionally or gradually. There is always a hesitancy or a shove to bring about change. Those who built resist those who move in and adapt. Those who move in, a second, third and fourth generations resist knowing their heritage. Residents lose sight of a city's history and value. It becomes just a place where people live. So goes the circle of a city's life. It goes round and round. Sometimes it comes around to its origins, original meaning and historical beauty. The Rockefellers rescued Williamsburg Virginia, that 17th and 18th century city of America, from oblivion. The Canadian and Provincial governments revived Louisborg on Cape Breton Island, bringing it back to its 17th century grandeur by using original architectural drawings discovered in the archives in Paris, France.

While Saint John slept, time took its toll. Fog obliterated and clouded what the city had been. Residents were unable to financially maintain buildings buffeted by harsh winters, driving rain, seeping fog, industrial smells of oil refineries and pulp mills. Paint can only resist so much abuse. Money can only solve some problems. The spirit of a city fades. No Commission on Urban Renewal, with good or ulterior intentions can revive what once was during glory days.

Marigolds fade into winter. They leave behind a path as barren as the vacant land along Main Street. Marigolds cannot bring back what was torn down. The city slept. For those old enough to remember, mourning takes over. Desperation and resignation sets in. Sometimes mourning serves as an opportunity for the spirit to awaken and arise. History is found.

Evelyn Crandall is not some maudlin sentimentalist. Her family was one of the founding generations of the once great city. She remembers stories told to her by her elders. Her stories, many that have become spiritual, relate back to 1784 when the Loyalists landed at the foot of King Street. It wasn't King Street then. It was the place that represented a new home and a new beginning. What they planted, what they built, what they preserved, The Old Loyalist House on the corner of Union and Wentworth Row for instance, became for them and their generations, home.

The founding fathers and mothers of Saint John were people of vision. They saw with spiritual eyes and heart. They instilled into their children a spiritual connection to the land and the city they built. Their vision became romantic. Living in their Saint John was a spiritual experience. In contrast, people like Commissioner McLennan and members of the Commission of Urban Renewal are far removed from what once was and what the city had become. They lack soul, or at least a spiritual sense of what was and what could become again. For them, a row of marigolds down the center of a street that once was the heartbeat of the city is enough. Marigolds are perceived as a way of atoning and caring for the city. They don't see urban renewal as preservation. In the wake of their destruction and degradation they hope for a future. There is a sense that once what was is gone forever. It is only to be found in picture books and on old glass photographic plates. Memory fades.

Tourists come to see what is left. They leave wondering what it was they saw and what was so special about their visit.

While the people of the city slept, the city ground along. Those not asleep worked their trade of urban renewal, until suddenly the sleepers in the city awaken to find their special, historic city is gone.

The famous fog and pulp mill smell lumbers on covering all sorts of sins of renewal. For those like Noll Huggard, the fog provides a canvas upon which to paint from memory a scene of the city that was and is no more.

The city sleeps.

CHAOS

Commissioner McLennan had no inkling of what was happening nor of what was to transpire. He hadn't even considered that he might be the catalyst and target for unfolding events. Mayor Blake had charged him with the task of bringing life back into the city. He was determined to do that at any cost. And he was finding out that the cost was dear. People's lives were being disrupted. Historic buildings were disintegrating or disappearing at an increasing pace. What he thought might be profitable for the city and his own pocket was turning out to be a nightmare of thick fog proportions. If he had designs on someday becoming the Mayor, or better the Premier of the Province, they were quickly disappearing.

McLennan called the meeting of the Commission to order and quickly learned that there was going to be no order. He had prepared an agenda detailing his expectations of each commission member. Included in his charge to each was an expectation that each would be responsible for a specific section of the city. He anticipated that urban renewal would go forward at a fast pace. The Commission had already accomplished much in various pockets of the city.

McLennan furiously slammed his gavel on the table to call the meeting to order.

"Where'd you get that toy?" asked Evelyn Crandall. "Think it's going to do you any good?" she asked in the most sarcastic tone of voice she could muster. Evelyn had situated herself right next to McLennan as much to take a gander at his notes as to intimidate him.

McLennan ignored her comment. He banged the gavel even harder. He banged it so hard on the table that it left a dent while causing Mary Jones to grind her teeth.

"Excuse me," said Barrister Bentley. "Lighten up a bit. You'll have us all on edge before we even have a chance to..."

"To do some more destruction?" mumbled Evelyn under her breath. She had placed her bright Easter hat right in front of McLennan. She had made it of artificial marigolds, tulips and hyacinth. Easter was a long way off. Evelyn wore many hats. This was her intimidate McLennan hat. If it weren't for the fact that the flowers were artificial, they would have laid down an aroma that would have obliterated any pulp mill funk and stench that McLennan was about to send out.

McLennan banged the gavel again on the table. "I demand," he said, "that we come to order."

Mary Jones shuddered at the thought of order. She was all about dis-order. That is, any order that would disturb her neighbourhood into noticing she was THE Mrs. Jones.

Annalee Gaudet pulled her pencil out of her black hair that she had wrapped into a convenient pencil holding bun. "I'm ready," she said.

"I bet you are," replied Albert Parlee. Albert was usually reticent with his comments, but the gavel banging had gotten his attention. Father Sweeney reached across the table to console Albert while Sam Greene, Edna Boyle, and Benjamin Northrup in unison pushed their chairs away from the table as if to be ready to run.

"I am calling this meeting to order," said McLennan with a final bang of his gavel.

"You like your new toy?" asked Evelyn. "What else did you get for your birthday?"

McLennan ignored her. Instead he shuffled his papers in an attempt to control his anger. He shoved Evelyn's blooming hat aside. The marigolds were reminding him that Evelyn was the first to criticize his Marigold Project. "No amount of your blooming cover-up," she had said, "will make up for all that you have destroyed. The city's so-called urban-renewal is on your head."

Father Sweeney was near enough to Evelyn that he could reach her hand just as she was about to start waving it in the air. His wordless touch stopped her for the moment. "Continue," he said to McLennan.

"I am happy to report," said McLennan, "that the mayor is impressed with our progress. He has been concerned for some time about businesses moving out of town and areas of the city turning into burned over zones. He doesn't want to have another fire like the Great Fire of 1877."

"We don't need a fire to …" quipped Evelyn. Sweeney squeezed her hand. She stopped in mid-sentence.

"I have been considering how to proceed," continued McLennan. "We don't want our work to go on for decades, yet we don't want it to come to a conclusion before we have made a difference in the future of Saint John."

"If there is a future," mumbled Evelyn.

"I suggest," continued McLennan, "that each of us be responsible for a small section of the city. If, between now and our meeting next month, we can inventory our assigned sections of the city, I think we can make some progress. That seems to be a sensible way of dealing with the charge we have received from the mayor and city council. Once we have done that, we can set priorities."

"I don't need to do much walking about," said Edna Boyle. "I know my neighbourhood like the palm of my hand. Without looking I can tell you what needs…"

McLennan interrupted Edna. "Make a list and we'll hear your report next meeting. Better yet," he continued, "put it in writing so we all can see it."

"I don't need to do a walkabout either," said Evelyn. "We've already done that."

"We?" asked McLennan. "Who is 'we?'"

Annalee Gaudet began to furiously write in her archival notebook. "This is getting good," she mumbled to herself. "I must make sure I get this down for posterity."

"What?" said Sam Greene.

"Nothing," said Annalee as she turned the page. She was making sure she got everything down, word for word.

"You said, 'we,'" said McLennan. "Who is we?"

"She is referring to the clergy in the city," said Father Sweeney. "We began to meet after the loss of St. Paul's Anglican Church in the Valley. We knew that Rev. Davies was missing. We watched as your Commission workmen displaced many people and tore down much of the neighbourhood. We thought it would be a good idea for us to meet as united clergy. We are concerned about our city and its people."

"And?" said McLennan.

"And," said Evelyn, "We have made a lot of progress."

"What kind of progress? We have been successful, in getting rid of the blight of many decaying buildings in the Valley." said McLennan. He was starting to get nervous. It appeared that he was losing control of the Commission. But, more importantly, he sensed that he was losing control of his own future and benefit. "What kind of progress?" he repeated.

"I'll answer," said Father Sweeney to Evelyn. "We have been meeting regularly to discuss the future of our churches, our buildings, and other historic buildings of the city."

"And?" asked McLennan.

"And," continued Sweeney, "We have engaged the free services of an architect, Ella Osbourne from Montreal. She's a friend of Rabbi Rosenfeld. He was able to get her to come and walkabout with us."

"Walkabout?" said McLennan. He began to turn red in the face. He grabbed for the gavel as if he were going to bang it once again in an attempt to restore order to the Commission. Instead he held it poised over the table while he twirled it in a fidget.

"Stop doing that," said Edna Boyle. "You are making me nervous."

McLennan put down the gavel. "And?" he repeated.

"And," said Evelyn, "We have walked about the city with Architect Osborne. She has been very helpful in identifying the remaining buildings of historic value, how other buildings could be restored, and where repurposing might be appropriate."

"For instance," said Sweeney. "She was impressed by the possibilities of restoring the North End. In her eyes, she could see it becoming one of the most beautiful and desirable neighbourhoods in the city. Robertson Park by the water, Indiantown to the locals, could be resurrected as a place where riverboats could dock. Victoria Square could be a venue for music in the summer, farmer markets and all sorts of activity. The houses that look so forlorn have hiden within their walls magnificent Victorian craftsmanship, design and possibility. Remove the boards that cover some of the windows of the houses and bring the neighbourhood back to life."

"And," said Evelyn, "Saint Luke's Anglican Church will remain the sentinel of Main Street. Urban renewal may have torn down much of Main Street, but Saint Luke's will NEVER be torn down. I bet you have never even been in it."

"Where?" said McLennan.

"Saint Luke's at the head of Main Street," replied Evelyn. "Just as I thought. You have no idea what treasures this city harbours alongside its streets. You're just bent on…"

McLennan slammed the gavel on the table. He suddenly realized that his financial and political future in the city was quickly being taken over by a renegade group of clergy.

"And when did you intend to fill us in on this architect?" shouted McLennan.

"Whenever," said Evelyn. "Whenever."

Evelyn's 'whenever' drove McLennan over the edge. He stood up in an attempt to regain his authority. It was no use. His crash and burn of many beloved parts of the city had brought about the demise of his authority.

"Many in the city," said Sweeney, "are perplexed by the seemingly unsympathetic attitude toward the history of the city and its residents. There is much grumbling. People fear that they may be displaced. It is no surprise then, that Calgary, Toronto, Moncton, Ottawa and other places west hold a hope for a better and more lucrative life. If the Commission is truly interested in urban renewal, then you will guide us to caring for the people as much as the city and infrastructure. In addition, Rev. Gwyn Davies is still missing. Rumours are circulating. It is even reaching into the Commission on Urban Renewal and your leadership."

McLennan was brought to silence. He sat down. Evelyn had reached for the gavel just in case McLennan had decided to wield it again. She moved her colourful hat to the middle of the table. "There. Isn't that pretty," she said satisfied with the chaos she had brought about.

"Pretty numbing," said McLennan. "You could have brought your concerns to the Commission," he said to Sweeney.

"Would you have listened?" said Sweeney. "I think not. For some reason you seem to have your own agenda."

Evelyn appeared to be ready to slam the gavel down on the table. Sweeney reached over and gently placed his hand on her arm. He didn't need to apply pressure. His hand stopped her from reacting.

"And," said Evelyn, "Architect Osbourne has mapped out a plan. We'll share it with you if you want. If you don't want, we will proceed in haste. And you can continue your crash and burn. Maybe you'll get what you want. Maybe you won't."

McLennan could feel his political and financial life whither right before his eyes. He wasn't sure what he was going to do but he was going to do something. And he wasn't going to warn them ahead of time.

"We're finished here," said McLennan as he grabbed his gavel. "Your mission, if you are willing," he paused, "is to be carried out over the next fortnight."

"You've been watching too much "I Spy," said Albert Parlee.

"Your mission," repeated McLennan, "is to complete these tasks I've printed out for each of you." He called each by name and handed them their task.

"I don't need one," said Evelyn. "Nor does Father Sweeney. We've already done your work for you. You'll see next meeting. Get your ducks in order," she paused, "before your goose is cooked."

Annalee Gaudet stifled a laugh but managed to write down Evelyn's comment for the archives.

Evelyn stood. She put on her hat, adjusted her skirt and prepared to leave.

"I'm happy," said McLennan, "to declare this meeting adjourned."

"I'm happy, for once," said Evelyn, "that you are happy. Prove it. Let's go Father," she motioned to Father Sweeney as she headed for the door.

"The hungry are in need of a good noonday meal," she said as she held the door for Father Sweeney. "We'll see you all over at the Soup Kitchen on Union Street, if you dare to venture out to do something meaningful."

McLennan sat down. There was no point in banging his gavel on the table. He knew when he'd been told. He didn't know that he had been found out. "Don't let the door hit you on the way out," he mumbled under his breath.

FIRE

Fog shrouded the buildings, streets and haunts of the city like a fisherman casting his nets in search of the mourning catch. It didn't take much for the correct mix of air temperature, Bay of Fundy waters and late autumn to spread a pall over the city. Fog was always lurking around the corner.

Noll Huggard was the first to know. He had arisen early. It was his custom to wend his way down Main Street, stop at Reggie's for a coffee and then proceed to make sure the streets of the old city and its Victorian buildings were still intact. He didn't trust the Commission on Urban Renewal. Nor did he trust the local residents with the history of the city. Too often he had come upon an empty lot where a grand Victorian building had been the day before.

Transplants to Saint John, for whatever reason, usually saw the city as dank, foggy and old. They had arrived in the city two centuries after the Loyalists landed at Market Slip. Their vision was self-centered. "It's an okay place to live," they would say, "but."

"But," whispered Noll to himself. "But for them it's just a place to live. They always have something to grumble about. Times are tough, Work is menial. Pay is low. The fog is wet. The pulp mill stinks. There's nothing in particular to do but watch the Bay of Fundy ebb and flow while cruise ships dock for a day or two in their attempt to satisfy their passengers and bring some dollars to the realm. They are destroying my city."

Noll took his usual path. Early morning with fog was a special time for him. The damage done by urban renewal wasn't as evident in the foggy dusk of the morning. With his peak wool cap pulled down to his ears, a warm woolen coat pulled tight around his neck, and a pink wintergreen mint or two in his pocket, he was all set for the day.

Noll walked downhill from Reggie's to King Street. He made his usual stop at the corner to look up and down. What he hoped to see was the bustle of a city in full regalia. Buses going up and down. He always saw in his memory cars from the 1940's; a DeSoto, Hudson or Meteor. It was a strain for those old cars to make the grade to the top and turn around Kings Square. He remembered the gnashing of gears as drivers maintained heavy pressure on the brake pedal, finessed the clutch and ground the gears. More than once, Noll had seen a car roll backwards into the car behind. King Street hill was a challenge for the novice driver in the middle of bustle. Noll saw through the fog into an earlier time when all was good with the world and Saint John.

"Thank goodness for the fog," he whispered to himself. "I don't have to look at the awful destruction urban renewal has done. They think they've done such good by tearing down and leaving enough to remind me of what was."

The fog covered up what urban planners called renewal. Noll loved the fog. It provided a canvas for him to paint in his mind the city he had grown up with. The city he loved.

The plaintive fog horn sounded off in the distance. He counted, "One, two, three four," between blasts. The horn echoed off the surrounding hillsides of the harbour. The fog made the sound even more ominous and thick. Noll saw his grandfather's three mast schooner, The Golden Ball, come around Partridge Island and head to safe harbour. The fog horn sounded again, "one, two three, four," interrupting his historical sight.

"There's no use looking up and down King," he said to himself. "I know what used to be there. I know what's there now." He hurried along in his mourning pace that was more a saunter than a hurry.

Noll had his favorite places in the city. Germain Street was one of them. For some unknown reason, people had decided to make Germain one of the posh residential streets. The trees on either side provided a canopy for pedestrians. Cars never speeded. The magnificent buildings on either side demanded that passersby stop and notice. Beveled glass doorways sparkled in the fog light. They reflected the images of those who stopped to look. Flower boxes in warmer weather overflowed with nasturtiums, geraniums, petunias and begonias. There was life, a vibrant life.

"What's the matter with the rest of the city?" said Noll to himself. "If the residents here can display pride for this street, why can't the rest of the city do the same?" Just then the fog horn disturbed his thought with another "one, two, three, four." He stopped to listen as it echoed. He imagined ships taking heed out in the Bay of Fundy.

"Good thing that fog horn works," he said to himself. "The shoals out in the Bay have taken more than one ship trying to make harbour. The fog didn't let him see but he could imagine that the Three Sisters Light was also flashing its warning. Between the "sisters" and the "horn," the city was safe for another day.

Noll had passed by Princess Street and was deep in thought when he came upon the Church of Saint Andrew and Saint David. The fog was so thick that it covered all but the multiple steps leading up to the front entrance. The clock in Trinity Church steeple chimed the hour. He counted the chimes. "Seven," he repeated. "Soon the city will awaken to some form of life."

As he continued down Germain toward the sea, Rev. John Bruce of Saint Andrew and Saint David, and Elder Laurence Colwell of Germain Street Baptist emerged from the fog.

"Morning, Noll," said Bruce. "You're out bright and early this morning."

"Early," said Colwell, "but not so bright. A typical Saint John morning."

"My favourite," mumbled Noll. "I like this kind of mourning. It stops urban renewal from their work. It also keeps the tourists at bay. Or should I say 'in the Bay.'" He laughed.

"Funny," said Colwell. "We would like them to appreciate our city. It's hard when you can't see the city because of the fog."

"Works for me," said Noll. "I can see the city more clearly when there's fog than when there's not."

"Have a good walkabout," said Bruce. The two continued down Germain each to their own church. "I wouldn't want to touch that comment with a ten foot pole," said Bruce. "Who knows what he is up to."

"He's harmless," said Colwell. "Here's my stop. Walk again tomorrow?" he asked.

"For sure," said Bruce as he watched Colwell climb the steps to Germain Street Baptist.

Noll had long disappeared into the fog. He walked along as if covered by a pall. Every step he took was a way of mourning. "And when I'm dead and gone and they bury me in my grave over there on Manawaganish road," he thought, "I'll go home to see my city and be free."

Walking this part of the old city comforted Noll. The Great Fire of 1877 had destroyed everything burnable in its path. Many grand Victorian homes had risen from the ashes. They marched up and down the many streets named for British royalty or that which reminded the 18th century Loyalists of their reason for settling there.

He whispered their names as he passed by: Queen Street, Duke Street, Saint James Street, Britain Street, Carmarthen Street and Wentworth.

Just as he rounded the corner and headed for Queens Square he heard it. The sirens were blaring. They were mingling with the sound of the fog horn with its plaintiff call. He knew.

"Another fire," he cried. "Another fire!"

He knew. He could see a glow several blocks away on the northeast corner of Queens Square. The fog horn sounded another mourning cry. Noll tingled all over at the thought of another pile of ashes and a vacant lot. He headed toward the red glow that was being disbursed through the fog. It created an artificial sunrise.

"A fire!" he whispered. "Where?" He had just passed through that corner of the square. There had been nothing unusual. Just fog. Just a restored Victorian house or two among the ones waiting for some tender care. Just...!

The fire engines raced by. The fog didn't slow them down. They always had thoughts of another great fire. "Get to the address," yelled the fire fighters as they blew past Noll and others who had also heard the sirens. Others had been awakened by the sirens. Many could be heard yelling as loud as they could.

"Fire! FIRE!"

Noll knew. At least he thought he knew.

Evelyn Crandall's Victorian home was engulfed in flames. A moment ago all was calm. Now urban renewal was working its mission.

"Fire!"

A DAY IN THE PARK

It was Ella Osbourne's last day in the city. On the morrow she would drive back to Montreal. Rabbi Rosenfeld had a Rabbi's conference to attend there so it was convenient for him to drive her. Plane flights were few and far between. Travel scheduling by train from Saint John was inconvenient for the Rabbi. .

"I remember," said Truly, "when you could take a train from Saint John to anywhere in the world. In fact there was even a steamship, the SS. Saint John that had a regular schedule. It sailed from Saint John to Boston and back."

"Really?" said Ella.

"Yes, really," said Truly. "My parents were regular passengers. It was nothing for them to visit relatives in the Boston states. I had one relative who used to take the train to New York City. She would check out the latest fashions and come back with fashion plates. She lived up country. Most people think of upcountry as the middle of nowhere. But she brought the city to the country. My folks two hundred years ago settled up there. They brought their city culture to the country wilderness."

"It's true," said the Rabbi. "People don't often associate Jews and the culture of the big cities with Saint John or upcountry. These early settlers were far from being country bumpkins. They knew what was happening down in the States. People in Boston and New York knew the latest news from Saint John. It was even reported in our local newspapers."

"Really!" said Ella.

The little group had gathered on one of the promontory cliffs of Rockwood Park. It overlooked the city.

"On a clear day," said Rev. Hatfield, "you can see the entire city and the harbour on both sides. Unfortunately the fog doesn't let us see today.

"Over there to the left," he pointed, "is the dry docks. It was one of the busiest in the world. You can tell it's there because you can see the glow of the refinery chimneys burning off gas. Once this fog burns off you can see."

"And," said Truly, "you can kind of see a glow over the city. Over there," he pointed indicating the Centre City perched between the two harbours.

"And," continued Hatfield, "over there to the right is the main Harbour. That's at the foot of King Street. It's called Market Slip." He pointed. "That's where the Loyalists pulled their boats up on shore. I can always hear them saying, 'We're home.'"

"Well," said the Rabbi, "let us walk a little. Evelyn Crandall was supposed to join us today. Evidently she has been waylaid. The fog hasn't shrouded Rockwood Park in a pall so let us do our walkabout. We'll also have to ride about because it is a very large park. This is one of the largest parks in Canada. It was designed by Calvert Vaux. He is best known as the co-designer, along with his protégé and junior partner Frederick Law Olmstead, of Central Park in New York City."

"This park," said Truly Morrell, "is 890 hectares. It is upland Acadian mixed forest. It is one of the untouched treasures of our city. One could spend all day here, and many do. When I was a boy my mother would bring us out here during blueberry season. We would spend the day picking blueberries. When we got home, she would make the most wonderful blueberry bang belly.[14] Sometimes she made blueberry grunt.[15] There's nothing like wild blueberries."

"I'd like some right now," said Ella.

"This park," said the Rabbi, "is made up of many hills, caves and freshwater lakes. There is an extensive trail network, golf course and the city zoo."

"It is the one place," said Truly, "that has been allowed to exist undisturbed. The Commission on Urban Renewal wouldn't dare touch this park. There would be hell to pay. It's one of the few places where

---

[14] There are numerous recipes for blueberries. I asked for recipes on the Saint John North Ender's Facebook page. Several came up with blueberry bang belly. Two people, Carrol Thorne of Cambridge Narrows, and Vicky Saunders of the North End. The recipe for Blueberry Bang Belly and others are included in the appendix of this book.

[15] Following was provided by Carrol Thorne: **Blueberry Grunt** – an Acadian delicacy was originally made by French settlers in a pot over an open hearth. Blueberries are cooked with molasses, sugar, and spices to create a sauce, which is then topped with dumplings and cooked on the stove in a covered skillet. The name "grunt" refers to the baking process. As the dessert steams, there's often a grunting sound. Every family in Atlantic Canada seems to have its own blueberry grunt recipe, and while it's a sweet dessert, it's often eaten for breakfast.

people can totally get away from the hustle and bustle," he paused, "and the disaster they call urban renewal."

The fog was beginning to dissipate. The glow over the city was intensifying. The sun was beginning to work its deed of awakening the city to a new day. The little group didn't presume that it was more than the sun that was creating the glow in the sky.

"I suggest," said Rev. Hatfield, "that we park the car by the squirrel feeding station and walk that circular trail. It's a short trail that will give you some idea of the variety of the flora and fauna of the park. Then we'll drive through and you can see Lilly Lake. There's also Long Lake, Harrigan Lake, Fisher Lakes and Mayflower Lake."

"This park," said Truly, "has played a prominent part in the city's life. The World Speed skating Championships were held in the park in 1926. Twenty five thousand fans came to watch. There's a monument over in King's Square. Charles I. Gorman was our celebrity. He competed in the 1924 and 1928 Winter Olympics. He dominated the sport of speed skating in the 1920's. He was often called "The Man with the Million Dollar Legs," and "The Human Dynamo.""

"So now I see," said Ella, "a part of Saint John that has been untouched by urban renewal. It would be a mortal sin if the Commission on Urban Renewal aimed its sights on this land. I hope it will always be protected for the use of people who come from all over the world."

"It needs some tender loving care," said Rev. Hatfield.

"But," said Ella, "there's nothing here than can't be enhanced and restored. The Pavilion at Lily Lake, the pathways, the auto road," she paused, "these can all be renewed without destroying the natural beauty of this place."

"We will keep an eye on this place," said Truly.

"And," continued Hatfield, "if anyone makes any suggestions about destroying the natural beauty and resource here,.."

"They will hear from us," said the Rabbi.

"Evelyn Crandall will see to that," commented Truly.

"I'm disappointed she couldn't make it today," said Ella, as the little group climbed into the Rabbi's car. "She is a walking advertisement for this city."

"Indeed," said the Rabbi as he started the car and eased it out on to Mount Pleasant Avenue. "And she is our only hope on the Commission. This is one of the nicest streets in the city. It will never change. The people on this street have the money and influence to keep it just as you see it."

"Beautiful!" said Ella.

Just as the Rabbi eased the car onto Somerset Avenue headed toward his home two fire trucks raced by with sirens screaming.

"Fire!" said Hatfield. "Another fire! It looks to be over town!"

"Urban Renewal," muttered Truly under his breath.

"What?" said Ella.

"Urban Renewal," he continued. "It seems to be the way to get rid of old buildings and build new around here. Evelyn Crandall will have something to say about this!"

FIRE!

It didn't take long for Truly to follow the glow in the sky. Saying goodbye to the Rabbi, Hatfield and Ella, he headed post haste across the city. Sadness and anxiety filled his heart. "Is this another one of those urban renewal fires," he thought to himself as he raced as fast he could from Wentworth Row, across King Street and down Germain. "I love this city so much," he said out loud, "that it breaks my heart. Just look at these magnificent old buildings on Germain. How could anyone think of destroying them?"

The closer he got to the red glow in the sky, the brighter it became. The brighter it became, the heavier his heart and the descending smoke that was mixing with the remnants of the morning fog. The fog was causing the smoke to linger even longer, refusing it permission to ascend into the morning sky that was beginning to appear crystal blue with a hint of the moon's light. The moon had tried to dispel the fog throughout the night.

Truly stopped to catch his breath. As he leaned up against the corner of Keirstead Florists on the corner of Charlotte and Princess Streets, Noll Huggard passed by. He too had been interested in the fire.

"Where you going?" said Truly. "The fire is that way."

Noll was headed toward King's Square.

"Can't stand it," muttered Noll. "Just can't stand it."

"Can't stand what?" said Truly.

"Can't stand it," he repeated. "Can't stand it. They've done it again."

"The fire?" said Truly.

"You figure it out," muttered Noll, as he continued on. "Can't stand it. The Crandall House."

Truly was stunned by what Noll had said. The Crandall house, Evelyn Crandall's house, was one of the premier historic buildings on Queen's Square. Evelyn was in the process of having it designated as a local historic place. She had applied to Trinity Royal Heritage Preservation.

The Crandall house was a brick two-and-a half story Second Empire Home on Queen Square. Truly knew it well. Evelyn had served him afternoon tea on many a day when she had seen him passing by on the way to home.

"It's such a beautiful home," whispered Truly to himself as he watched Noll disappear into what fog was left. "Heaven forbid this beautiful home with its Queen Anne Revival influences, its hexagonal tower, brick exterior, mansard roof, pediment dormers and bay windows is destroyed." He paused to wipe away a tear that had formed. It wouldn't be the first or last that Truly would shed.

"That house," said Truly to himself, "was built by a lumber manufacturing family after the Great fire of 1877. In 1892, the builder moved in and lived there until Evelyn bought it in the 1940's. She lovingly made sure every detail inside and out of the home was preserved."

Truly quickened his pace. As he got closer to Queen's Square the sky got redder, the smell of the burning flesh of an historic building intensified and the fog turned to smoke. He covered his nose and mouth with his red bandana. Police lines had been erected to keep the fire bugs from getting too close. Truly didn't need to get close to see what he hoped he would never see. He stood in the center of Queen's Square by the Samuel de Champlain statue. The square is heart of the historic South End neighbourhood. It was one of the reasons Evelyn Crandall wanted to live there. The area of the history made her feel as grounded as ever a Loyalist could feel in a country that had been home for more than 200 years. Evelyn could also see the Harbour and Bay of Fundy from the tower of her house. To her it was no widow's walk. It was a place where she retreated after an especially disheartening Commission on Urban Renewal meeting. She could see the city.

"Little did she know," whispered Truly as he stood by the Champlain monument. "Little did she know," he repeated.

As he watched the fire fighters wage a losing battle, he noticed that all the windows of the home had been blown out. The magnificent bay windows on the second floor stood blind to the world. Others watched. Their interest was more in the excitement of a fire than the loss of an historic building. Fire chasers have a maudlin fascination with what was, what might be, and what is discovered in the ashes. Not so for Truly.

Truly searched the crowd. Most of the people he saw were local. He noticed Mayor Blake huddled off to one side. Commissioner McLennan was with him. He could only imagine what they were talking about. Evelyn was nowhere to be seen.

"I hope, dear God," said Truly, "that she's off doing some charitable work. She will be devastated to find her home gone."

Just as he spoke the words, the fire fighters yelled at the top of their lungs. "GET BACK, GET BACK. SHE'S ABOUT TO GO."

The crowd obeyed. Even though they were quite some distance from the fire, they huddled together, closer to the Champlain Monument.

No sooner had the fire fighters yelled their warning, the mansard roof of the home buckled and came crashing down inside taking out what was left of the pediment dormers and hexagonal tower. Once the fire had reached the tower, all was lost. The fire fighters knew it. Towers, chimneys and spires involved in a fire act like a chimney that just feeds oxygen. The fire fighters knew that. They stood back. They continued to stream water onto the structure. But all was lost.

All that remained once the roof fell was a façade of what once was. "Another historic piece of Saint John, no doubt," said Truly, "will be torn down by in the name of urban renewal."

"I hope the Commission on Urban Renewal is happy," he said into the air. "I hope," he repeated, "that they are happy. Fire is doing their work. Evelyn will be homeless. Now she will really be on a campaign to save the city's historical buildings."

Truly didn't know. No one knew. Only the ashes of the fire as they cooled knew. And they didn't even know until…

COMFORT FOOD

There was no use hanging around to watch the fire fighters wage a losing battle. Once the roof of Evelyn's house crashed down there was nothing to do but make sure that the blazing fire turned to embers and the embers to cold ash. For some the result might be hoped for cold cash!

Commissioner McLennan seemed overly interested in the fire. It was well known that he didn't much like Evelyn. She had been a thorn in his side and he in hers. Still he saw some value in making sure she continued on as a member of the Commission. McLennan was always ready to use others for his own purpose. He was truly a snollygoster. Truly loved words and snollygoster was one of his favorites.

"That snollygoster," whispered Truly under his breath. He repeated it with a little snarl that only he could perceive. "That snollygoster," he repeated. "That McLennan is just a shrewd bastard who wants to be in office regardless of party, platform or principles." Truly paused. He didn't often use such words, but this situation required that he stoop almost as low as McLennan. It made Truly feel as if he was doing some good by being present all around the city. Truly was no snollygoster. He was, like Evelyn, a man in love with the city. He was a man in mourning for what had been destroyed. And he was a man who was looking out for what remained.

"Snollygoster," he whispered to himself. "That's a good word for this snark. McLennan is one of the shrewd, unprincipled people in the city who are in it for themselves. A highbinder who is more swindler and corrupt politician that honourable citizen. They don't care about the city, the population or our history.

"Snollygoster," Truly snorted to himself one last time as he headed back down Charlotte Street toward King Square. He had pumpkin pie and Margaret Greene on his mind. Comfort food is always good any time of day or night when a catastrophe of whatever proportion hits home. He could taste the pumpkin pie with every step he took.

But it wasn't just the pumpkin pie he was interested in. "Maybe," he thought, "just maybe Margaret will have some inside dope on what is going on in the city. She has a keen sense of hearing. She filters out the rubbish and keeps important information to herself. Probably someone who had sat at her Woolworths lunch counter must have let slip something or other."

As he walked along, Truly became aware that if he was going to learn anything from Margaret, he would have to make sweet. Her family mansion had been burned to the ground several weeks prior but that didn't particularly disturb her since she was estranged from her family. But she wasn't estranged from her customers. There were many. And every one had a story to tell.

Noll Huggard was sitting at the far end of the lunch counter chowing down a bowl of clam chowder.

"He got here fast," said Truly to Margaret.

"He can be quick on his feet when he wants to be," replied Margaret. "Harmless, I suppose. Just a lonely old man with his peak cap, woolen coat, scarf and the city to himself as he walks along."

"Maybe," said Truly. "But he does seem to appear out of the fog and disappear into the fog. He reappears in the strangest places. What do you make of it?"

"Nothing really," said Margaret. "I suppose the morning chill caused him to want some warm chowder. He'll be gone shortly."

"He doesn't need to be gone," said Truly. "I'll have some of that pumpkin pie and a hot cocoa. It's a hot cocoa kind of morning."

"Putting on the pounds, are you?" said Margaret, as she set down the pie. "You'll be ready to play Santa. I knew you'd be here so I saved back a piece for ya. Want some whipped cream or marshmallows on that?"

"Nope. Just the pie and cocoa," said Truly. "Tell me," he continued. "I bet you hear a lot of stuff working this counter."

"Sure do," she said. "Nothing you need to know."

"Aw, come-on, Maggie," said Truly. "Let me in on a little of what you hear."

"Don't call me Maggie," she said. "My father called me that and I hated it. It's 'Margaret' to you, Mr. Truly."

"Okay, Maggie, err.. Margaret," said Truly with a glint of a chuckle in his eye. "What have you heard lately?"

"Well," she said, "For one I hear the tourists are always questioning what there is to see around here. They go to the Old Market and love that, but..."

"But," he finished, "there's been a lot of renewal and destruction. Right? Tourists don't know what they are seeing because so much of what they would have seen 30 years ago is gone. Every time a privately owned business closes some more of the city moves out and urban renewal moves in. The city shuts down and dies a little."

"Exactly," she said. "I tell them what they are missing. That makes them sad because many of them are coming from areas of the world where historic areas are gone. They are on a cruise to see history as much as a different country. And what do they see?"

"A city in decline," said Truly, "and a city that has lost its Victorian uniqueness. We've become just another stop on the cruise lines itinerary. Sometimes," he continued, "the ship they are on is more historically interesting than our city. Take for instance, the Queen Elizabeth 2 that visited port this past summer. That ship is history on the sea, even if it is a new version of the old ocean liners. It reminds the passengers and our citizens of when crossing the Atlantic by ocean liner was the only way to go."

"Exactly," she said. "I watched that ship turn around when it was in port. It was quite a sight to see an ocean liner fill our harbour from side to side as she turned to leave."

"I bet the old sea captains who still live here," he said, "were thrilled to see that. But tell me,…"

"Tell you what?" she said.

"Tell me," he continued, "what do you hear about this Commission on Urban Renewal? I've been doing walkabouts with the clergy and an architect from Montreal. Evelyn Crandall has been involved with the Commission and the Clergy group. The architect has helped us identify what remains of our historic city."

"I've heard a few rumours about that," she said.

"And?" he continued.

"And," she commented, "Commissioner McLennan has been in cahoots with a commissioner or two. One day he even cornered Noll Huggard over there," she pointed toward the end of the counter where Noll was finishing up his chowder. "They had their heads together. Some kind of secret was going on. Made me think that the Commissioner is nothing but a highbinder. You know, a swindler or a corrupt politician. I heard something about fires and destruction. I'm sure Noll hasn't been very happy with what the Commission has been doing. He walks this city and knows every nook and cranny. I bet he could paint a picture of the city with his eyes closed if he had any talent other than walking."

"Do you think they were up to anything?" said Truly.

"Nah." Said Margaret. "I doubt it. I'm sure they were up to something but probably nothing very important. Maybe the commissioner was trying to get on Noll's good side in case he needed him for his own purposes. You know," paused Margaret, "that commissioner is…." She paused. "What is it you called him?"

"A snollygoster?" he replied.

"That's it," said Margaret. "He's a snollygoster." She put a finger to her ear as if to listen for an explanation. "What is that anyway?" she asked.

"A snollygoster," said Truly, "is a shrewd, unprincipled person. It's someone who wants office for the sole purpose of self-aggrandizement and winning. They want to see what they can get out of any position for their own gain."

"That's it," said Margaret. "I don't trust him. Nor Noll now that he's had his head together with McLennan. The two of them were whispering."

"You don't think," asked Truly, "that they were whispering sweet nothings?"

Margaret laughed as she wiped down the counter. "You finished with that pie?" she asked.

"What do you think?" he said. "Not a crumb left. You can take the plate. I'll finish this cocoa and be on my way."

"To where?" she asked.

"I don't know," he replied. "Maybe back to the fire. I'm sure that they will be sifting through that mess soon. Maybe the homicide detective will get involved just in case…"

"Just in case what?" said Margaret.

"Just in case Evelyn Crandall was in that house when it burned to the ground," replied Truly.

Noll heard that. He had a startled look on his face. He had not thought far enough ahead that as he watched the house burn he might have been watching Evelyn burn up in it. Noll pulled down his cap, buttoned up his wool coat and headed for the door farthest away from Margaret and Truly.

"There he goes," said Margaret. "At least he paid when I served him. He'll be walking around the rest of the day, I suppose."

"I hope," said Truly, "that he finds everything in order in the city. Perhaps we ought to tail him. Maybe he has some ideas about urban renewal."

"Nah!" said Margaret. "The man hasn't had a productive thought in all the years he's been wandering around. If he had, no one would know it. Keeps to himself. Occasionally breaks out of his wool coat and peak cap and let's someone in, like that McLennan fellow a day or two ago. Odd bunch some of the people in this city."

"And it gets odder by the day," said Truly. "Maybe the oddest thing I can think of at the moment is that you and I seem to hit it off. We seem to think alike."

"So?" said Margaret. "What's that mean?"

"It means," said Truly, "that maybe we could end up being sweet on each other."

"Hrumpf," shrugged Margaret. "That'll be the day. We may think alike, but that's about all is going to be."

"Really?" said Truly.

"Really," said Margaret. "Keep me posted if you hear anything about Evelyn.

"And you," said Truly, "keep me posted if you hear any good dirt that might be helpful to the clergy group and…"

"And?" she said.

"And," he replied, "if you have any thoughts about sweets?"

ASHES TO ASHES, DEATH TO DUST

Evelyn hadn't been seen since the fire. Nor had Rev. Gwyn Davies. Two mysterious disappearances caused the city fog to be thicker than ever. Rev. Davies had just disappeared before St. Paul's Anglican Church in the Valley had burned to the ground. He left the congregation just at a time when they ended up with no church and no priest. They still didn't know where he was. They were beginning to be annoyed with his absence. The longer he was missing the less they cared. They were even having thoughts of just merging with Old Stone Church and be done with the whole building thing. Their neighbourhood was gone. They might as well be gone too.

Evelyn's absence was a different matter. It was unusual since she had been nominated for the honour of Citizen of the Year for all her volunteering at the Soup Kitchen and her involvement on the Commission on Urban Renewal. She would never just disappear and leave the city unattended. Even if she had decided to resign from all her volunteer activity, she would have made it official. Evelyn was missing.

Several hours had passed since Truly had left Queens Square for pumpkin pie at the Woolworths. "Might as well go back and see what's happening now," he said as he headed down Wentworth Street. He never took the same route twice. It was his custom to make sure that he kept an eye on the various streets of the city just in case. "Just in case," he said to himself, "that McLennan guy decides it's time to pull the rug out from under Centenary Church, the Hayward Mansion, or some other significantly important, historic part of the city."

Truly passed by where the Greene Mansion, Margaret's old home, used to stand. "That fire," said Truly, "sure left a hole near Centenary Church. One less church family. One less historic home. One less...." he whispered. Before he could finish the rest of his thought, Noll Huggard came strolling around the corner. He was also headed toward Queen's Square.

"Cheers Noll," said Truly as he waved to him from across the corner of Wentworth and Princess.

Noll just looked. He pulled his peek cap down almost obscuring his eyes as if he didn't want to be seen or he didn't want to see. Truly noticed some form of acknowledgement that Noll had seen and heard him. But Noll was such an odd fellow, a fixture in the city, that any form of acknowledgement was seen as a sign that Noll was Noll.

"Where you headed?" shouted Truly, as Noll quickened his pace, his back to the shout.

"Hey," yelled Truly, "where you headed!"

Noll pointed in the direction of the South end. There was no use in pursuing Noll or a conversation. Noll knew ever alley. He knew every place where he could step into thin air and disappear. It was one of the creepy things about Noll. And just as usual, Noll did just that. Before Truly could get close enough to tail Noll, Noll had stepped into nothingness as if the fog had returned to protect and surrender him to the Victorian city he mourned.

Truly shook his head. He continued on down Wentworth Street, crossed over toward Queen's Square on Saint James Street to arrive at the Square's corner, Saint Andrew and Sydney. From that vantage point he was able to look across the square to Evelyn Crandall's burned out home. Smoke was still filtering into the air but the ashes had cooled.

Truly could see that the RCMP, Fire Inspector and other officials had arrived. There was great interest in this fire, not only because of whose house it was, but because it was a significant anchor for the historic district around Queen's Square. There was also a CBC mobile truck parked along Queen Square North. Constable police cars were everywhere.

"It'll be all over the news," said Truly. "All over the news. That's all we'll hear for days. Another building burned and…"

Before he could finish that thought he noticed the arrival of an ambulance. Emergency personnel hopped out but seemed in no hurry. There was no point in being in a hurry. If that fire had consumed man or beast, there would be nothing but ashes.

"Ashes to ashes, dust to dust," whispered Truly to himself. "ashes to ashes. That's where we'll all end up," he repeated. The phrase spoken at gravesides always made him grin. "I guess there could be worse fate than to burn up into ashes in your own home. Maybe in your own bed."

Truly's worst fears were that Evelyn Crandall had been in the house when it caught fire.

"If she burned up in that house," he said, "I hope to God she succumbed to smoke before fire got to her." He shuddered at the thought of Evelyn with her colourful hat being reduced to ash.

Truly walked over to the Champlain monument to get a better look through the trees and jam of vehicles. From there he could clearly see the burned out façade of what was once one of the most beautiful and pristinely restored Victorian homes in the city.

Noll Huggard was leaning up against a tree closer to the front of the house. He was far enough away but close enough to…

"Close to be an accomplice to this scenario?" thought Truly. "Or just another fire chaser." Noll had suffered the loss of his family mansion over on Douglas Avenue and been relocated to Metcalf Street. The cause of that fire had never been determined. It haunted Noll almost as much as the dynamics of his family haunted him.

Evelyn's house had been watered down enough that the Fire Inspector and his assistants were able to do some searching. It was no time before they found what they were looking for, and it wasn't the cause of the fire.

Inspector Belyea motioned to the men standing by the ambulance. There was too much rubble to wheel a stretcher much closer than the front door of the mansion, so they gathered up a white body bag and picked their way to where Belyea was standing.

Noll stood at attention as if to see better what they were looking at. Truly stepped up onto the first level of the Champlain monument pedestal. That gave him a better view from there than Noll could ever see at ground level from his tree.

The four men and the inspector blocked the view of whatever it was they were looking at. Truly knew. They had found what they were looking for. They had found her. Of course they couldn't say it was Evelyn until an official autopsy, but, Truly knew. Who else would be in her home late at night when fire broke out?

"Evelyn and…?" whispered Truly. "Evelyn and…" as if he instinctively knew that there was more to this fire than fire.

Noll seemed particularly interested in the activity in the middle of the pile of ashes. Mayor Blake had also arrived with Commissioner McLennan in tow. They stood off to the side, far enough to see, but not close enough to be repulsed by the sight of something that looked like the form that once was a human being. Homicide Detective Black had joined them.

"I wonder," said Truly to himself, "if this will end up as urban renewal. Knowing Evelyn's opinion of the Commission on Urban Renewal, THAT would be ironic. Either this will get the attention of people in this area of the city and spark restoration or it will make renters and home owners suspicious of what lurks in their buildings that might cause a fire. Old wiring, soot filled chimneys, fireplaces with faulty brickwork, wood cook stoves, you name it, and there is a cause for many a fire. Mrs. O'Leary's cow kicked over an oil lamp in Chicago that sparked that great fire. Evelyn Crandall's fire could metaphorically be the cause of another great fire in Saint John, or at the least, an excuse for the Commission on Urban Renewal to accelerate their program of crash and burn.

Truly watched as the medics gently carried out what he believed to be Evelyn in a white body bag.

"Poor Evelyn," he whispered to himself. A tear ran down his cheek. He mourned for Evelyn as much as he constantly mourned for every historic building that disappeared in the city.

There was nothing more to see. The fire was out. Whatever they had found was taken off to the morgue. The magnificent façade of Evelyn's home that once looked out from its bay windows toward the Bay stood blind. No beveled glass doorways nor sparkling windows remained. The life of the house had been snuffed out. The light on that side of Queen Square with the loss of Evelyn's home dimmed.

THE FIRE WORKED

For the time being, the fire of Evelyn Crandall's home worked. It served as a wake-up call to the city. One by one historic portions of the city were being destroyed by fire, urban renewal, and innocuous restoration or bulldozing. Parking lots filled in blank spaces around King's square where businesses once thrived. Every time a privately owned business closed, the Commission on Urban Renewal saw an opportunity to tear down. The life of the city gradually moved out and businesses thought to bring renewal moved in. It didn't work. The people who made Kings Square and Centre City moved out along with the businesses that closed.

Fires worked to the advantage of the Commission, or so they thought. Fire scared people. It put the city into confusion. And fire, that involved the death of a prominent citizen, Evelyn Crandall, made the citizens even more nervous. Evelyn was a topic of discussion throughout the city, at Welsford Drugs, at the Woolworths, the Old Market and St. Luke's Church. Rumours abounded.

As for Commissioner McLennan, he was relieved that Evelyn, who was constantly calling his motives and leadership into question, was gone. The investigation into the fire had just begun when McLennan called a meeting of the Commission to discuss the possibility of taking over Evelyn's burned out property and using it as an excuse to bring about some renewal to Queen's Square.

"The fire," he said at the next meeting, "has given us an opportunity." He paused. "Another opportunity to move forward with our charge to bring about urban renewal."

Mary Jones for once put her own self-interest aside and chimed up. "I think you are totally inappropriate," she said. "Here we are a week away from Evelyn's fire and you are talking about an opportunity. Have you no heart?"

McLennan ignored Mary and proceeded to his agenda. "Opportunities come our way," he continued. "Sometimes it's a fire. Sometimes it's a business moving out. Sometimes it's just..."

"Sometimes," said Mary, "it's just not appropriate to take immediate action to any opportunity. There hasn't been a conclusive report if Evelyn was toast in that fire. And if she was, there hasn't even been a funeral."

"Well," said McLennan.

"Well, what?" said Albert Parlee who had been listening with some sense of amusement and relief that Evelyn wasn't there to chide McLennan. In fact, Albert was more than amused that Mary Jones got off her high horse and rode in on a steed of another colour. No members of the Commission ever thought that would happen.

McLennan didn't know what to say. He had charged each of the members with inventorying various parts of the city, so he quickly moved from an "Evelyn fire agenda," to something less controversial. At least he thought the reports from each commission member would be less controversial. His thinking was wrong. When McLennan charged each member with taking responsibility for assessing the status of various areas of the city, he had not thought in advance that he was giving each commission member the opportunity to be like Evelyn and become advocates for more of the history of the city instead of crash and burn.

McLennan suddenly witnessed that his opportunity to make a name for himself while lining his pockets with some graft was slipping away.

This fire had indeed worked wonders. And it was just the beginning.

HEADLINES

"Good to see ya, Truly," yelled Harriet from behind the high top counter at Reggie's. "What'll you have today? How about some toast?" she laughed as she brought over his coffee. "How about this?" she asked. "Toast!" She plopped the newspaper face down in front of him.

Truly turned over the paper.

Evelyn Crandall Murdered
Gunned down before the fire!!

The newspaper headlines splashed across the whole top half of the Saint John Evening Times Globe hit the city like a winter's unexpected blizzard.

"How do you like that!" she said. "Now we don't only have urban renewal, we have fires and murder! That ought to put this city on the map. Bring in the tourists. Give 'em something to look at and talk about!"

"Toast!" said Truly.

"You want toast?" asked Harriet. "Toast? And anything to go with the toast?"

"Toast!" repeated Truly. "And try not to burn it to a crisp. If you do, you'll have to start calling it "Evelyn Toast." Might be a hit. A tourist attraction. I can see it now. "Reggie's – where that famous Evelyn Toast is served!"

"That's not funny," said Harriet. "Not funny at all."

"I know," said Truly. "But sometimes life situations are so sad that there's nothing to do but laugh. Who would have ever thought that Evelyn, our beloved Evelyn, our Evelyn who represented all the best the city had to offer, would end up on the ash heap with the rest of the work of the Commission on Urban Renewal. Who would have thought it?"

"Here," she said as she dropped the plate of toast down in front of Truly. "If it's too dark scrap off some of the ash!"

"Sick," said Truly.

"Sick," said Noll Huggard who had been sitting off some distance in his usual corner. "Sick."

"I heard that," said Truly. "What do you mean sick?"

"Nothing," said Noll. "Just sick. I'm sick."

"Don't pay no attention to him," said Harriet. "He's always sick of something. If it's not his family, it's something else. The mayor. The commission, the bus route, whatever. He's always sick of something."

"Maybe," said Truly, as he motioned for Harriet to come closer so he could whisper. "Maybe we ought to pay more attention to him. Maybe," he paused to look over at Noll. Noll was paying attention to his oatmeal. "Maybe," continued Truly, "that man knows more than we think about..."

"Murder?" said Harriet.

"Or fire," replied Truly. "He was acting mighty strange after that fire was put out. Appearing and disappearing up one alley or another. I mean, he acts strange to begin with, but..."

"You don't think?" said Harriet.

"I don't think anything," replied Truly. "I know we ought to keep our eyes and ears open to the heartbeat of this city. It has many stories to tell us. There's a story out there about that newspaper headline. Someone knows it."

"What story?" said Rev. Hatfield who had just arrived. Rabbi Rosenfeld was quick behind him along with Monsignor Sweeney. "May we join you?" said Hatfield.

"Please do," replied Truly as he plopped the Saint John Evening Times Globe down in front of him.

"What!" exclaimed Hatfield. "Murder? I'm not surprised but I am surprised. We haven't even had Evelyn's Funeral Mass and now we have murder on our hands." Hatfield fingered the newspaper as if it were something to be caressed. "Murder." He repeated.

Sweeney reached for the paper. Rosenfeld leaned in as the two scanned the article.

"No suspects have been identified," said Rosenfeld. "That will be a difficult one for Homicide to solve," he commented.

"How so?" said Sweeney.

"Ashes to ashes, dust to dust," said Hatfield. "If you didn't have a ..." he stopped short of finishing his comment for fear that he would offend the others.

"I'll finish it," said Harriet. She had come over to get their order. "Coffee, Evelyn toast, and?" she asked. "And," she continued, "the little clergy joke, known only to clergy is known by many. Ashes to ashes, dust to dust,.."

"Stop," said Hatfield.

Harriet didn't stop. She repeated what she had started. "As I was saying, Ashes to ashes, dust to dust, if you didn't have an asshole your belly would bust!" she didn't miss a beat. "Evelyn toast, or just plain toast?" she asked.

"What?" said Sweeney. He wasn't laughing. He had heard that little inside clergy ditty before, but he wasn't laughing. He didn't want to reveal that he really thought it funny. In fact, there were times when at a graveside committal, he had almost said that 'ashes to ashes' quip. "What do you mean Evelyn toast?" he asked

"Burnt or normal?" asked Harriet with a grin.

The little group couldn't resist. Truly had tried to stifle but he was the first to double over in laughter. The rest followed.

"It's not funny," mumbled Noll from his corner of the room. He had been listening all along.

"Not funny what?" said Truly.

"Nothing," mumbled Noll. "Just not funny." They thought he was referring to the "toast" joke. In reality he had been fixated all along on how sad he was about urban renewal. "My city is disappearing right before my eyes," he whispered, as he got up, pulled on his peak cap and headed toward the door.

"Don't let it hit ya on the way out," yelled Harriet after him.

"You're in a rare mood this morning," said Hatfield. "What brought that on?"

"Toast," said Harriet. "If you can't cry, you gotta at least laugh. What else is there to do?"

"I'll answer that," said Rosenfeld. "I think it's time we crashed the next meeting of the Commission on Urban Renewal. Now that Evelyn has filled them in that the clergy have been meeting. Now that they know Ella Osbourne has been here, it is time for us to crash that meeting and ..."

"And bring some accountability to that group," said Sweeney. "I'm all for that."

"But," said Hatfield, "first let us get Evelyn's Funeral Mass out of the way. We don't want to dishonour her by not honouring her. The city, I am sure, will come out and fill Saint Luke's. I have the service partially mapped out. I'm even going to ask Mayor Blake and Commissioner McLennan to bring some words."

"I hope they bring some good words," said Truly. "We've already heard and seen enough results of their words."

"Here's your toast," said Harriet, as she sat down a plate piled high with enough toast for the group. "And it's not burnt," she quipped.

"Marmalade please," said Sweeney. "Can't have toast without marmalade. Evelyn loved Marmalade. When's the service?"

"Sunday evening, this coming," replied Hatfield. "That way everyone can come. Might be the first, or last time, Saint Luke's sees a full house."

"Then," replied Rosenfeld, "we can be at the Commission meeting the following Thursday. I pray nothing more in the city gets destroyed before then."

SAINT LUKE'S ANGLICAN CHURCH

The multitudes poured into Saint Luke's. They had come to honour Evelyn as much as to witness what seemed to be dying all around them; their beloved city. To many citizens of the city, Evelyn had represented the last hope of stopping destruction. She had spoken for them. She had stood up for them. She had encouraged them when there was nothing but despair and discouragement. She represented what had been and their hope of what might be.

Evelyn was the splash of colour and flash of fire that kept the restoration and preservation going until a real fire consumed her.

"She went down in a blaze of glory," said Truly to Margaret Greene as they found a seat toward the front. Margaret had closed down the lunch counter at the Woolworths in honour of Evelyn. She had gotten some resistance from her manager but she insisted. Other businesses in the city had also closed for two hours during the service that was to begin with the noonday chime of the clock in St. Luke's bell tower.

"She did indeed," whispered Margaret. "She did indeed. And in her own house that she dearly loved and preserved."

The organ music soared to the Victorian rafters of the vaulted ceiling and bounced from every cranny down to the worn floor polished from the feet of years of the faithful. The altar guild had made sure that the brass communion rail, the Eagle gospel lectern and the free standing candelabra were polished beyond mirror bright. The brass shine multiplied the candle light. The flames flickered each time with the opening and closing of the front doors. The stream of people was nonstop.

"What's that the organist is playing?" whispered Margaret to Truly.

"It's 'The Arrival of the Queen of Sheba," answered Truly. "By Handel!" [16]

Margaret nearly choked on her attempt to stifle an outburst of laughter. Her hand over her mouth, a natural reflex in time of need, caught the laugh just in time. She hoped no one had noticed she was

[16] https://www.youtube.com/watch?v=ey_8VSD7fgc – "The Arrival of the Queen of Sheba" played on a pipe organ.

laughing.

"You think it's funny?" asked Truly.

Margaret nodded.

"I suppose," He continued, "one could think that. There will be people here who will think that. But I think it is quite appropriate. I bet Rev. Hatfield chose that just for Evelyn. I can hear him now as he consulted with the organist. "Evelyn was the queen of our hearts and this city," he probably said. "We must usher her in to this service and out into eternity with appropriate music."

"Really?" said Margaret.

"Yes, really," said Truly. "Evelyn and Rev. Hatfield had a relationship that rarely happens between a parishioner and priest. He knew he could rely on her for support and advice. She knew she could rely on him for encouragement and prayer. They were not to be reckoned with when it came to things that effected the preservation and future of Saint John. No siree, you didn't want to get in the way of Evelyn or Rev. Hatfield when it came to what was and what wasn't."

"It will be interesting, I suppose," said Margaret, "to see how the Commission on Urban Renewal proceeds now that they don't have her to contend with. Most of them are here. And look." She indicated with a nod. "Did you notice the constable and homicide detective in the back pew? Undercover."

"Wait and see," said Truly. "The RCMP are all up and down Main, standing guard. Hey, Maggie," he said.

"Don't call me Maggie," she replied above a whisper. "I told you…"

"I know," he said. "You told me never to call you Maggie. Shhh. People be noticing us whisper sweet nothings. Margaret."

"Shhh yourself," said Margaret. "And keep your sweet nothings to yourself. Evelyn wouldn't approve."

"You don't know that," he replied. He put his finger up to his lips to emphasize that they had just shhhed each other and that perhaps it would be best to watch and be seen rather than be heard. He nudged her again with his elbow.

"Stop!" she said.

"Watch," he replied. The music for "The Queen" soared to full volume just at that point to announce the Queen's arrival. Instead its volume covered up a multitude of gasps and aha's from the people entering who had never been in Saint Luke's.

"Watch," he whispered.

"I'm watching," said Margaret. "And I am noticing."

"You know what?" said Truly, "Evelyn has extolled the importance of this church and it's architecture for decades and no one paid any attention. It looks like it took a fire and her death to get them to come in here. Just look...."

"I'm looking," she said.

"Just look," said Truly, "to a person the moment they walk in here their eyes are drawn to the ceiling. They've never seen anything like this. Maybe now Evelyn will have her final say about St. Luke's. And they will hear. And that it will never be touched by urban renewal."

"Glory to God in the Highest," whispered Margaret with more than just something to say. She meant it. The architecture had reached down into her soul and pulled out a belief she didn't know she had. Architecture that is done properly can do that.

"Glory, for sure," said Truly. "I'm happy so many people have come. Their reason for coming doesn't matter. All that matters is that Evelyn is honoured."

"And that this magnificent church is standing strong," said Margaret, "is a testimony to her persistence."

"A sentinel on Main Street," whispered Truly. "That's how she referred to St. Luke's. Not much to look at on the outside. Beauty to behold on the inside. A lot like Evelyn. A sentinel that shall endure for as long as St. John embraces these shores of the Bay of Fundy."

He put his finger to his lips and nodded toward the front pews. "Mayor Blake and Commissioner McLennan have arrived." He said. "Let's watch."

"And pray," replied Margaret as the "Arrival of the Queen of Sheba" came to a close. The verger was ready to process with the Acolytes, Crucifer, the Choir and Rev. Hatfield in tow.

They heard the ancient words intoned from the back of the sanctuary, "In the name of the Father, Son and Holy Ghost."

"AMEN!"

The sounds of the processional hymn soared out of the organ pipes to the ceiling and descended down over the congregation bringing them to their feet and transforming them into one body gathered for one person. Evelyn.

THE BURIAL OF THE DEAD [17]

Rev. Hatfield intoned the opening scripture from the back of the sanctuary as the procession was about to move down the aisle.

"*WE brought nothing into this world, and it is certain we can carry nothing out. The Lord gave, and the Lord hath taken away; blessed be the name of the Lord.*" (I Timothy 6.7, Job 1.21)

Truly leaned over and whispered in Margaret's ear. "I could have a big debate on that one."

"Shhh," she said. "I know. The whole city is debating that one. Everyone knows it was more than "The Lord" taking Evelyn away."

Rev Hatfield's intonation wavered a little off-key with the ancient words.

"*I AM the resurrection and the life, saith the Lord: he that believeth in me, though he were dead, yet shall he live: and whosoever liveth and believeth in me shall never die.*" (I St. John 11.25, 26.)

The organ soared to life to lead the procession and congregation in the opening hymn. It was one of Evelyn's favorites.

Praise, my soul, the King of heaven;
to his feet your tribute bring.
Ransomed, healed, restored, forgiven,
evermore his praises sing.
Alleluia, alleluia!
Praise the everlasting King!

Angels, help us to adore him;
you behold him face to face.
Sun and moon, bow down before him,
dwellers all in time and space.
Alleluia, alleluia!
Praise with us the God of grace! [18]

The procession slowly made its way down the aisle. Rev. Hatfield had solicited the assistance of members of St. Paul's Anglican Church in

---

[17] Portions of the service liturgy quoted are from "The Book of Common Prayer" Anglican Church of Canada, 1962
[18] Henry Francis Lyte (1834)

the Valley. Truly was pleased to see that some of his friends were serving in honour of Evelyn. Abner Short, Senior Warden of St. Paul's was the crucifer. He was followed by, of all people, Barrister Bentley and Mary Jones. Truly remembered hearing Rev. Hatfield say that "since the members of the Commission on Urban Renewal didn't seem to be of much earthly good, perhaps they might be of some heavenly good by serving in Evelyn's funeral." Truly nudged Margaret and whispered, "Hatfield meant what he said. Look who's in the procession!"

"I know, I know," said Margaret with a somewhat amused and stunned look on her face. "There is justice for the guilty." She replied.

"Guilty?" said Truly as the urn bearer drew up behind Jones and Bentley.

"Yes, Guilty," said Margaret. "We all know this funeral didn't need to happen. If not for the guilty, and that bullet," she said with emphasis, "Evelyn might not be in this position. Look at that urn!"

"Do you know something I don't?" asked Truly.

It didn't' surprise Truly nor anyone else in attendance that Evelyn's black as coal corpse had been further reduced to ashes and was stored in a magnificent floral urn that mimicked her trademark hats.

"Where'd they get an urn like that!" quipped Truly.

"Probably Hayward and Warwick," whispered Margaret. "I guarantee you Brenan's Funeral home didn't have anything like that in stock. I bet Evelyn is smiling down on us right now. She's processing in a blaze of colour."

"Ayah," said Truly, "And it's a good thing she's in an urn and not a casket. When my mother was buried from here, they had to close the doors to the narthex and the street. There's so little room for a casket that the funeral director is always afraid the deceased might end up on their head or the ground the way they have to turn the coffin at right angles and up a half set of stairs. They didn't want anyone there if anything happened."

Truly stifled s chuckle as the choir passed by.

"They look so holy," whispered Margaret. "But…" She paused in stunned mid-thought.

"But!" said Truly. "What is Noll Huggard doing walking in the middle of that choir!!! Psssst! Noll," he loudly signaled as Noll passed by.

Noll paid him no attention. His peak cap, as usual was pulled down to his ears and shielded his eyes from the congregation. Everyone knew it was an act. Noll might look like he was oblivious to everyone but...

"He's watching us all," said Margaret. "What the..."

"Hell is he doing in that procession?" said Truly. By the time he got that out, Noll had passed by, and pushed in to the pew where Mayor Blake and Commissioner McLennan were seated. He forced them to move over just enough so Noll could hunker down. He sat with a thud disappearing out of sight while the rest of the congregation remained standing and singing.

The procession continued on with their usual ritual of bowing to acknowledge the altar and split off, each heading to their side of the choir stalls. Basses and Sopranos on the left. Tenors and Altos on the right.

"What the..." repeated Truly as the organ soared to a great 'amen.' "I guess there's not much you can do," whispered Truly in Margaret's ear. "Once the liturgy and processional starts, ya just go with it. No point in Rev. Hatfield stopping the whole procession just because Noll jumped into the middle of the choir. Just ignore and continue."

"Shhhh!" said Margaret, giving Truly a real good poke to emphasize that it was time to listen and obey.

Most parts of the liturgy were familiar to the Anglicans gathered for the service so the Books of Common Prayer remained in their pew racks. Familiar words were mumbled or stumbled over. Others were just ignored as the congregation let the Priest do all the bidding.

'There was no point," it was heard said by some, "to bother to participate. Evelyn's brilliant coloured floral urn and her priest, Rev. Hatfield can do all that needs to be done."

The Liturgy proceeded as Evelyn had planned some years before. She knew the music she wanted played. She had instructed Rev. Hatfield to keep it simple and to the point. He obliged except for one detail. Since Evelyn was such a prominent figure in the city he felt it appropriate to ask that one or two persons bring a word of celebration. He had chosen Commissioner McLennan to be that person since Evelyn was really the driving force and catalyst for much of the good work, little that it had been, that the Commissioner was doing in urban renewal.

"Before I ask Commissioner McLennan to come to the lectern," said Rev. Hatfield, "we shall spend a few moments in meditation, listening to one of Evelyn's favorite pieces of music. Her mother used to play "The Lost Chord," on the old pump organ in her parlour. Our organist searched the archives and found a copy. Mary Jones will sing the words. Let us listen."

Mary was thrilled to have been asked to participate in Evelyn's funeral. It was her opportunity to be THE MRS. JONES for the entire city to see. She rose and stood in full view next to the organ console as the organist began to play. Mary sang.

Seated one day at the organ, I was weary and ill at ease,
And my fingers wander'd idly over the noisy keys;
I knew not what I was playing, or what I was dreaming then,
But I struck one chord of music like the sound of a great Amen.

It flooded the crimson twilight like the close of an Angel's Psalm,
And it lay on my fever'd spirit with a touch of infinite calm.
It quieted pain and sorrow like love overcoming strife,
It seem'd the harmonious echo from our discordant life.

It link'd all perplexed meanings into one perfect peace
And trembled away into silence as if it were loth to cease;
I have sought, but I seek it vainly, that one lost chord divine,
Which came from the soul of the organ and enter'd into mine.

It may be that Death's bright Angel will speak in that chord again;
It may be that only in Heav'n I shall hear that grand Amen! [19]

Mary was very pleased with herself. Her voice, such as it was, had not left her. Nor had her ability to make sure people noticed THE MRS. JONES. She took a bow as if she had just finished an aria from Madama Butterfly. Mary's husband, who for once got to hear her sing, stood to applaud. An elderly gentleman sitting beside him yanked on his sport blazer and forced him to sit. Rev. Hatfield intoned the canticle.

"*I HEARD* a voice from heaven, saying unto me,…"

"Good God in heaven," whispered Truly to Margaret. "I hope that's the last time we heard that voice. And…" Margaret poked him real hard. She knew what he was going to say.

"It was no voice from heaven," she growled into his ear. "Now sit up and behave," she ordered. Truly had never heard her speak to him

---

[19] Music by Sir Arthur Sullivan; words by Adelaide Anne Proctor

like that. It rather pleased him because he thought just maybe, just maybe she was getting sweet on him. At least she cared enough to order him to behave. Or was it that she just didn't want to be embarrassed. Didn't matter. He was tickled, and in the middle of Evelyn's funeral yet!

Rev. Hatfield continued: "*saying unto me, Write, from henceforth blessed are the dead which die in the Lord: Even so, saith the Spirit, for they rest from their labours.*"

"Before I invite Commissioner McLennan to the lectern, I have several announcements. In the spirit of Evelyn's giving of herself, she requested that we have an alms box at the back of the sanctuary. Any monies you wish to donate will be given to the soup kitchen to feed the hungry. Following the service there will be a time of fellowship in the Undercroft. You are all welcome. Any food leftover will be donated to the Sisters of Charity for their meals program. Finally," he paused, "I wish to express my gratitude to the participants in the service from churches all over the city and to you, the citizens who have come to honour Evelyn. I am grateful."

With the announcements out of the way, Rev. Hatfield offered time for Commissioner McLennan to speak.

THE WORD

Commissioner McLennan pushed his way past Noll Huggard who had been sitting next to him in the pew. The Commissioner made sure that he wore his medals of authority and honour. He wanted the people to know that he was official. He had no thought that this time allotted to him would reveal a scandal of an unexpected politician. He had good intentions. They just weren't intentions that related to eulogizing Evelyn. Evelyn knew it. In short order, the rest of the congregation would also know. There would be headlines splashed all across the top of the Saint John Evening Times Globe in the morrow. The Commissioner was too self-centered and dimwitted to even think that far in advance. A light bulb flickered on one of the chandeliers, perhaps confirming that he wasn't the brightest bulb in the room.

Rev. Hatfield took his cathedral like seat facing the lectern. The choir angled their bodies so that they could hear. Truly and Margaret leaned in. They didn't trust this man nor did he. McLennan didn't trust anyone. Sometimes he didn't even trust himself. This was one such occasion. He knew he was supposed to eulogize Evelyn with kind words. He really wanted to tell the truth about how he felt. But, he had determined, that he would behave and stifle.

He began: "I can't believe such a wonderful person with such a big heart can be reduced to ash in that little urn."

"Believe it," whispered Evelyn in his ear.

McLennan paused and looked around. He thought he had heard Evelyn's voice. But, since McLennan had no idea what it meant to be spiritually in tune with the Lord, no less with Evelyn or a deceased person, he figured it was just his mind playing tricks on him.

"Believe it," whispered the voice again.

"Believe it," said McLennan in a somewhat hesitant and squeaky voice. "Believe it," he repeated.

"Believe what?" whispered Margaret to Truly.

"How should I know," said Truly. "The man has issues. Maybe this is one of them. Maybe he's never been in a church before. Maybe this is the first time that he's seen the inside of this magnificent architectural treasure. Maybe he's going to believe, finally, what Evelyn has been goading him about all along."

"We'll see," said Margaret.

"Evelyn Crandall," continued McLennan, but pausing as if to gather his thoughts. He heard the voice again.

He continued. "Evelyn Crandall was the only person on the Commission who knew what urban renewal was supposed to be all about. She was a thorn in my side."

"There, you've finally told the truth!" whispered the voice in his ear.

"The truth," the voice whispered. "Tell the truth."

"Evelyn Crandall," said McLennan this time with some hesitation as to what would come out of his mouth.

"Evelyn Crandall," he paused...

"You've already said that," whispered the voice. "Get on with it. Tell the truth."

"I'm going to tell you the truth," said McLennan.

The constable and homicide detective shifted their considerable weight on the back pew. It creaked as they did so. "This is going to be good," said one to the other.

"Evelyn Crandall," continued McLennan, "was the loveliest person we had on the Commission on Urban Renewal." He paused. "Except for Mary Jones. Now she is really THE MRS. JONES! What a wonderful woman to build such a big mansion in such a decrepit section of Saint John!"

"There ya go, McLennan," said the voice. "Tell it like it is."

Mary Jones sat up straight. She looked around to see if anyone was noticing that she, MRS. JONES was right there in front of them. No one noticed. She deflated herself back into just being.

"I am so pleased that Mayor Blake appointed me to be the Commissioner of Urban Renewal, because..."

"Because I found a way to make some extra money while at the same time climbing the political ladder," whispered the voice in his ear.

McLennan blurted it out! "Because I found a way to make some extra money while at the same time climbing the political ladder!"

Truly and Margaret sat up straight. Mayor Blake hunkered down and tried to disappear into the creaky old pew. Noll had heard enough. He pulled his peak cap down as far it would go, gathered his scarf up around his neck and headed for the door.

"Noll Huggad and I," whispered the voice in McLennan's ear.

"Noll Huggard and I," said McLennan before he had a chance to stop himself.

"Go on," said the voice.

"Go on," said McLennan. He had a frightened look on his face. He didn't' know which way to turn, or if he should turn and run as fast as Noll had run up the aisle.

"Go on," said McLennan. People leaned forward to hear what the "go on" was going to be. McLennan waited for the voice, Evelyn's voice to tell him what the "go on" was.

"Tell them about this church," said the voice. "Tell them about all the buildings you have torn down. Tell them."

"I, I," stuttered McLennan, "have never been in St. Luke's before. I apologize for not seeing how magnificent some of the historical buildings in this city really are."

"There ya go," said the voice. "Lay it on thick."

"How could we ever think of tearing something down like this treasure?" continued McLennan. "I will never again tear down something without taking a good look."

"Yeah right," whispered Truly to Margaret. "Believe that one and I'll sell you the Queen Mary."

"Evelyn Crandall," continued McLennan, "was the happiest member of our commission.

"No I wasn't," whispered the voice in his ear. "You were the happiest when you were tearing down parts of our beloved city."

"She," continued McLennan, "was the happiest watching me celebrate and profit from all of the urban renewal I was responsible for."

"There ya go," said the voice. "Tell it!"

"And," he continued, "I looked forward to our meetings with anticipation of what Evelyn would say next. She was a thorn in my side."

The congregation gasped. The constable and homicide detective made notes. Truly and Margaret sat in disgust. They knew what McLennan was like but they never expected him to admit it. Everyone wondered what in heaven's name had gotten into McLennan to further destroy his reputation and bring himself down.

Rev. Hatfield leaned forward in his chair and indicated to McLennan that he needed to wrap it up before he, like Evelyn, made an ash of himself.

"In the name of the Father, Son, and …." Said McLennan

"And snollygoster," said the voice.

"SNOLLYGOSTER," repeated McLennan with a stunned look on his face.

The congregation didn't immediately react. They had never heard the word before. Sirens punctuated the gloom of the moment, offering a distraction.

"Snollygoster" he repeated.

"Good job," said the voice in McLennan's ear. "You've finally said it. You are the lowest politician of the low. You are a good-for-nothing puppet being yanked by the Mayor. But most important, you have let your integrity and ethical behavior lapse, if you had any at all. You are what you just said you are. A scandal of an unexpected politician. You are a snollygoster preying on our beloved city, our residents, and our future. SIT DOWN," the voice shouted in his ear.

"SIT DOWN!" he yelled. "I'M GOING TO SIT DOWN!"

The congregation was stunned. Those who were mildly amused were now salivating to spread the story of what had just happened.

"I'm sorry, Evelyn," muttered McLennan as he turned to bow at the altar.

"Don't bow," said the voice. It was now clear the voice he was hearing was Evelyn. Even in death, she wouldn't let up on her attempts to call McLennan to account.

"Don't bow," said the voice again. "Your bow is fraudulent. No amount of show now will help your cause. "Don't bow! You're a fraud!"

McLennan crept back to his pew. He tried to disappear into the woodwork. He was almost successful due to the fact that the magnificent interior of St. Luke's could make almost anything holy and sacred. It didn't work. Mayor Blake slid far away from McLennan. He didn't want to be associated with McLennan or his words. It was too late. Once guilt by association is established, rumours run rampant. McLennan had confirmed rumours about urban renewal. The truth came out.

OUT OF CHAOS

With Commissioner McLennan duly chastised, and by Evelyn no less, Rev. Hatfield in his gentle and firm pastoral way brought the service around from snollygoster to benevolence.

"We thank Commissioner McLennan and Mayor Blake for coming today to honour Evelyn," intoned Hatfield. "We are grateful for Evelyn's life and all that she has offered to us. Let us pray."

AMIGHTY God, with whom do live the spirits of them that depart hence in the Lord, and with whom the souls of the faithful are in joy and felicity: We praise and magnify thy holy Name for all thy servants who have finished their course and kept the faith; and committing our sister, Evelyn, to thy gracious keeping, we pray that we with her, and with all those that are departed in the true faith of thy holy Name, may have our perfect consummation and bliss, both in body and soul, in thy eternal and everlasting glory; through Jesus Christ our Lord. **Amen** [20]   Hatfield continued:

THE LORD bless you, and keep you. The LORD make his face to shine upon you, and be gracious unto you. The LORD lift up his countenance upon you, and give you peace, both now and evermore. **Amen**. [21]

With the Benediction said, the entire congregation stood to sing. The choir recessed.

"Welcome, happy morning!" age to age shall say:
hell today is vanquished, heaven is won today!
Lo! the dead is living, God for evermore!
Him their true Creator, all his works adore!

Earth her joy confesses, clothing her for spring,
all fresh gifts return with her returning King:
bloom in every meadow, leaves on every bough,
speak his sorrow ended, hail his triumph now.

---

[20] The Book of Common Prayer, Anglican Church of Canada, 1962
[21] Ibid.

"Damn that Evelyn," muttered McLennan as the procession passed by. "She just won't let up on that 'happy' bit!"

Months in due succession, days of lengthening light,
hours and passing moments praise thee in their flight.
Brightness of the morning, sky and fields and sea,
Vanquisher of darkness, bring their praise to thee.

Maker and Redeemer, life and health of all,
thou from heaven beholding human nature's fall,
of the Father's Godhead true and only Son,
mankind to deliver, manhood didst put on.

Thou, of life the Author, death didst undergo,
tread the path of darkness, saving strength to show;
come then, true and faithful, now fulfill thy word,
'tis thine own third morning! rise, O buried Lord!

Loose the souls long prisoned, bound with Satan's chain;
all that now is fallen raise to life again;
show thy face in brightness, bid the nations see;
bring again our daylight: day returns with thee! [22]

"That's Evelyn," said Truly as the processional passed by. "Evelyn was determined to have the last word in regard to this church and our beloved Saint John. The hymn is appropriate."

"And" said Margaret, "one of her favourites."

The ushers opened the doors to Main Street as the procession reached the Narthex. A sudden hush came over those gathered. For as the doors were opened, a rush of fog entered. But it wasn't fog. The sirens heard in the distance during McLennan's talk only seemed at a distance because of the thick church doors. Now that the doors were open the sirens belied the confusion that was occurring down Main Street and around the corner on Metcalf Street.

Once again, while the city slept, even while the city mourned the murder of Evelyn Crandall, the city burned.

---

[22] Venantius Fortunatus, cir-ca 590 (Salve, festa dies); translated from Latin to English by John Ellerton, 1868.

"I bet," said Truly, "McLennan will have something to say about this. A whole block of houses on Metcalf Street is on fire. More urban renewal for him to grovel about. How convenient for that snollygoster!"

McLennan and the Mayor were nowhere to be found. They had snuck out the vestry door, avoiding the crowd in the undercroft. Evelyn had done enough for them that day.

31 METCALF

Noll Huggard crouched down on the sidewalk some distance away from 31. His head in his hands. "What will I do, what *will* I do?" he kept repeating to himself as he rocked back and forth. He held his peak cap in his hands as if it would bring some comfort. The flames were so hot as they licked out the windows of 31 and surrounding houses that he had removed his heavy wool coat, scarf and tie. Tears streamed down his face and mingled with the sweat from the fire's heat. Smoke choked the air mimicking the fog that often shrouded the city. It protected perpetrators of crimes.

"My house, my house," cried Noll.

When Truly realized what was happening a short distance from St. Luke's, he grabbed Margaret's hand and yelled, "Let's go!" They ran as fast as they could over to Metcalf Street. Rev. Hatfield followed. He didn't bother to remove his robes. He ran, hoping beyond hope that this fire wouldn't result in another death.

The quickest route was straight down Main. They passed Adelaide, Durham and Elgin Streets and crossed over Albert Street. It was there that they found Noll crouched down on the stoop of a corner house. His body was wracked with shock and sorrow as he watched his house burn.

"I'm done, I'm done," he muttered through the sobs. "I'm done. I'm homeless. It is finished."

Rev. Hatfield gathered up his robes and sat down beside Noll. Truly and Margret stood beside them.

"It's another Great Fire of Saint John," whispered Truly. "Another great fire. One hundred years later."

"This time," said Margaret, "It is the North End."

"And this time," said Truly, "McLennan and his Commission on Urban Renewal will be delighted. They haven't known what to do with the North End for decades. Now they will have an excuse to tear it all down. The incentive to transform this area, like Architect Osbourne suggested, into a posh, upscale neighbourhood, will be gone. Who is going to want to live with a gash of burned out and boarded up buildings?"

"No one," cried Margaret. "No one. Our city is disappearing

before our eyes."

"And," said Truly, "while most of the city sleeps. Doesn't anyone recognize what a treasure of Victorian architecture we have here?"

"No one." Said Margaret. "Well maybe some. After what McLennan said, maybe he's going to get it after all."

"Yes," said Truly, "but did the congregation hear what he said? Was the murder of Evelyn and St. Luke's architecture enough to get the attention of the citizens of St. John? Only time will tell."

Just then the woodshed on the back of 31 Metcalf came crashing down like thunder over the Bay.

"It is done," cried Noll. "It is done. How can I ever live there again? Look what's been done!"

Rev. Hatfield tightened his arm around Noll's shoulder. For once, Noll didn't resist the caring of another human being. Hatfield had sensed all along through the years that there was more to this man than just walking the streets of St. John all hours of the day and night.

"Still waters run deep," Hatfield had often said about people who were overly private. His comment was true when it came to Noll Huggard. He had come from a close-knit family of Loyalist origin. But as most families, the Huggards had their secrets. One daughter had married and then ignored her husband by giving total care and loyalty to her elderly parents. The eldest daughter married and moved out of the country. The first surviving son, Harold, was a spider-like little fellow who knew every nook and cranny of the city and always had a trick up his sleeve. He sowed his wild oats in Chicago but never revealed what he did there for five years. Eventually he married a young girl he'd impregnated. His mother saying, "You've done this one too many times. This one you're marrying." He did and was married for 74 years.

The biggest Huggard family secret had been hidden for years. Their namesake had emigrated from Ireland in 1824 and integrated into a Loyalist household. The Irish were the minority back then. They were less than Loyalist.

And then there was Noll.

Noll was the still waters of the family. He walked the city streets day and night. He observed the rhythm of the city. He made mental notes of what had been and what remained of the Victorian city he loved. He sat at King Square on brilliant summer days and watched the tourists gawk. And he wondered what they were seeing because what he saw could be only seen when the fog was thick and shrouded the city. It was then he painted in his mind's eye the picture of the city he remembered and had grown up with. Most of it was gone. And more of it was going. He mourned the loss of anything Victorian and historical. That's why he attended Evelyn's funeral. He wasn't so much interested in Evelyn. He wanted to see one more time the magnificent interior of St. Luke's Church. It reminded him of his father and grandfather who had sailed three mast schooners out of St. John Harbour to all points around the world. He felt close to them when he was in St. Luke's. The church had not only been there since his childhood and before, it had also been a go-to place where he could reflect on those bygone days and dream.

St. Luke's remains. The sentinel of Main Street. As for 31 Metcalf Street. All had changed.

Noll sobbed into the arms of Rev. Hatfield. Truly and Margaret were surprised at the scene. The constable and detective from the homicide squad had arrived with half the congregation in tow. They weren't merely fire chasers. They were taken by what McLennan had said and how Evelyn was memorialized.

Instead of her service calming down the city and bringing to a close her life's chapter and her involvement with the Commission on Urban Renewal, the service re-ignited the rumours that had been running rampant for weeks.

Where had Rev. Gwyn Davies of St. Paul's in the Valley disappeared to?

Why did the Huggard Mansion on Douglas Avenue burn, leaving Noll homeless. His sister used the fire as an excuse to exclude him from any welcome back into the family!

Why did the Greene Mansion near Centenary Church end up in ashes?

And, mystery of mysteries, who shot Evelyn Crandall and then tried to cover the murder by burning down her mansion. Or was that fire just a coincidence?

"There's too many coincidences than.." commented Truly.

"Than what?" asked Margaret.

"Than.." he hesitated. "I don't know." He replied. "There's just too much going on here that doesn't make sense."

"It doesn't make sense," sobbed Noll. He had been sobbing and listening at the same time. Rev. Hatfield had been whispering sweet nothings and platitudes in his ear. It was his attempt to deal with his own shock of Evelyn's murder and now another fire.

"Noll," he said, "There's nothing we can do here. 31 Metcalf, even if they save the front of the building, is over. You can't live there again. The firefighters will finish what the fire has begun. Looks like some of the block is going to survive."

"But, But," sobbed Noll. "My home."

"Your home is gone," replied Hatfield. "For now, your home is with me. You can stay with me at the Rectory until some plans can be made for where you can live."

"But, But," repeated Noll.

"Never mind the buts," said Hatfield. "The Commission on Urban Renewal will take care of Metcalf Street. I'm also part of a city-wide clergy group that has been meeting to explore ways of stopping urban destruction and bringing about restoration and renewal. Let the "buts" take care of themselves. We need to help you now."

Margaret, Truly, the homicide officers and gawkers watched as Hatfield helped Noll up and supported him as they walked toward the Rectory located on a cliff overlooking Main, Robertson Square and the St. John River.

Noll looked back with great sadness in his eyes as if he hoped the thick fog would descend so he could once again see what had been.

They walked in silence.

31 Metcalf Street – Mid 1960's

THE HEADLINES

Truly walked Margaret back to Woolworths. Since he was there, he thought he might as well have a piece of pumpkin pie. Evelyn's funeral, the fire and Noll, made him think that he deserved some comfort himself.

Margaret didn't have much to say. If she knew more than she was letting on, only she knew. The lunch counter at Woolworth's was a perfect place to hear gossip. Too much gossip was more than Margaret could take. She tuned it out. She dismissed most of it as rumour. "It's people's way" she said to Truly, "of trying to come to terms with so much that has happened: the mysterious fires, murder, urban renewal and loss. Another fire. Noll at the rectory.

"Did you notice," asked Truly, "how fast Noll disappeared during the funeral service. Maybe McLennan said something that hit home."

"Dunno know," said Margaret. "Don't much care."

"It is confounding," he replied. "It is confounding that so much is happening that seems connected but not. And that speech by McLennan. That was something. What the …"

"Hell got into him?" she finished Truly's sentence. Margaret wasn't prone to use profanity but she couldn't help herself.

McLennan's speech heightened suspicions and rumours throughout the city. Before the ink had time to dry the Saint John Evening Times Globe put out a special edition. They had been investigating the Commission on Urban Renewal, McLennan, Mayor Blake and the events of the past two months. They didn't have many specifics regarding involvement of individuals. They did have some opinions and possibilities about what was causing all the events that seemed related to urban renewal. The headline in the special edition was:

ANOTHER FIRE:
MURDER – ARSON – URBAN RENEWAL?

The paper implied that the fires were confusing investigations going on by the clergy group, the homicide division, the RCMP and one or two persons inside the Commission on Urban Renewal. It seemed to be more than coincidence that significant historical buildings in the city were being burned down in the wake of urban renewal or in relationship to persons who either lived in them or had a history with the buildings. The Huggard Mansion on Douglas Avenue had been slated as an anchor building for renewal of all the homes there. The Greene mansion near Centenary Church was looked upon as a possible restoration project that might have some saving influence for Centenary Church and the other churches in the area. The fire of Evelyn Crandall's home resulting in her murder or because of her murder was the most suspicious. And now, Noll Huggard's home!

The paper implied that none of these, except for the fire at St. Paul's Anglican Church in the Valley, were coincidences. All seemed to be tied to urban renewal. And once the urban renewal gang moved in to clean up after a fire, destruction continued beyond the fire's footprint. Someone was making a fortune out of the clean-up. Someone was taking advantage of empty land for their own purposes. The paper alleged that graft was involved and perhaps running rampant throughout the Commission on Urban Renewal.

All this, and more, was also part of Truly and Margaret's whispered discussion at the lunch counter. Truly smoothed his beard down so as not to catch any pumpkin pie. Margaret busied herself with cleaning and closing down the counter. It was getting late in the day. Both of them were exhausted from attending the funeral and watching the fire. Sometimes days like this are better left to quiet thought, a night's sleep and awakening on the other side of dawn. The newspaper correctly concluded, "the city is confused, frightened and on edge."

"I'll be going," said Truly. "Thanks for the memories we just made."

"What do you mean?" she asked.

"You held my hand a lot today," he replied. "It felt good to be connected to another human being. I've missed that. Thank you. Maggie," he chuckled.

"Truly!" she said in an admonishing tone.

He knew what she meant. "I know," he said. "You don't like being called 'Maggie,' but I like it. It makes me feel like we might be more than friends."

"Don't get any ideas," said Margaret. "It's still 'Margaret' to you. I do have to admit, though, that my hand in yours was comforting. It made me a little less confused. It made me more comfortable being in a crowd of people at a time that could easily have erupted in a riot when they heard what McLennan had to say. I admit..."

"You admit you liked it?" he asked. "I like that you liked it. Maybe we can do it again sometime. Just for fun. Just because."

"Just because?" she replied.

"Just because," he said. "I'll be going now that I've had my cake, … ah … pie and ate it too." He winked at her as he got up and headed for the door.

"Adios, Bonos Nachos, A-river," he yelled with a wink and a grin. She laughed.

Truly did his best thinking up at Fort Howe when the fog was its thickest. The fire at 31 Metcalf was nearly out. There was just enough smoldering ashes to create smoke and smell that mingled with the late evening fog. There was something about the fog that delighted Truly. It was one of the few things remaining that the Commission on Urban Renewal was unable to change. No amount of planning by the Commission could change the fact that Saint John was famous for its fog, the Bay of Fundy and The Reversing Falls. And, in his thinking, murder and fire was not going to destroy the city he loved.

THE LAST COMMISSION

It had been a week since Evelyn Crandall's funeral and the 31 Metcalf Street fire. The newspaper headlines and subsequent articles had spooked the city. Some chose to go back to sleep. Others opted for curiosity. Some took it upon themselves to play the part of a Victorian sleuth. Most, however, at least the ones who had heard McLennan at the funeral, chose to come to their own conclusions about what was happening. To them, fire was arson. Murder was cover-up and retribution. And graft was defining the future of the city. They were pretty close to being correct, but there was little way of proving those conclusions, unless. Unless someone broke down and confessed to the various crimes.

Commissioner McLennan called the meeting to order with his usual attempt at inflicting upon the members his propaganda. "I'm happy to be here," he said. "And," he continued, "I'm happy to see you all present and accounted for."

"Except Evelyn," said Annalee Gaudet as she positioned herself across from McLennan so she would be sure to take accurate notes for the Archives at the NB Museum. Annalee was dressed in her signature archivist outfit: black skirt and jacket, black pumps, white archivist gloves, bright red lipstick and white blouse. Her black hair was pulled back in a bun. But for this meeting, in honour of Evelyn, Annalee had purchased a bright red artificial flower. She wore it in her hair. It could not be missed. Annalee rarely wore anything different from her "archivist" attire.

"That's quite a flower you have in your hair," said Edna Boyle.

"In memory of Evelyn," said Annalee. "She may be gone, out of sight and off this committee..." she hesitated as if to consider what she really meant. "But she is still here with us, in this room, in our hearts. Her dedication to our city, preservation and restoration will live on through each of us for a long time. I'm making sure we have good archival notes."

"I hope." said Edna. She had brought a small bouquet of artificial flowers that was quite similar to the ones painted on the urn that held Evelyn's ashes. She had noticed. "Between your flower and this little bouquet, we can honour Evelyn's work with us and call her into our presence." She paused. "Just in case."

"Just in case what!" said McLennan. His tone of voice revealed that he was anxious, angry and annoyed all at the same time. "Just in case what!" he repeated.

"Don't use that tone of voice," said Benjamin Northrup. "It will get you in more trouble than you're already in."

That made McLennan even more antagonistic toward the group. While this banter was going on, Constable Priestly and Homicide Detective Gunnerson had quietly entered the room and found a seat. McLennan's back was toward the door so he didn't notice them enter. It was as they wished. They had been seated in a couple of chairs behind McLennan for most of this small talk. But it wasn't really small talk.

"I'm glad that you have come," said Barrister Bentley addressing Priestly and Gunnerson. He was sitting next to Annalee. He had been prompting her to vocalize her concerns. "Make sure," he wrote on a note and passed to her, "that you get down every word that is said this morning at this meeting. You may need it in court." She understood. She nodded.

"I'm glad I came too," said McLennan, not realizing that Attorney Bentley was addressing the constable and detective.

"Not you," said Bentley. "Turn around and look. You might want to choose your words carefully today." Bentley had been at Evelyn's funeral and heard McLennan's speech. He had listened carefully to what McLennan had to say, some of which confirmed his suspicions about the Commissioner.

McLennan turned around to see who was sitting behind him. His reaction to the presence of the Constable and Detective was clearly visible. And, while Bentley was talking, to make matters more complicated, Truly Morrell and Noll Huggard had also arrived. Noll had a vested interest in urban renewal since his home had burned. Truly had his own motivation for being present. Restoration, preservation and Margaret were on his mind so much that they almost became his "god."

McLennan turned back to the business of the meeting. He shuffled his notes and tried to make some sense of authority and order out of his intent for the meeting. He knew that somehow he had to regain control of the Commission and his reputation after the damage he had done to both at Evelyn's funeral. Evelyn was intact, even if she had become an urn of ashes. She was still an influence to be reckoned with. The Commissioner, on the other hand, was teetering on the brink of a political and criminal cliff.

"I'm happy to be here," he said. "And I'm happy that you all came."

"We wouldn't miss this for the world," said Father Sweeney. "There is too much at stake for our city. Evelyn's murder seems to have awakened many people from their proverbial slumber and sleep."

"I agree" said Mary Jones. "Evelyn's funeral was the first time many people had ever seen the inside of historic St. Luke's. I know some were stunned when they walked in."

"I know I was," said McLennan without thinking.

"It's about time you were," said Truly from the sidelines. He couldn't help himself. He wanted to have his say, even if it was only an aside from the created visitor gallery of chairs lining the walls of the room. The commission members were seated around a big long table.

The bouquet of flowers, the artificial bouquet in the middle of the table, seemed to grow by the moment.

"Look," said Edna Boyle. "Look. The flowers." The flowers were quivering as if a gentle breeze were blowing across them. The daffodils swayed alongside the tulips. The roses appeared to begin to open to full bloom. And a scent of Evelyn's favourite perfume hung in the air. "Look," she repeated.

Stunned silence. A chill as cold as an iceberg seemed to envelope Commissioner McLennan. Evil, cold evil made him shudder. The rest in the room felt a gentle warmth. It comforted them. It made them feel a sense of peace and purpose. However they participated in the meeting, they knew it would have Evelyn's approval.

"Look," repeated Edna. This time it was in a whisper. The visitors seated alongside the wall leaned forward to look around McLennan to see where Edna was pointing. They also felt it. They smelled the hint of perfume. Mystery and clarity mixed together and descended into the room.

Each person in the room noticed that when they directed their attention toward Commissioner McLennan a chill as cold as the St. John River frozen over in winter made them shiver. When they looked one to another and at the bouquet in the center, a warm glow surrounded them.

"Evelyn is here," whispered Benjamin Northrup. "Evelyn is here."

"Yeah, whatever," said McLennan. He knew what Benjamin said was true. He had experienced it during his speech at the funeral. He thought that was the last he would hear from Evelyn. Evelyn had another agenda. "Yeah, whatever," he repeated this time with an attempt to regain authority and control. It didn't work. He knew his authority, political future and financial profit was quickly slipping away. Evelyn was going to see to that. Her presence refused to leave him. It caused him to shiver in the icy cold. Others watched. Those along the wall were especially interested.

"I'm happy to see you all," he repeated.

"You said that," commented Albert Parlee. He generally was the most congenial member of the commission but he was beginning to feel the meetings were a waste of time. He was annoyed. "You said that," he repeated. "Let's get on with this meeting so we can get on with our lives. You're going to do what you want to do anyway."

"No he isn't," whispered Evelyn in McLennan's ear.

McLennan looked startled. "The jig is up," whispered Evelyn.

"I like jigs," said McLennan.

"What?" said the group in unison.

"Jigs," he repeated.

"Now you're getting it," whispered Evelyn. Her whisper had become more of an aside. It wasn't quite loud enough for the rest to hear but they all knew something important was going to happen.

"Yeah, well," said McLennan. "Our agenda today is to discuss the future of the North End."

"Tear down some more buildings," blurted out Noll. "So that I won't be the only one homeless." He pulled his peak cap down over his eyes as if to hide from being chastised for his comment.

Rev. Gwynn Davies had also quietly entered the room and was seated next to Noll. He reached out to him the way his congregation had wished he would have if he had been there for them after the fire of St. Paul's Anglican.

"Where'd you come from," said Truly, as he leaned forward to look around Noll. Those seated with their backs to the door turned around to see who Truly was talking to.

The air was sucked right out of them when they saw who it was.

"Rev. Davies," said Albert Parlee. "Where in hell, or heaven, have you been all this time?"

"Around," said Davies matter-of-factly. "Around."

"I know it sounds absurd," said Davies, "but when St. Paul's burned to the ground I made a decision to disappear for a time. You know how Jesus was tempted in the wilderness? I decided that I would disappear for a time to test the faith of the congregation. Would they rally and survive? Would they give up and close? What would they do? I had full support of the Bishop. He was as curious as I to see what a congregation would do if their priest disappeared. He had no idea, nor did I, that the test would involve the church burning to the ground and the Commission on Urban Renewal complicating the test by tearing down the entire neighbourhood!"

"Did we pass the test?" said Albert Parlee.

"You're working on it," said Davies. "We will know your grade, pass or fail, when I show up to preach this Sunday at Old Stone Church! If you all can keep the secret!"

"I can keep a secret," said McLennan.

"I bet you can," said Constable Priestly. "And what would that secret be?"

"We have business to attend to," said McLennan trying to ignore the asides that were getting out of control. "We need to get on with hearing reports from each of you responsible for your neighbourhood."

"And," said Homicide Detective Gunnerson, "what each of you think is really going on with this commission."

"Murder," said Truly. "Murder of our beloved city. Murder of the lives of residents. Murder of..."

"Evelyn," whispered "Evelyn in McLennan's ear."

"I heard that," said McLennan.

"You heard what?" asked Noll.

"Evelyn," whispered McLennan.

Mary Jones began to cry. She caressed the bouquet of artificial flowers that were within her reach.

"Stop the blubbering," chastised Edna. "You are still THE MRS. JONES. Nothing has changed that. For heaven's sake, stop!"

"Evelyn," whispered McLennan with a glazed look in his eyes. "Evelyn," he repeated. He looked as if he was going to burst out in tears.

Homicide Detective Gunnerson and Constable Priestly stood and moved to either side of McLennan. They blocked his escape just in case he had any ideas.

"Commissioner McLennan," said Gunnerson, "I am taking you into custody for questioning. You can either come willingly or I can arrest you for suspicion of murder. We'll get the truth out of you."

McLennan slumped over in his chair. His head brushed the table.

"Told ya," whispered Evelyn in his ear. "Told ya."

"Oh shut up!" yelled McLennan.

"Never," whispered Evelyn. "The truth will set you free. But more importantly, the truth will set this city free. I hope you have a nice forever."

There was nothing more to say. The Commission members and spectators were as stunned as McLennan. That's not saying much since McLennan knew all along why the Constable and Homicide detective were there.

He knew.

Evelyn knew.

Soon the entire world would know.

REGGIE'S CLERGY MEETING

Two days after MacLennan was hauled off to the precinct for questioning the Clergy group gathered at Reggie's in mid-morning while all was quiet. Once McLennan was in the custody of the Homicide detective, he squealed. He revealed that he wasn't as brave and hard-nosed as he liked to appear. It didn't take them long to get the confession out of him. McLennan had been confronted one too many times by Evelyn's questions. He felt the noose tightening around him. He suspected that she knew he was taking money off the top of all the urban renewal projects. He was lining his own pockets while contracting with several corrupt construction firms who obliged to cooperate.

The Saint John Evening Globe headlines screamed the truth!

COMMISIONER MCLENNAN CHARGED WITH MURDER!

The newspaper reported that McLennan confessed to having shot and killed Evelyn Crandall while she slept in her bed. As for the fire, he denied any responsibility. "It was just a coincidence he said." But that fire was too convenient. The newspaper alleged that McLennan had set the fire after murdering Evelyn, or that he had encouraged someone else to come behind his murder to cover up. McLennan had told more than enough. He clammed up.

All of the clergy gathered at Reggie's for an evaluation of their work in progress. They reviewed Ella Osbourne's architectural report. And they were overjoyed to welcome and celebrate Rev. Gwyn Davies' return. They were most curious about how he had arranged a disappearing act just when his church burned to the ground.

"How in God's name did you convince your Bishop," asked Monsignor Sweeney, "to go along with your disappearing act? I think my name would come before the Pope if I tried anything like that!"

"It wasn't easy," said Davies. "I had been considering for some time how to light a fire that would metaphorically burn throughout the congregation. They needed something to get their attention. They needed to move beyond putting all their faith in a building, altars and rubrics. I considered disappearing for a week or so but…"

"Then the fire happened," said Hatfield. "Gwyn told me some time ago that he was thinking of doing something like this. He made me promise silence."

"I knew about it too," said The Rev. Canon Jacob Wentworth of Old Stone Church. "We had been talking about his disappearance for some time. The fire, as devastating as it was, provided the perfect opportunity for him to disappear. I had agreed that when he disappeared I would assist St. Paul's while they grappled with how to continue. The fire just provided even more cover for Gwyn's prank."

"It wasn't a prank," said Gwyn. "It was a real life object lesson. You know. There are some things that a priest can say in words. There are some things, like the bread and wine that must be acted out. No words can substitute for partaking of the bread and wine."

"Aha!" said Rev. Somerville. "And the disappearance of the leader of a church who has taken on, or been designated as the main catalyst for the church's ministry..."

"Is a real life object lesson," said Gwyn.

"Did it work?" asked Elder Laurence Colwell of Germain Street Baptist.

"In a variety of ways," said Wentworth. "We shall see how the congregation of St. Paul's reacts when Gwyn walks down the aisle to do the sermon. They don't know he's reappeared."

"They'll either surround me with love," said Gwyn, "or they'll riot and lynch me."

"I can't wait to hear about this," said Sister Honora Collins. "So you've been around all the time?"

"All the time," admitted Davies. "Incognito. I've been watching. I've even had lunch a number of times with your community, sister, and at the Soup Kitchen. It's amazing how much one can get away with when you're not expected to be around."

"I bet," said Hatfield. "I didn't blow your secret."

"And," continued Davies, "I've seen more than my share of what's been happening with the Commissioner and urban renewal. I saw him sneaking around Evelyn's neighbourhood in the thick fog several nights before the murder. I just figured he was scoping out some more areas for urban destruction. And that Noll Huggard guy. He's been lurking around lately. But as for him, that's nothing new. Everyone knows he appears and disappears when there's fog as thick as pea soup.'

"Can't you come up with a better metaphor," laughed Somerville. "How about 'fog as thick as swamp water?'"

"That doesn't work," said Wentworth. "But it does explain the proverbial swamp urban renewal has been creating lately."

"And McLennan," whispered Sister Collins, "slithered out of that swamp and tried to drain it."

"Easy Sister," said Sweeney, as he placed his hand on hers to calm her down. She was beginning to see red!

The morning was getting on to lunch hour. The gathering agreed that they had duly reported in. They decided to continue as a self-appointed group to monitor the Commission on Urban Renewal. They also agreed to maintain Gwyn Davies' cover. Once the congregation of St. Paul's in the Valley welcomed back their priest, the whole story could be told.

"I hope," said Wentworth, "that once the truth about all that has been going on comes out, we can encourage the city to have a massive celebration. We need to celebrate our city. We need to celebrate that one of us was lost and has returned. We need to celebrate the future of our city. But…"

"But," continued Hatfield, "with caution. We must be ever vigilant about our city. We must preserve what Victorian architecture and Loyalist history we have. If we fail, our city will fail."

THE RECTORY

Rev. Hatfield usually took the fifty wooden steps with a small landing part way up the cliff and ending on Waring Street. It was good exercise. He liked the view. He usually stopped on the landing to "survey his kingdom," as he would say. From there he could see up and down Main, St. Luke's Church, over the roof tops across Main, and all the way to Spar Cove, Rowan's Point and The Reversing Falls. On a clear day when the Pulp Mill wasn't pumping out its fumes and the fog had rolled out, he could see the tops of a ship or two in the harbour.

The rectory was just a short walk from the top of the steps. It was perched on the edge of the cliff between Holly and Bridge Streets. The house, a luxurious two and a half story brick Second Empire home with a three and a half story off-centre tower proclaimed to the world that it had been built by a family a century before who wanted to be known as THE JONESES. Rev. Hatfield chuckled every time he walked home. It made him think of Mary Jones and her desire to be THE MRS. JONES in her neighbourhood. He was just the Rev. Hatfield to his neighbours.

The Rectory with its mansard roof and ornate bracketed cornices and stone quoins utilized throughout the front façade had been a landmark overlooking Main Street. It seemed, forever.

Noll Huggard had followed Rev. Hatfield home the fateful day of the fire at 31 Metcalf.

"My rectory," said Hatfield, "is way too big for just me and my wife. It was even too big when our children were at home. Now that they are grown, we are rattling around in those sixteen rooms. I am happy to be able to share it with you."

Noll was so devastated by the fire at 31 Metcalf that he could only nod. He was exhausted from the climb up the fifty steps. Hatfield showed him to a room that was just below the tower. It overlooked Noll's beloved city. It was perfect. He felt that he had finally found a home.

"You can stay with us," said Hatfield, "as long as it takes for you to get your bearings. You are free to come and go." He handed Noll a key to the front door. "Our home is your home now."

Hatfield's kindness to friend and foe was well known throughout the city. It was no surprise that he would offer his home, especially to some such as Noll who had been through so much in his life. The loss of the family home on Douglas Avenue, his rejection by his family, the fire at 31 Metcalf and his wandering the city streets, a homeless person of sorts, was touching that he had finally found a home.

Noll gradually felt more comfortable living with the Hatfields. The news of murder in the city began to die down. The Commission on Urban Renewal was in the process of being reconstituted and made into an effective advocate for restoration and renewal. The march toward destroying many areas of the city seemed to be over. Noll still walked the city, but now with a different mood in his step.

Noll could see as far as his historical vision could see. He was the happiest when the fog rolled in and enveloped the house. He couldn't see beyond the window sill of his room on those days.

Rev. Hatfield noticed Noll's fascination with the fog. "You spend a great deal of time," said Hatfield, "at your window on a foggy day. There's not much to see but fog. What do you see?"

"I see," said Noll, "I see…" he hesitated for fear that Hatfield would think him a little daft. "I see," he continued, "the city. I see our home on Douglas Avenue. I see 31 Metcalf." He paused. "I see clear over to Centenary Church, The Greene Mansion,…"

"You see," said Hatfield, "the old city. What was. What still is. What has burned?"

"I see." Said Noll. A tear rolled down his cheek.

Hatfield had invited himself into Noll's room. Noll had been spending a lot of time on foggy days sitting at his window. So Hatfield gently approached Noll.

"You see," said Hatfield. He had pulled up a chair next to Noll as they sat watching the fog swirl outside the window and the mist gather and drip down the pane of glass.

"I see," said Noll. He quietly cried.

"Noll," said Hatfield. "You can tell me anything you wish. You are safe in my house. I am a priest. Whatever you tell me stays with me, under the stole."

"I don't," he stuttered, "I don't understand."

"I am a priest bound to keeping close to my heart and soul the confidences people tell me. Call it the privilege of the confessional. I am bound by the seal of the confessional. I must keep all confidences inviolate."

"Violet?" whispered Noll.

"Inviolate," said Hatfield. "It means that whatever anyone tells me stays with me. Only God, I and the person know. No amount of law, court, and writ can get it out of me. You can trust me."

Noll and Hatfield sat quietly watching the fog. Slowly as their hearts warmed to each other, Noll began to tell his story.

"I, I..." he stuttered. "Rev. Hatfield. "I have spent my life searching for love and acceptance. My parents loved me beyond what any parent can. But I have experienced confusion, rejection and loss."

Hatfield pulled out his small purple confessional stole that he always carried with him. He placed it around his neck and set his small vial of anointing oil on the window sill. He turned his chair to face knoll. They sat knee to knee. Noll's room became a safe place. He knew he could say anything and it would still be home.

"I have done things," continued Noll, "I ought never have done and I have left things undone I ought to have done."

Hatfield knew the words by heart. Every Sunday the people prayed together the same words. Hatfield grasped Noll's hands. Noll had not felt the warmth of the hands of a caring person since his mother cradled him in her arms. They sat for a moment face to face. Hatfield began to pray the familiar prayer:

ALMIGHTY and most merciful Father, We have erred and strayed from thy ways like lost sheep, We have followed too much the devices and desires of our own hearts, We have offended against thy holy laws," Hatfield paused for a moment of silence after which Noll prayed:

"I have left undone those things which I ought to have done, And I have done those things which I ought not to have done; And there is no health in me."

The words of the Prayer of Confession was readily on Noll's lips. Hatfield sat listening to the beat of his own heart. He considered how those words were meaningful to his own life. He was hearing directly from Noll the confession of his heart.

"But thou, O Lord," continued Hatfield, *"have mercy upon us, miserable offenders. Spare thou them, O God, which confess their faults. Restore thou them that are penitent; According to thy promises declared unto mankind in Christ Jesus our*

Lord. And grant, O most merciful Father, for his sake, That we may hereafter live a godly, righteous, and sober life, To the glory of thy holy Name." [23]

They sat in silence. Finally Noll spoke through the tears.

"You didn't say the 'amen.' He whispered.

"Because," said Hatfield, "I sensed that there is more to say."

"I can say anything," said Noll, "and you won't think less of me?"

"Anything." Said Hatfield. "You are one of God's beloved."

As they sat there in the quiet of the moments only the tick of Noll's alarm clock punctuated the silence. Gradually the fog began to roll out toward the Bay of Fundy. The fog horn that had been keeping time in the distance had silenced.

"Anything?" repeated Noll.

"Anything!" said Hatfield.

"I am so grateful," said Noll, "that you have welcomed me into your home. I have spent years wandering the streets of this city. My own sister finally found a way to turn me out of her heart and home. And…"

"And?" said Hatfield.

"And the pain was so great," said Noll, "that I set the fire and burned our house down. I didn't know what else to do. I had no place to go so I might as well finish it off."

Hatfield listened.

"Then," continued Noll, "When the Commissioner started tearing down the city I love, it was as if the rest of my world was being torn down. I walk the streets not because there is nothing else to do. I walk so that I can remember. The fog helps me to remember. It covers up the destruction that time and urban renewal causes. I see in my mind, as if it is painted on the fog, the city as it was. My beloved Victorian city with its magnificent buildings, trolley cars, bustling King Street and Square. It's all gone."

"And then there were fires," said Hatfield.

"Fires," whispered Noll. "When St. Paul's Anglican Church in the Valley burned," he paused, "and then I saw what the Commissioner did in the name of urban renewal," he began to cry. "I knew," he continued, "I had to do something. I couldn't let him continue to destroy what I loved. So…"

---

[23] Prayer of General Confession, Book of Common Prayer, Anglican Church of Canada

"So?" asked Hatfield.

"So," continued Noll, "I decided to take matters into my own hands before the Commissioner did any more destruction. At least," he paused, "at least if anything else was going to be torn down, I would control it." He paused.

"And?" said Hatfield.

"I burned down those buildings before anyone else could." He continued. "I figured if I burned down a building or two or three maybe the Commissioner and the city would wake up from sleep. Maybe, just maybe a good fire or two or three would wake up everyone to see what they have and don't have anymore. How could I know?"

"Know?" said Hatfield.

"Know," continued Noll, "that the Commissioner would find out I had set those fires. That he would use me for his own evil deeds."

"Find out?" said Hatfield.

"Yes," said Noll. "He found out that I set the Greene mansion on fire. He thought I set St. Paul's on fire. I didn't. That happened on its own. Probably the workmen restoring the building set it on fire by accident. But,"

"But?" said Hatfield.

"But," continued Noll, "The Commissioner discovered I had set our house on Douglas Avenue and the Greene Mansion on fire. He said that unless I cooperated with him, he would make sure I ended up in jail. I am already in jail. The loss of so much of my beloved Victorian city has me in jail."

"So what did he do?" asked Hatfield.

"Blackmail." Said Noll. "He told me to be at Evelyn Crandall's house the night she was murdered. I didn't know he was going to murder her. I just thought we were going to put a scare into her. I loved Evelyn. So I agreed."

"And?"

"And," continued Noll, "I set her house on fire. I had no idea she was already dead! And then, when I heard McLennan speak at her funeral," he paused. "That bastard. Liar. I ran out and set 31 Metcalf on fire. I had no idea it would burn down along with half the block. I didn't give it a second thought that I'd end up homeless."

They sat in silence.

"I am sorry for the sins of others," said Hatfield, "that you have endured. Forgive me for not being observant enough to reach out to you. Our sins often turn around and bite us. Commissioner McLennan's mean spirit, his greed and his eventual murder of Evelyn came back to haunt him. He will spend the rest of his days in the Provincial penitentiary. And…"

"And?" asked Noll.

"The city has been awakened to see what they have to treasure and preserve." Said Hatfield. "The clergy have been hard at work to influence the Commission, the politicians and the citizens. And…"

"And?" said Noll

"And," continued Hatfield, "even though you were at a loss as to how to deal with all that was happening and your family, your arson fires have in a sense turned into fires that have helped cleanse the city of graft and greed. You have a forever home with us. There is no judgement here. Just love. And what you have said in this room, stays in this room."

"And" said Noll, "Now the "amen?"

"You," said Hatfield, "have confessed before God and me. In truth there is new life. You are safe here. Like the old hymn says, "you once were lost, but now are found."

"One of my favourite hymns," whispered Noll. "I hum it often as I walk. Now the "amen?"

"But first," said Hatfield. "Let us pray:

" ALMIGHTY God, the Father of our Lord Jesus Christ, who desireth not the death of a sinner, but rather that he may turn from his wickedness, and live, hath given power and commandment to his Ministers, to declare and pronounce to his people, being penitent, the Absolution and Remission of their sins. He pardoneth and absolveth all them that truly repent and unfeignedly believe his holy Gospel Wherefore we beseech him to grant us true repentance and his Holy Spirit, that those things may please him which we do at this present, and that the rest of our life hereafter may be pure and holy; so that at the last we may come to his eternal joy; through Jesus Christ our Lord." [24]

"Now?" asked Noll.

"Now!" replied Hatfield.

"Amen!"

---

[24] Ibid.

THE SCANDAL

Sometimes the negative becomes positive in the scheme of things. McLennan had started out with good intentions. He loved Saint John just as much as any in the city. But he loved money and power more.

McLennan had no intention of destroying the city. But when he discovered he could make money from his appointed position as the Commissioner of Urban Renewal his true nature began to appear. It turned into a scandal of an unexpected politician.

Politicians often find themselves in office with good intentions that have turned to personal intentions. The temptation of the power and opportunity in office becomes their purpose. The real reason for their appointment disappears.

It was no different for the Commissioner and the Commission on Urban Renewal.

Mary Jones was delighted to have been appointed by Mayor Blake to the Commission. Her first intent was to assist in the restoration and renewal of the city. But, as with McLennan, her acquired intent became her self-promotion. She couldn't resist announcing to the Commission and the world that she was THE MRS. JONES with the big mansion in a less than desirable neighbourhood. Instead of her big mansion sparking urban renewal, it caused much contentious feelings among the community. People were jealous. Mary became haughtier as the days wore on. She didn't dare walk down the street in her neighbourhood, nor would she want to. She preferred to drive by in her Mercedes. Even her car proclaimed that she was better than the rest.

Father Sweeney and Sister Honora learned an important lesson by their membership on the Commission. Buildings, to them, had always represented their purpose for being. Of course the Cathedral and the Soup Kitchen ministries were mixed up with their buildings. As a result of serving on the commission and the clergy gatherings, they learned that buildings represent people, not the other way around. As a result, their focus for the city was to honour in many ways, the lives and legacies of the people of Saint John. People were honoured. Historic areas and buildings of the city became, for them, representations of what was and what could be. They could be heard saying, "Before we tear down any more buildings, we must consider the effect it will have on people. And we must consider the people's wishes. We must preserve, conserve and renew our city for generations to come."

Annalee Gaudet had been a benign observer throughout the course of the Commission. She had dutifully recorded every jot and tittle for posterity. As a result, her notes became important evidence in the trial of Commissioner McLennan. They were evidence that revealed the complicity of many of the commission members. Most importantly, they revealed McLennan's guilt by implication. Annalee was glad to go back to her archives where she continued to sift through the debris of centuries of dust and mortar. Some of the city may have been destroyed over the centuries, but for her, it remained for all to see. Her work was important in providing guidance for a reconstituted Commission on Urban Renewal. In fact the mayor had renamed the Commission. It was now the Commission on Urban Renewal and Preservation. Its membership incorporated the Clergy Group as well as several of the original members. To everyone's surprise, The Rev. Gwyn Davies was designated as the new chair.

Rev. Davies sudden return on Sunday morning at Old Stone Church had stunned and delighted. As he walked down the aisle reading the Gospel for the day, everyone gasped. Their stunned silence turned into cheers of joy. He was reading from the story of the lost son. Truly and Margaret were in attendance. Together.

Truly nudged Margaret and said, "Maggie. He once was lost but now is found." For once she didn't correct Truly. She had become quite comfortable with him calling her 'Maggie.'

Truly was appointed to the Commission and designated the muse, or the one person who could observe and comment upon their work without judgement. He was charged with helping to keep the Commission focused. His comments were to be noted, appreciated or not. He could say anything. They were to listen and consider.

Noll Huggard lived out the rest of his days with the Hatfield's. Because his memory of the city was so keen, he was appointed to be a memory archivist. He was to work with Annalee Gaudet. Both were charged with reviewing the state of the city, maintaining memories and monitoring the renewal and restoration work. Noll was appreciated for his photographic memory of the city. Before any building was torn down, restored or repurposed, he was consulted for what he remembered. His knowledge was used in many effective ways that honoured the old city and looked to the future. His confession remained under Rev. Hatfield's stole for eternity. The truth had set him free.

Becoming unexpected politicians for some, like McLennan, had led to scandal. For others, becoming unexpected politicians, like Truly, Noll and even Mary Jones, had led to renewal and new purposes in life.

CELEBRATION

The city had learned an important lesson. Its citizens learned that they could no longer sleep through their days, years and decades. While citizens sleep, cities decay and politicians take advantage of situations. The fires, the demolition, the murder of physical and emotional lives of citizens, buildings and history had shaken the city back to life.

The city would think twice before any more historic buildings or neighbourhoods were destroyed in the name of urban renewal.

Rev. Davies had learned that the faithful could endure the loss of a building and still be a church. His disappearance, while causing great stress, had resulted in the congregation of St. Paul's circling the wagons and drawing closer together. In the process, they came to appreciate the guiding hand of the Spirit upon them as they discussed how to continue. Their decision to remain a congregation without a building permanently worshiping at Old Stone Church brought new life to both congregations. Old Stone Church found new life. St. Paul's found ways to be an effective church without walls.

There was much to celebrate in the middle of murder, fire and destruction. Out of the ashes, a city with vigor and vibrancy began to emerge. History was honoured rather than dismissed. Children discovered an excitement knowing from where they had come and to where they were going. The past became the future. Citizens stopped letting the degradation of the past become their present. Instead, all that was good about the past, buildings, history, culture, Loyalist, became things to treasure and learn from.

King Square once again teemed with people. But now the people weren't sitting there watching the city, and tourists, parade on by. Citizens paused on a park bench or two to watch the vibrancy of the city coming back to life.

Woolworth's, which had been on the verge of closure, found new ways of in gathering people around its lunch counter. Margaret hummed joyous songs as she served. Truly had become more than her customer. He had convinced her that his use of 'Maggie' was a term of endearment. She was falling for it. She no longer complained when he called her 'Maggie,' instead she saved special pieces of pumpkin pie for him, serving it with a wink and a blown kiss.

"Maggie," he had been heard to say, "I'll pick you up at eight. We can walk over to Fort Howe. Maybe the fog will roll in. I'll show you," he continued, "the city I love. We both love Saint John. And perhaps..." he paused.

"Perhaps," she finished his sentence, "perhaps, just perhaps, it will be our special place. Our special time. The city will be ours. Forever."

EPILOG

I have by no means exhausted the subject of urban renewal, nor did I intend to. As I drove through the North End in the summer of 2017 I was shocked to see so many buildings that have been boarded up. I can only imagine that they are slated for demolition. In wonder what will be left in their wake. Blank hills? Rubble? Non-descript new housing? Lost History? Homeless people? I can only imagine.

In my on-going research about Saint John while I wrote the story, I found many resources ranging from the North Ender Facebook Page to the New Brunswick Museum, to various blogs. Saint John has a fascinating history that is being preserved by many people. Some of that history is still stashed away in the minds, hearts and attics of residents. I would encourage anyone who loves this city to unpack memories, chests and attics. The past must not be lost. We must not relive depressions, war, or great fires without remembering and learning from them.

Dr. Robert McKinnon, (Dean of Arts, UNB Saint John and Co-Director, The Industrial City in Transition Community-University Research Alliance Project) concisely comments on the city. I quote him:

Although identified as Canada's oldest incorporated city (1785), the city's contemporary urban structure owes a considerable legacy to the industrial age. Following a disastrous fire in 1877, the waterfront and central business district were redeveloped. The urban residential and commercial structure was altered by the vigorous rebuilding of a large portion of the downtown which resulted in one of the best, contiguous collections of Victorian architecture in Canada. In 1893, an electric streetcar system replaced a horse-drawn street railway, and promoted the expansion of suburbs in the western fringe of the city.

The First and Second World Wars stimulated Saint John's economic and demographic base. The shipbuilding industry was rejuvenated in these eras, and many Saint John companies engaged in goods for the war effort. Following World War II, a variety of large-scale industrial enterprises emerged as the backbone of the City's economy: pulp mills, a sugar refinery, an oil refinery, and shipbuilding facilities.

Among the most noteworthy urban changes in the post-war era were housing developments in the City's north end, and an extensive post-war urban renewal programme. These significantly altered the face of several of the City's neighbourhoods.

An ambitious master plan for the City was designed in 1967 (Merrett Report) that outlined new suburban neighbourhoods … and proposed areas for redevelopment. [25]

Ronald Jack in his blog "thelostvalley.blogspot.com" writes that in 2009 there was an estimated 120 boarded-up buildings in the city. I observed that much of that has not changed in 2017. He comments that "this is a huge problem in a small city like Saint John, yet the City staff do not seem overly concerned."

My yearly visits to Saint John since 1944 have left an impression on me that perhaps destruction is more important than preservation. The Harbour Bridge was controversial for a moment until it was built and people would whiz from one side of the city to the other. Haymarket Square, with its smoke from cars and buses succumbed to viaducts. The Saint John Hospital sat dormant for decades before implosion. Its disappearance left a blank spot on the Saint John skyline. Churches have either closed or been razed or left to decay. Centenary Church, a 1200 seat historical structure stands as a warning sign to the city. When left to its own devices and desires, buildings take care of themselves. They rot, decay and disappear. Beyond a certain point, citizens become more apathetic, fall deeper into sleep or are resigned to the disappearance of structures that might have been saved.

Much of the city exists in the memory of its oldest citizens or has been passed down to younger generations. I both remember what the city was like in the 1950's and remember my father's stories of his memory of the city from the very early 20th century. He delivered newspapers all over the city. He knew Walter Pidgeon. He remembered music stores with Victrola's, pianos, and salespersons who would help with the selection of new music. He remembered and passed those memories on to me.

I know the past and the city of my memories will never return. Like Noll Huggard and Truly Morrell in the story, I sit at Fort Howe. When the fog rolls in and obliterates the 21st century version of the city, I also see the old city through the fog. Main Street is gone. Penny candy now comes in bags at Sobey's, the Great Atlantic Store, or the Old Market. Buses no longer lay down exhaust fumes that created a blue haze over King's Street.

---

[25] Saint John: An Industrial City in Transition, New Brunswick Museum, Educational Resources, Dr. Robert McKinnon, (Dean of arts, UNB Saint John and Co-Director, The Industrial City in Transition Community-University Research Alliance Project)

As long as I can, I shall return yearly to Saint John. I will remember. I will rejoice that my father, and my relatives in NB, instilled in me a love for the Bay of Fundy, the Maritimes, the Old City Market, the streets and haunts of old Saint John, and the ability to see what is no more.

APPENDIX

MEMORIES

In the course of writing this book I developed a significant pile of notes and resources. Many, many people have shared memories. Some of the memories were just place names. Names of businesses that no longer exist were a big part of the sharing. Here, in no particular order, are some of the places and names people have shared. I am leaving a blank page or two for you to add your own list of places and memories.

Manchester, Robertson, Allison
Scovil Brothers
Mr. Erb in the Old Market
Calp Department Store
Narins Store
Welsford Drugs
Victoria Street Baptist Church
Centenary Church
Germain Street Baptist Church
St. Paul's in the Valley Church
Main Street
Customs Houses
King Street
The Riviera Restaurant
Reggie's
Haymarket Square
The Saint John Hospital
Poncho's Variety
Robichard's Corner Store
Shorts Variety
Polly's Convenience
    Metcalf and Durham
The YMCA
Woolworth's
The Train Station
Jelly Bean Houses
Odeon Theatre
Paramount Theatre
Simpson and Sears

Dominion Stores
The Old Kiwanis Grounds
Red Rose Tea
The Pidgeon's store
Simm's Brush Factory
Stephen's Drugstore
Duffering School
St. Peter's School
Holder's Music Store
Riverboats at Indiantown
Jackie's Fish & Chips
    On Main
Bank of Nova Scotia
Woodhouse
Colby Smith
McCready's Pickle Factory
North End Pool Hall
Dot's - Cor. Albert & Main Sts.
Fran's Grocery
Jim Flynn's Taylors
Pitt's Barber Ship
    Near Bridge Street
Gault's Store
Hoffman's
Main Street Baptist
Morris Drugs
Sam's Smoke Shop
Smith's Barber Shop
Honest Joe's Pawn Shop

The Diamond Grill
Snowflake Lime Office
Art McGuire's store
    Bridge/Spar Cove
Titus Bakery
    Corner of Main & Elgin
Mahoney Drug
    Adelaide & Main
Maritime Electronics
    Main & Adelaide
Hoffman's
Pirie's Blacksmith Shop, Main
Garvin Funeral Home on Main
Phil's across from 82 Victoria

Taylor's Meats off Newman St.
Flash Muffler on Metcalf St.
Two restaurants on Main St.
    Hicksons & Grahams?
Martins Store, Main St.
Pridham's Photograph
Wiezel's
Kennedy's Shoes
Taffy Tom's, as known as
    Phillip's- On Main St.
The Princess Dress Shop
MacArthur's Wallpaper & Paint
Salty's Candy Shop

Every time a privately owned business closes a little bit of the city moves out of the city to the suburbs and the city begins to close. Every time something closes in town, the town shuts down and dies a little.

A BIG "Thank you" to the many people who responded to my questions on Facebook and by email. Their input helped to generate the above partial list of businesses and places remembered.

ADD YOUR MEMORIES TO THIS LIST

YOUR MEMORIES

BLUEBERRY RECIPES

BLUEBERRY BANG BELLY
Recipe provided by Carrol Thorne and Vicky Saunders
Recipe is also called Mrs. Williston's Blueberry Bang Belly

INGREDIENTS

Filling
4 cups blueberries
1 ½ cups sugar (or less if desired)
3 tablespoons of flour
Topping
2 cups flour
1 teaspoon salt
2 teaspoons baking powder
2/3 cup butter or shortening
½ cup of milk.

INSTRUCTIONS

1. Combine the blueberries, sugar, and flour in a saucepan.
2. Cook together until the mixture bubbles.
3. Spread the filling in a greased 9 by 13 inch cake pan
4. Preheat the oven to 400 degrees.
5. In a bowl, whisk or stir together the flour, salt & banking powder.
6. Cut in the shortening until the flour looks like coarse corn meal.
7. Add the milk and stir until the dough forms a ball.
8. Flour a board lightly and roll the dough out about a half inch think or slightly less, sufficient to cover the berries and lay on top of the blueberry mixture.
9. Bake for 20 to 30 minutes or until the crust is golden brown.
10. 10 cut in squares and serve from the pan.[26]

---

[26] Recipe by Taste Buds oat //tastebuds bangordaily news. Com

CARROL THORNE'S BLUEBERRY GRUNT [27]

Mix together in a large sauce pan on top of the stove, cover and bring to a light boil
4 cups Blueberries
1/2 cup white sugar
1/2 cup water

DUMPLINGS

Mix the following dry ingredients all together with a fork in a medium small bowl and make a well in the center
2 cups flour
4 teaspoons baking powder
1 Tablespoon sugar
1/2 teaspoon salt

Mix together in a measuring cup
2 Tablespoons oil
1 cup milk
Pour all at once the milk and oil mixture in the well of the dry ingredients. Stir gently with a fork just until all the dry ingredients are absorbed in the liquid. Drop small portions on top of the hot blueberry mixture, cover and cook 15 to 20 minutes like for dumplings/doughboys on top of a stew. Serve warm with Ice Cream on top ENJOY!!!!!!

PS: NOTE: 2 Tablespoons of shortening or butter can be used instead of the oil, BUT it would need to be blended into the dry ingredients before the milk was added and stirred in.

---

[27] Carrol Thorne of Cambridge-Narrows, NB Canada.

BLUEBERRY CREAM MUFFINS [28]

INGREDIENTS

2 eggs
1 cup sugar
½ cup vegetable oil
½ tsp vanilla
2 cups all-purpose flour
½ tsp salt
½ tsp baking soda
1 cup sour cream
1 ½ cups blueberries

1. Preheat oven to 400 degrees & Spray 12 large muffin cups or line with cupcake papers.
2. In a separate bowl stir flour, salt and baking soda
3. In large bowl whisk eggs and gradually add sugar, continue whisking until pale yellow in colour.
4. Continue whisking while slowly pouring in oil and then vanilla.
5. Stir dry ingredients into egg mixture, alternating with the sour cream.
6. Gently fold in blueberries
7. Scoop batter into prepared muffin cups
8. Bake in preheated oven for 20 minutes

[28] Patricia Bacon's sister's, Monica Parlee, recipes.

BLUEBERRY STREUSEL COFFEE CAKE [29]

INGREDIENTS

Streusel Topping
    1 cup packed brown sugar
    2/3 cup all-purpose flour
    1 teaspoon ground cinnamon
    ½ cup butter
Cake
    1 ¾ cups all-purpose flour
    2 teaspoons baking powder
    ½ teaspoon salt
    1/3 cup butter, softened
    1 cup white sugar
    1 egg
    1 teaspoon pure vanilla extract
    ¾ cup buttermilk
    ½ cup sour cream
    1 ½ cups blueberries (Fresh of frozen tossed with 1 tbsp., flour
        If using frozen DO NOT THAW, toss with flour and
        store in freezer until ready to use.

INSTRUCTIONS
1. Preheat oven to 350 degrees and spray 9 " spring form pan with cooking spray
2. **Streusel Topping**
3. Mix born sugar, flour, and cinnamon in a medium bowl. Cut in ½ cup of butter until mixture is well combined and crumbly. Set aside.
4. **Cake**
5. Whisk together flour, baking powder, and salt, set aside
6. Beat together butter and sugar until fluffy and creamy
7. Add egg and beat well
8. Stir in sour cream
9. Add vanilla to milk

---

[29] Ibid. and recipe by Monica Parlee, Author of Mommy Still Yummy at //oldermommystillyummy.com

10. Add 1/3 of the flour mixture at a time and alternate with the milk mixture, beating well after each addition.
11. Spread half of the batter into the prepared pan. Cover with ½ streusel mixture followed by all the blueberries. Add remaining batter, spread carefully. Cover batter with remaining streusel topping.
12. Bake at 350 (175 C) for 55 – 60 minutes, until deep golden brown and set.
13. Remove pan to wire rack. Cool completely before removing outer ring.
14. Store in airtight container or cover well with plastic wrap.

BLUEBERRY LOAF [30]

1 ½ cups of sugar
¼ cup of Rogers golden syrup.
2 tsp. Vanilla
5 tsp Baking Powder
2 cups of blueberries
2 eggs
1 cup of milk
4 cups of flour
1 tsp of salt.

Preheat oven to 350 degrees. Grease two loaf pans.

In a large bowl beat eggs, stir in sugar and syrup. Add milk and Vanilla and mix. Combine flour, baking powder, and salt and stir into egg mixture. Mix well. Fold in Blueberries. Spoon into loaf pans. Bake 1 ¼ hours (or until toothpick comes out clean) Cool for 10 minutes in pan. Then unmold on rack to cool. Wrap and store. Freezes well.

---

[30] From Vicky Sanders of North End of Saint John.

ACKNOWLEDGEMENTS

The writing of this book has involved decades of vacations and observations of the city through those decades. I could not have written this book without the valuable help of Sandra and Richard Thorne of Hampton. Upon several occasions, Sandra has guided me away from naming a character or area that actually existed. With her guidance I changed, for instance, the pastor's name of St. Paul in the Valley to Gwyn Davies, thus suggesting that he was of Welch descent. She has also been instrumental in clarifying for me Canadian terms in the Anglican Church, building names, site names etc. Her help has been invaluable as I plagued her, almost daily, with email questions.

Various Facebook pages encouraged me to keep writing. The Saint John North Enders page was particularly helpful. Whenever I asked a question, answers were replete with examples and information. I have included that information in the text and the blueberry recipes in the appendix.

Then there is Vern M. Garnett. I met Vern by chance in August 2017, in the middle of Kings Square, and then again on the same day in the Old Market. Both times we chatted about the city. We mourned the loss of so much that was beautiful and historic. Vern has also been mourning the loss of his beloved wife. I was so intrigued by his conversation and physical appearance that I made him the muse in the story. His name in the book is Truly Morrell. It's a name that I changed in my writing because the original name I came up with from my imagination was actually the name of a local writer!!! Writing is a mystery.

Vern is a lover of all things Saint John. I am too. Our conversations ranged from historical facts to commentary on the state of the city. Many of his comments are incorporated in Truly Morrell's conversations in the book.

Several of the other characters in the book are based on my relatives I have known and loved. I will leave it to your imagination to identify which ones. No judgement is intended. Just fascinating characters included to make the story more real.

I am also grateful to friends, family and strangers who have listened to my rambling and put up with my sleepless nights and tired days as I worked on murder, arson, and historic preservation.

ABOUT THE AUTHOR

Thomas L. Shanklin is a direct descendent of Captain Thomas Spragg who arrived in New Brunswick in 1784. He is also a descendent of James John Shanklin who arrived in 1824 from County Donegal, Ireland.

He was born in New Jersey, vacationed in Saint John and UpCountry and spent many hours watching the rise and fall of the Bay of Fundy and the city as its heart beat. His love of the city, all things New Brunswick and Metcalf Street is rivaled by none.

He is a graduate of Fairleigh Dickinson University with a Bachelor of Science. And Drew University with a Masters of Divinity, and a Masters of Sacred Theology. He has done extensive post-graduate studies. His interests include: travel, music, oil painting, reading, history, writing, singing, photography and much more. He is ordained clergy of the United Methodist Church.

He has authored numerous books, all of which are available on Amazon, in the Saint John Public Library, Kings County Historical Society, Queen's County Historical Society, the Provincial Archives and the Canadian Archives.

His book, "Downeast-UpCountry," has received rave reviews for its preservation of stories from the first quarter of the 20th century. He has also authored "Finding Ireland," which tells the story of James Shanklin arriving in New Brunswick, and a small book of his Father, Harold Shanklin's World War I writings and poetry.

He regularly does readings at the Saint John Public Library and sells his books at the Queen's Square Sunday Farmer's market and Kingston Farmer's market and Amazon.

He resides in New Hampshire and Florida but can almost always be found wandering the streets of Saint John and Upcountry in August!

Thomas L. Shanklin
16114 Pennington Road
Tampa, Florida 33624
mysterywy@gmail.com

BOOKS BY THOMAS L. SHANKLIN

MYSTERIES
TRILOGY

A Soul to Die for – Vol. I
There's a Hearse in My Parking Space – Vol. II
Up from the Grave – Vol. III

EPILOG TO TRILOGY

The Missing Chapter
The Rest of the Trilogy Story

INSPIRATIONAL BOOKS

It's About Acts
Thoughts on the early church found in the book of Acts

Uncommon Thoughts
Readings to start some of your days

Spirit Thoughts
Poems and Other Writings To Feed the Soul and Body

NEW BRUNSICK – CANADIAN BOOKS

Downeast-UpCountry
A Place, A Family, A Time

Finding Ireland
The New Brunswick-Liskeran Shanklins

World War I Poetry and Writings
Writings of Harold MacKenzie Shanklin from 1916-1918

List Continued on Next Page

CHILDREN'S BOOKS

Willy Finds a Home
Every Home needs to be owned by a Cat

Geshnozzletoff
The Day a Pig Came to Dinner

ALL BOOKS AVAILABLE FROM THE AUTHOR
OR ON AMAZON

mysterywy@gmail.com